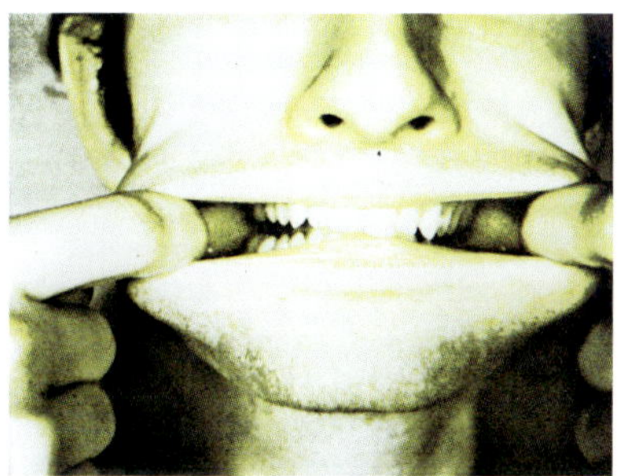

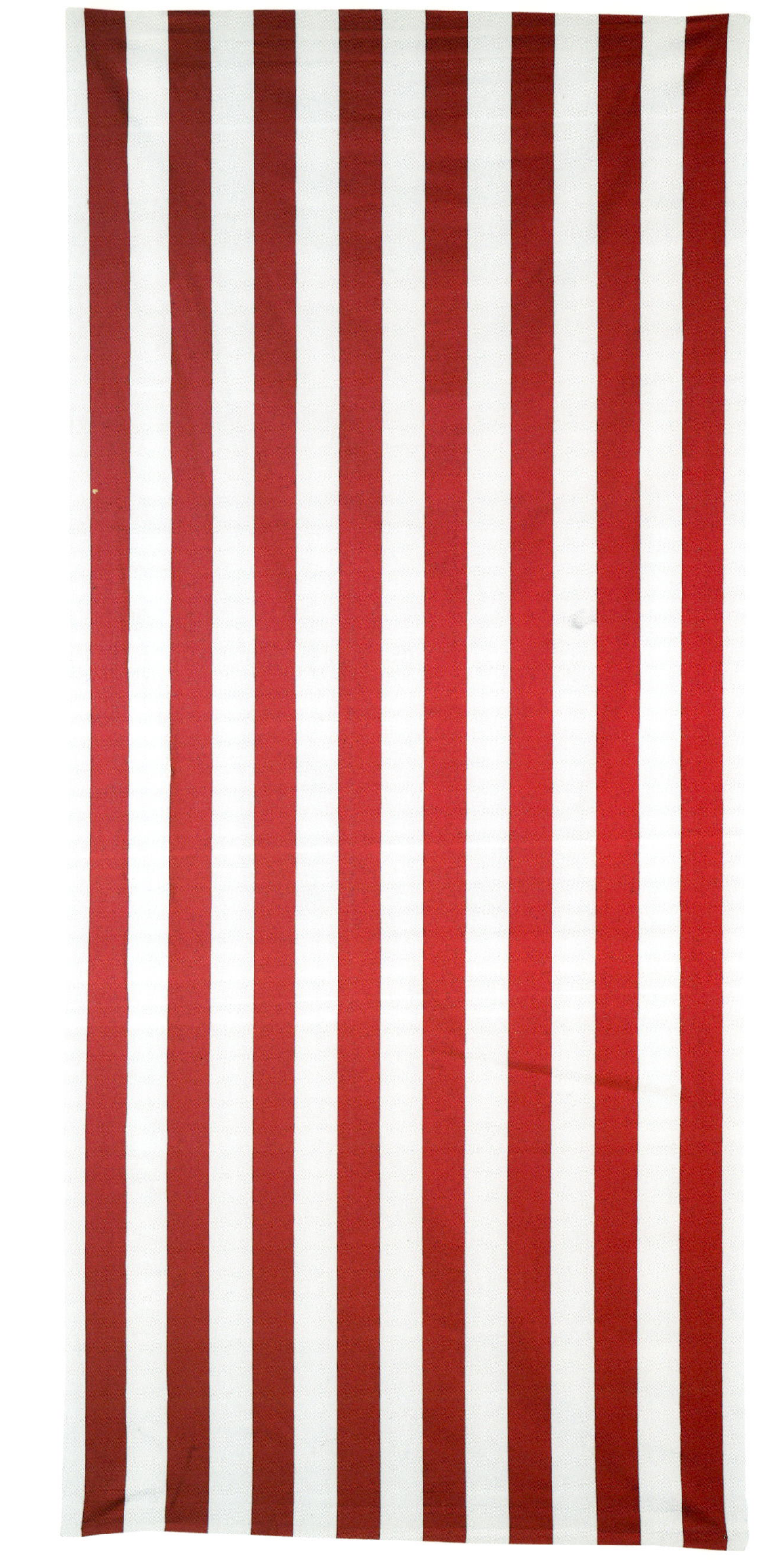

conceptual Art

DANIEL MARZONA
UTA GROSENICK (ED.)

TASCHEN

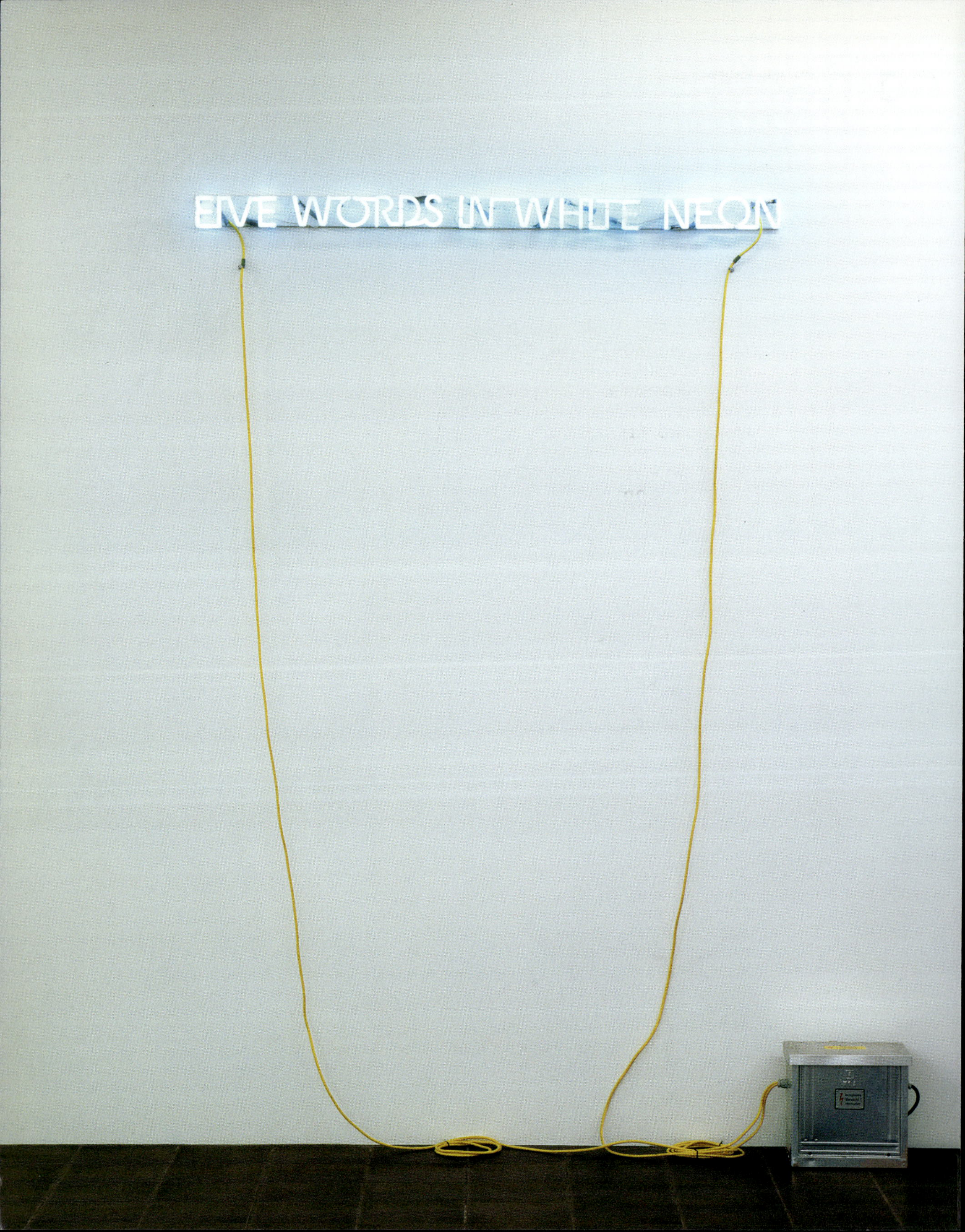

FIVE WORDS IN WHITE NEON

contents

ideas, systems, processes

What is art? How is its context to be defined? Can art be created or perceived when it is no longer bound to an aesthetic object? Can art be political or is art *per se* integrated into political contexts? Can the discourse about art itself constitute art? How can the authority to make appropriate judgements on art be extended from a small circle of insiders to a large number of "stakeholders"?

These and many other issues were raised by various works which in the late 1960s radically questioned the traditional idea of what art was, and which, more for want of a better name than anything else, are lumped together under the term of Concept Art – or more properly Conceptual Art. For in retrospect, the artistic approaches and intentions of the artists involved in the foundation of Conceptual Art prove to have been far too heterogeneous for us to talk of a unitary style or even of an artistic movement.

The expression "Concept Art" first cropped up in an American context in 1961. In his essay of the same name, published in 1963, the Fluxus artist Henry Flynt uses the term to refer to a kind of art whose actual distinguishing feature is the way it deals with language. A few years later, the term "Concept Art" had already been replaced by "Conceptual Art". This term was invented by Sol LeWitt, an artist whose works from the outset had not been exclusively language-oriented. His essays "Paragraphs on Conceptual Art" (1967) and "Sentences on Conceptual Art" (1969) brought the term to the attention of a broader public and in a sense specified what was to be understood by it. In 1969 the English artists' group Art & Language published the first number of the magazine "Art-Language", which was subtitled "The Journal of Conceptual Art", and that same year the young concept artist Joseph Kosuth declared: "All art (after Duchamp) is conceptual (in nature) because art only exists conceptually."

In other words the term was already internationally current by the end of the 1960s, but it was nonetheless the subject of controversy. Thus the first anthology on the novel forms of art was brought out by Gregory Battcock in 1973 under the title "Idea Art", while Lucy Lippard's annotated collection *Six Years: The Dematerialization of the Art Object* the same year referred cautiously to "so-called Conceptual Art". With one exception, the first large survey exhibitions, which revealingly first took place in Europe, bore titles which took account of the heterogeneous nature of the art production current at the time: "Live in Your Head. When Attitudes Become Form. Works-Concepts-Processes-Situations-Information" (Bern, 1969), "Op losse Schroeven: Situaties en cryptostructuren" (Amsterdam, 1969), "Prospect 69" (Düsseldorf, 1969).

So what is or was to be understood by the term Conceptual Art? One way or another, all the artists' essays, surveys and exhib-

---

1966 — Exhibition of Minimalist sculpture: "Primary Structures", Jewish Museum, New York

1966 — Mel Bochner exhibits photocopies of working material:

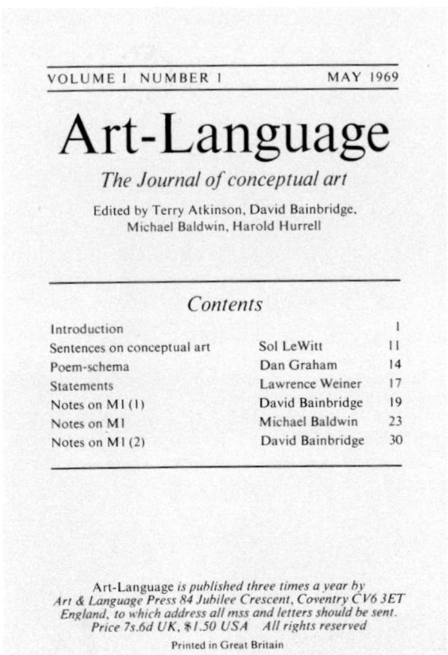

"Actual works of art are little more than historical curiosities."

Joseph Kosuth

blank [blæŋk] *a(dv)* blank, weiß, leer, ausdruckslos, offen; unbeschrieben; blanko ...; bleich; blaß; reimlos; *s* Weiße *n*; leerer Raum *m*; Blankett *n*; Niete (Los) *f*; Schrötling (Metallstück) *m*; in ~ in blanco.

itions mentioned above express the fact — and ultimately this constitutes the lowest common denominator — that within Conceptual Art there is an explicit emphasis on the "thought" component of art and its perception. In the course of the 1960s, normative definitions of art began to crumble, and thus younger artists, often with an excellent academic education, started to re-interpret the essence of art in extended analyses. Thus, not only art itself, but also its institutional context, became the centre of attention, subjected to comprehensive criticism in artistic practice. Many artists expressed their worries about traditional forms of marketing art, and so ways were sought of getting away from the idea of artworks as decorative objects for well-heeled buyers.

In these and other experiments, the idea, or conceptual structure, of the art work began in the late 1960s to liberate itself from the material realization, which was seen by many artists as subordinate or even superfluous. Accordingly new ways of presentation and distribution of this often "objectless" art had to be found, which significantly differed from traditional forms of display. Now a catalogue or invitation card could replace the traditional exhibition, and a telegram, an interview or a brief notice could be a valid contribution to an exhibition. At a stroke, art was understood as a special form of information, which was often presented as a combination of photography and text. The beholder was now finally being urged to take part in the art actively, and often at considerable expenditure of effort.

Conceptual Art has often been described as a theoretically top-heavy, over-intellectual art form. And it is certainly true that many artists, in the development and underpinning of their work, do indeed use theoretical models which have been developed in other disciplines. The later linguistic philosophy of Ludwig Wittgenstein, logical positivism, French structuralism and in particular the semiotic writings of Roland Barthes, the critical theory of Herbert Marcuse and much more besides all flowed into the matrix on the basis of which new forms of artistic expression were tried out.

Maybe even more significant than the diverse fragments of theory which are reflected in Conceptual Art was the merciless confrontation with aesthetics on the part of the art critic Clement Greenberg and his adherents, which claimed universal validity until well into the 1960s. Greenberg argued on a strictly formal plane: in an unmistakable affinity with the epistemology of the philosopher Immanuel Kant (1724–1804), Greenberg was of the opinion that it was the task of every artistic genre to question its fundamental conditions in order, self-reflectively, to arrive at its own essence.

The respective genres (painting, sculpture, etc.) were, in this context, to be kept strictly apart from each other. His reception theory,

---

"Working Drawings and Other Visible Things on Paper Not Necessarily Meant to Be Viewed as Art", New York

1966 — National Organization for Women founded in USA

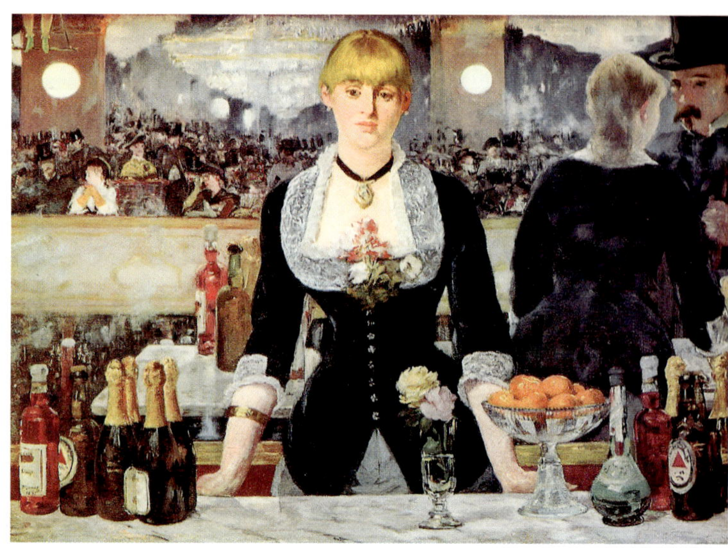

3. EDOUARD MANET

<u>A Bar at the Folies-Bergère</u>
1882, oil on canvas, 96 x 130 cm
London, Samuel Courtauld Trust,
Courtauld Institute of Art Gallery

formulated only in outline, seemed to be based on the assumption that in some inexplicable fashion, works of art emanated a significance that could only be intuitively understood by a few insiders in the context of a view of art beyond the bounds of time and space.

To oversimplify somewhat, it is indeed true that in each of the various manifestations of Conceptual Art specific "dogmas" of modernist aesthetics come in for criticism. For this reason, it seems useful to attempt a provisional taxonomy of Conceptual Art, geared to the central motifs of the formalist aesthetic. By a process of exclusion, the artistic techniques can thus be better defined and demarcated.

The Dialectic of the Modern – Early Approaches to a conceptual view of Art

Modern art is generally reckoned to have begun with the appearance of the work of Edouard Manet (1832–1883) and Paul Cézanne (1839–1906). It was then that painting for the first time reflected on its own conditions, adapting motifs to contemporary life (in the case of Manet), or setting a course towards an abstraction freed from the requirement merely to reproduce what could be seen (in the case of Cézanne).

Having come under substantial pressure from the dissemination of photography and the ever more rapid modernization of technology, science and the economy, and the resulting social contradictions which were becoming visible, the task of painting could no longer consist in the reproduction, as perfectly as possible, and affirmative confirmation, of reality. Thus, first, the classical perspective of the Renaissance was given up, and the pictorial space was visibly flattened. With the works of Cézanne, the significance of the means of painting began to dissociate itself from the significance of the depiction, albeit without painting becoming totally dissociated from concrete things.

A further step in the direction of abstraction was taken a little later by the Cubists, led by Pablo Picasso (1881–1973), Georges Braque (1882–1963) and Fernand Léger (1881–1955). At the start of the 20th century, this generation of young artists saw themselves confronted by the omnipresence of photographs, which were becoming increasingly easy to take and to reproduce. In the conviction that mechanically produced photographic images lacked the possibility of raising subjective, emotional contents above the object depicted, the Cubists sought to renew painting by throwing any naturalism of depiction overboard. What they wanted to paint was no longer a reproduction, but the image of an autonomous reality.

1966 — Cultural Revolution in China   **1966 — Founding of the "Extra-Parliamentary Opposition" (APO) in Germany**
1967 — Che Guevara killed in fighting with the Bolivian army

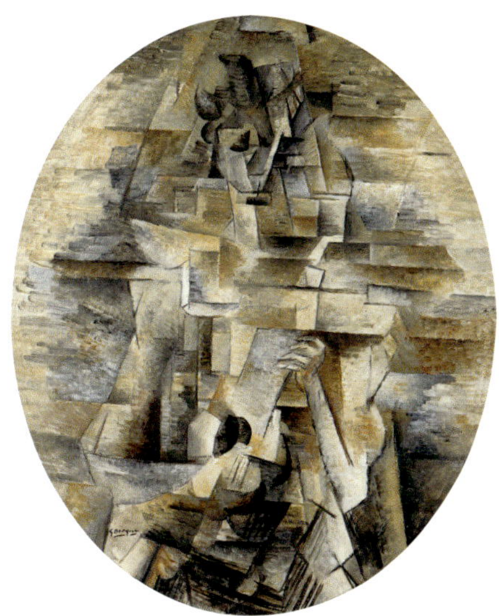

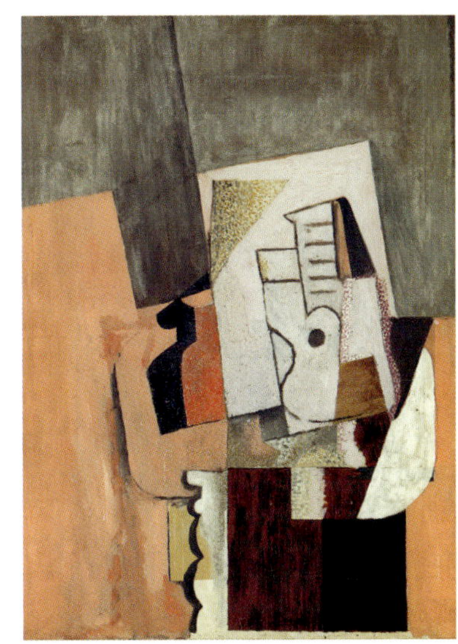

4

5

In the "simultaneous arrangement of the three basic elements of image design, namely line, form and colour" (Léger), the Cubists increased the degree of abstraction in their painting. Thus the poet and theoretician Guillaume Apollinaire could speak of a "peinture pure" (1913), a pure form of painting, and in his "Aesthetic Meditations" state: "Likeness has no importance any more, for the painter sacrifices everything to the truths, the necessities of a higher nature, which he presumes to exist, without discovering it. … Thus we are moving towards a totally new art, which will mean for painting the same as what we have hitherto seen as the function of music as opposed to literature. It will be pure painting, just as music is pure literature."

Almost at the same time as Cubism was developing in France, a group of artists in Russia, led by the painter and theoretician Kasimir Malevich (1878–1935), were pushing the development of Suprematism as a response to the output of the Cubists. With Malevich's famous picture *Black Square* (1915), abstract painting soon reached an early climax. In 1915, for the first time, a picture was exhibited in St Petersburg that lacked any reference to any object in the external world. Tellingly, Malevich justified the total renunciation of figurative depiction in Suprematism in very similar terms to Apollinaire, in that he too pointed to the project of a pure form of painting, in which a pure spirituality was to be expressed.

In the progressive experimentation with an abstract pictorial language, the art of the early avant-garde liberated itself not only from the duty of depiction, but also from any relationship to literature, religion and philosophy, such as had characterized the history of pre-modern art for centuries. The content-related aims of art gave way to form, in which the emotional, spiritual or expressive content was to be fulfilled. To many artists and theoreticians of early modern art it was precisely the dissociation of the visual arts from all linguistic traditions that seemed to constitute the essence of abstraction. They saw in the possibilities of the abstract formal language a pure and elemental expression which was far superior to the medium of language. Dominated by theoretical considerations of this sort, in about 1914, avant-garde painting, in other words Cubism and Suprematism, had nailed itself down very quickly to material-visual and formal aspects.

With the newly won freedoms of a truly abstract painting, however, serious problems soon however began to appear. What were the criteria for a "successful" abstract painting, and who was in a position to decide whether a particular composition had attained the status of "formal harmony" or "aesthetic maturity"? Could these criteria be objectivized, or was it dependent on the subjective judgement of the artist or art critic whether a picture was to count as good or bad?

1967 — Media theoretician Marshall McLuhan publishes "The Medium is the Message"

1967 — Art critic Germano Celant coins the term "Arte povera"

6. KASIMIR MALEVICH

<u>Black Square</u>
1915, oil on canvas, 80 x 80 cm
Moscow, Tretyakov Gallery

7. MARCEL DUCHAMP

<u>Fountain</u>
1917/1964, urinal made of sanitary porcelain,
61 x 48 x 36 cm
Private collection

8. GEORGE GROSZ

<u>A Victim of Society (Remember Uncle August,
the Unhappy Inventor)</u>
1919, oil, pencil and collage on canvas,
49 x 39.5 cm
Paris, Musée national d'art moderne,
Centre Pompidou

6

The Assault by Marcel Duchamp

It was the young artist Marcel Duchamp, who, in his post-painterly work, was to raise doubts concerning aesthetic judgements to the point where they could not be ignored. Before Duchamp decided in 1913 to abandon traditional easel-painting until further notice, he had within the space of a good ten years adopted modern painting in a process of imitation.

Through his two elder brothers Jacques Villon (1875–1963) and Raymond Duchamp-Villon (1876–1918), he came into contact with the work and the ideas of the Cubists. Presumably inspired by the early motion photographs of Etienne-Jules Marey, the young painter began to combine the Cubist idea of simultaneous different perspectives with an interest in the depiction of movement. Duchamp's important picture *Nude Descending a Staircase*, dating from 1912, which he entered the same year for exhibition at the Cubist-dominated Salon des Indépendants, was so strongly rejected by Albert Gleizes and other leading members, that it had to be removed even before the exhibition opened.

Irritated by the dogmatism of the alleged avant-garde, Duchamp began to doubt altogether the sense of any painting oriented purely towards the visual. While the Impressionists, Fauvists and Cubists had still been able to take up positions in opposition to the official Salon painting of the academies, after 1913 Duchamp developed an artistic programme that strictly rejected the basic principles of an avant-garde that was still in the process of formation. There were two strategies above all that Duchamp deployed in his attack on the principle of art for art's sake: the close link between linguistic and visual elements and the ready-made. In effect these established his position as pioneer of a conceptual view of art.

"People thought of nothing but the physical aspect of painting. No idea of freedom was taught, not the slightest philosophical idea was discussed," remarked Duchamp, looking back on the situation in 1912, and stressing: "I was interested in ideas – not just in visual products. I wanted to place painting at the service of the mind."

He succeeded in impressive fashion with his masterpiece *The Bride Stripped Bare by her Bachelors, even*, conceived between 1913 and 1915, whose realization he pronounced to be "definitively unfinished" in the USA in 1923. For this enigmatic work, which essentially represents the schematic and abstract hint of a complex sexual process, Duchamp used diagrammatic depiction techniques on a large two-part plate of glass. To this visually barely decipherable work he added, in 1934, after a considerable delay, a number of manuscript notes, which he had written while working on the so-called *Large*

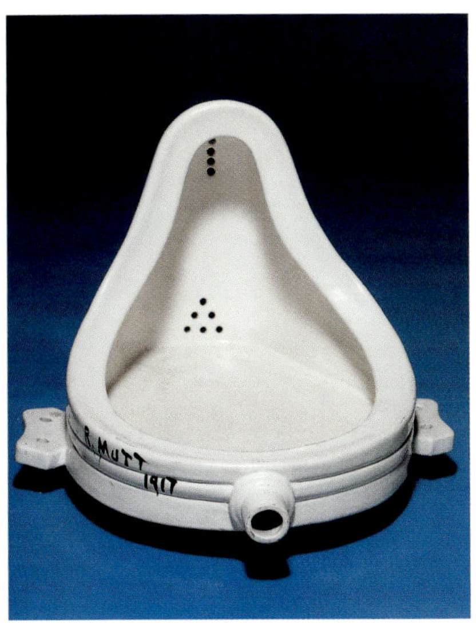

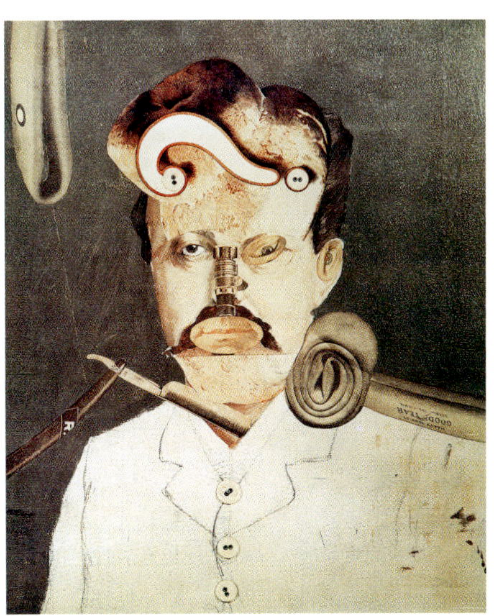

7

8

Glass. These elaborately reproduced notes, summarized in the multiple *The Green Box,* deal with an astonishingly broad spectrum of topics and ideas, revealing a versatility of language, and a tone which swings with ease from scientific sobriety to poetic multivalence. Ultimately the notes explain and transfigure in equal measure what is happening on the *Large Glass*. For in the combination of text and picture, Duchamp kept the focal point of meaning of his work deliberately vague, and invited the beholder/reader to take part in what are ultimately inconcludable reflections on the meaning of the work.

Duchamp's strategy of the "ready-mades", frequently interpreted as an anti-art gesture, is perhaps even more radical than the reverbalization of art as implemented in the *Large Glass*. This strategy can best be explained by reference to the urinal which has gone down in the annals of the history of art.

In 1917, under the pseudonym of Richard Mutt, Duchamp, who had been living in New York since 1915, entered a standard commercially available porcelain urinal for the exhibition at the progressive Society of Independent Artists, of which he was himself a member, giving it the title *Fountain*. As was to be expected, the exhibition committee refused to exhibit this "indecent" object, since it "could in no circumstances be considered a work of art". Thereupon Duchamp resigned from the Society and added to the affront by having his girl-friend Beatrice Wood write a caustic statement in their magazine "The Blind Man".

With this staged institutional scandal, the ready-made left the private sphere of mere intention – Duchamp had already selected and titled a number of objects, all of which had a more or less clear reference to the *Large Glass* – and took on the status of an object seriously challenging art-theoretical assumptions. It raises the question of the boundary between art and non-art, and insists that this decision cannot be dependent on an aesthetic judgement however formulated, but on convention. Duchamp evidently no longer regarded this convention any longer as given and immutable, but as flexible and continually redefinable in artistic practice. With the simple idea of interrupting the use-flow of everyday things, and in the choice and (re-)naming of a ubiquitous object, investing the same with new dimensions of meaning, the field of what could be counted as art was dramatically extended and on principle no longer susceptible to normative delimitation. The question of what is art becomes a question of the context in which ideas, objects, and pictures are produced and perceived. It is precisely this insight of the context-dependence of art, implicit in the ready-made, that was to make Duchamp so important for the development of the Conceptual Art of the 1960s.

1967 — Sol LeWitt publishes "Paragraphs on Conceptual Art"
1968 — Assassination of leading civil-rights activist Martin Luther King in Memphis, Tennessee

---

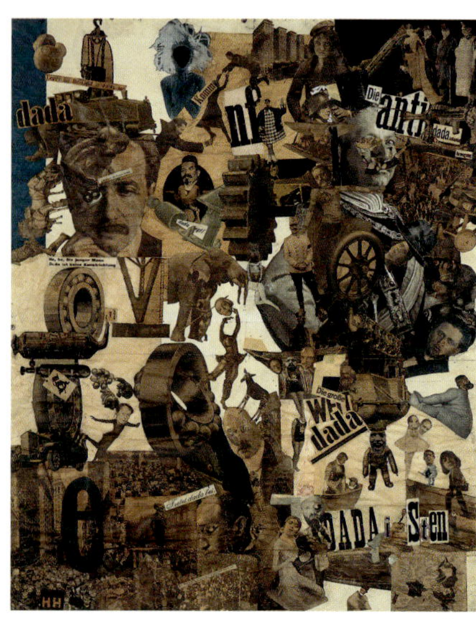

9. HANNAH HÖCH

Incision with the Dada Kitchen Knife through Germany's last Weimar Beer-belly Cultural Epoch
1920, collage, 114 x 90 cm
Berlin, Neue Nationalgalerie

10. VLADIMIR TATLIN

Model for a Memorial to the Third International
1919, wood, steel and glass, 420 x 300 cm
Photo of the original, Moscow (destroyed)

11. ALEXANDER RODCHENKO

Design for a kiosk, motto "Bisiaks"
1919, gouache and ink-wash on paper,
51 x 34.5 cm
Moscow, Private collection

9

Dada and constructivism

Alongside the work of Duchamp, two artistic movements should be singled out for special mention, both of which questioned the autonomy of art at an early date. Both Russian Constructivism and Dada have at their heart a fundamental critique of the paradigm of art for art's sake.

During the Great War, the political elite and the mostly monarchical social systems lost their credibility almost everywhere on the European continent. In strict opposition to the existing social order and the bourgeois view of art, there formed in Zurich, in 1916, the first Dada grouping in the Cabaret Voltaire. The leading protagonists included Hans Arp, Hugo Ball, and Tristan Tzara. The Dada movement soon took on international dimensions, and artists joined together in the spirit of Dada in Paris, Berlin and New York. As suggested by the very name Dada, the movement was characterized by irrationalist and anti-artistic tendencies. Dada was an art of doubt, of polemics, of irony, which had lost all its ultimate truths. While Duchamp, Francis Picabia, Man Ray and others were using their sharp wits to poke fun at the public's good taste, the Dada movement, especially in Berlin, grew increasingly politicized. After the collapse of the German November Revolution of 1918 – an outcome which disappointed many artists – and its seamless transition into the bourgeois Weimar Republic, art was deployed openly for political purposes. Alongside the production and distribution of pamphlets and manifestos were staged theatre and cabaret performances and other activities, in which artists passionately advocated a basic change in social conditions. Artists such as Raoul Hausmann, George Grosz, Hannah Höch and John Heartfield developed and refined the techniques of photomontage and photocollage, which in their hands became instruments of artistic-cum-political agitation.

In Russia the successful October Revolution of 1917 had already led to quite different social conditions from those prevailing in Germany or the United States. The victory of the Communists gave the Russian avant-garde, for a brief period at least, the opportunity of taking an active part in shaping a new Communist society. Artists such as Alexander Rodchenko, Vladimir Tatlin and the Stenberg brothers developed an art that quickly transcended esoteric Suprematism and pushed on from the surface of the canvas to the design of three-dimensional space. In the process, the so-called laboratory art of Russian Constructivism turned towards the trying-out of new materials whose artistic organization would benefit the whole of society. The new art was intended to be absorbed into revolutionary life, and in this spirit Rodchenko wrote: "Constructive life is the art of the future. Conscious and organised life, the ability to see and construct, that is modern art… Attentiveness, experience, purpose, construction, technology and mathematics, these are the fellow-travellers of contemporary art."

1968 — Massacre of Vietnamese civilians by American soldiers in My Lai
1968 — Major student unrest in Western Europe and North America　　　　**1968 — Death of Marcel Duchamp**

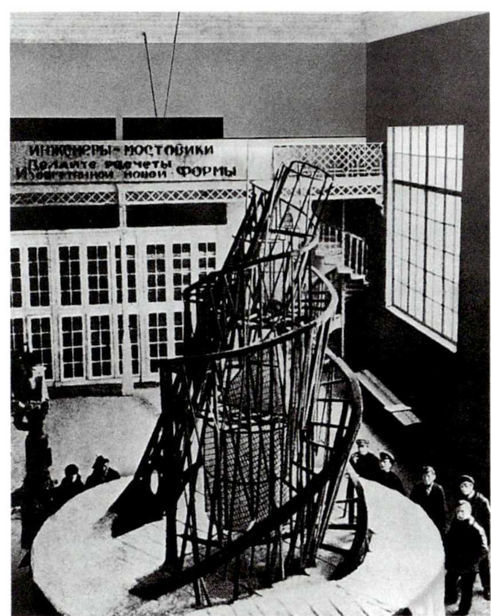

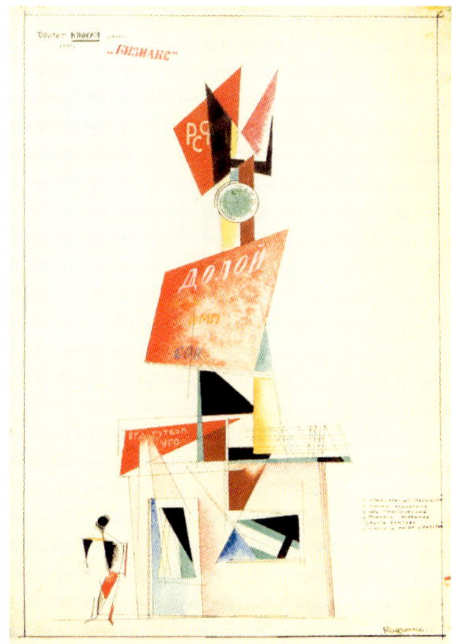

10   11

For a variety of reasons, the criticism of aestheticizing tendencies in modern art which culminated in Dada, Constructivism and a little later in Surrealism, was not successful. It was above all the unstable political situation in Europe that contributed to a failure of the avant-garde in the 1930s and 1940s. Under Fascism and Stalinism it was brutally repressed, and had to re-form in western Europe after the Second World War in totally changed conditions. In contrast to Europe, the United States saw a further delay in the reception of early avant-garde boundary-crossing, due largely to Social Realism, Abstract Expressionism and the dominance of Formalism à la Greenberg in the post-war period.

The Art of the 1960s and the crisis of Modernism

This brief outline of the early avant-garde is not meant to provide ammunition for a view of tendentious art history in which Modernism starts with Cézanne and necessarily leads, via Duchamp, to Conceptual Art in the 1960s. The very concurrence of different approaches in the art of the 1960s would take such a notion *ad absurdum*. The development of Modernism was, on the contrary, itself a story full of caesuras and contradictions. Thus artists were able, in the changed conditions of the 1950s and 1960s, particularly in the USA, to link up with the legacy of the "repressed" avant-garde, especially since there the paradigm of Modernism still continued almost unchanged in the shape of Formalism à la Greenberg.

The late 1950s saw the beginnings of a change in the social and political climate of Europe and the United States. After a decade which in the USA had been dominated by the Cold War, the McCarthy-led anti-communist witch-hunt, and bigoted prudery, the early 1960s the time seemed ripe for major changes in culture and society. In Europe, after years of economic growth, a new generation began to take a critical look at the role played by their parents' generation in the Second World War. Political utopias were revived, and vehemently debated in student circles. The social reality of bourgeois capitalism was no longer uncritically accepted on either side of the Atlantic, and on both sides, a search was started for alternatives or at least reforms. In this climate, art could no longer continue living in its ivory tower where the beautiful, the true and the good reigned supreme.

In Europe, the Situationists and the artists of the COBRA group forced a politicization of art, while in the USA the international Fluxus movement formed around the architect, artist and organizer George Maciunas. In the early 1960s, this movement explicitly took up the political utopianism of Russian Constructivism, and at the same time rediscovered the instruments of humour and irony which had been tried out by the Dadaists, in order to break open the fossilized formal-aesthetic view of art.

1968 — "Prospect 68", initiated by gallery-owners Konrad Fischer and Hans Strelow, at the Kunsthalle Düsseldorf
1968 — Douglas Huebler exhibits at the Seth Siegelaub Gallery in New York   **1968 — Richard Nixon elected President of the USA**

12

Pop Art, at about the same time, was making the banal motifs of advertising and mass consumption "art-worthy", and artists such as Andy Warhol, with the silk-screen printing process, introduced into painting the serial production techniques of highly developed capitalism. Minimal Art raised serious doubts about the fundamental assumptions of Greenberg aesthetics. Thus Donald Judd, in his influential 1965 essay "Specific Objects", threw out the strict separation of artistic genres when he wrote: "Half or more of the best new work in the last few years has been neither painting nor sculpture." At the same time, many Minimal Artists rejected any transcendental view of art. Their objects and the materials they used were no longer to point beyond themselves. A row of metal plates was suddenly wanted to be no more than a row of metal plates. In addition, the Minimal Artists started to theorize on the perception of their objects. Robert Morris, for example, referring to gestalt theory, assumed a whole-body, rather than a purely visual, perception of his extreme reductionist works. In this way, a temporal dimension was introduced to artistic perception, which in a different way also came about with the happenings of the Fluxus artists, having already been anticipated a decade earlier in avant-garde music by the artist and composer John Cage.

For a long time, Clement Greenberg ignored all these practices on the part of the neo-avant-garde that contradicted his theory. When he finally saw himself constrained to react, in his 1967 essay "Recentness of Sculpture" he simply wrote off the art forms in question as insignificant "Novelty Art". He obstinately persisted in his opinion that Modernism was to be understood as a progressive process of reduction, in which every artistic genre had to reveal its irreversible conditions in accordance with its own laws. Art for Greenberg was exclusively a matter of the visual, whereby the quality of a work of art was to be determined in a viewing divorced from any temporal or spatial context and in its objective materiality. For him, the work of art was autonomous and independent of any non-artistic influences.

In December 1966 the 25-year-old Dan Graham published a curious article in "Arts Magazine", which at first sight looks like a sociological essay and in dry descriptive fashion looks at the serial architecture of provincial America. On a double-page spread, roughly equal-sized blocks of text and colour photographs alternate. Among other things, Graham presented the individual building types, listed the male and female predilections regarding colour, listed the combinations of different building types possible in a block of eight buildings, and garnished this bald information with amateur photographs.

The importance of this unassuming article is not confined to the fact that in *Homes for America* Graham was applying a basic principle of Minimal Art the juxtaposition of identical elements to the typo-

Dan Graham

12. MEL RAMSDEN (ART & LANGUAGE)

Secret Painting
1967/68, Letraset on cardboard, acrylic on canvas,
two parts, each 31 x 31 cm
Berlin, Staatliche Museen zu Berlin – Preußischer
Kulturbesitz, Nationalgalerie, Marzona collection

13. DAN GRAHAM

Homes for America
1966, printed text and photos on paper,
each 101 x 76 cm
Courtesy Marian Goodman Gallery, New York

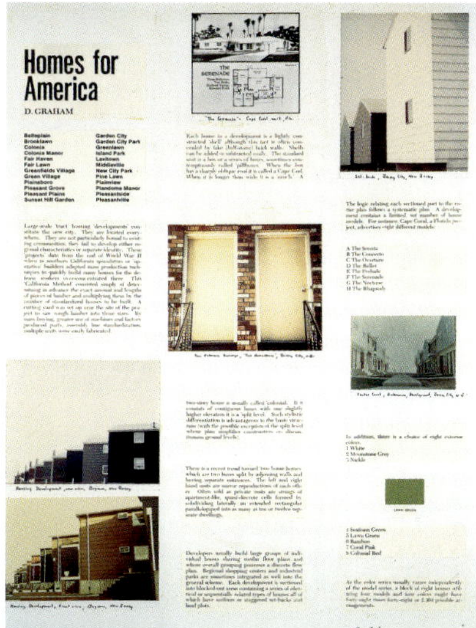

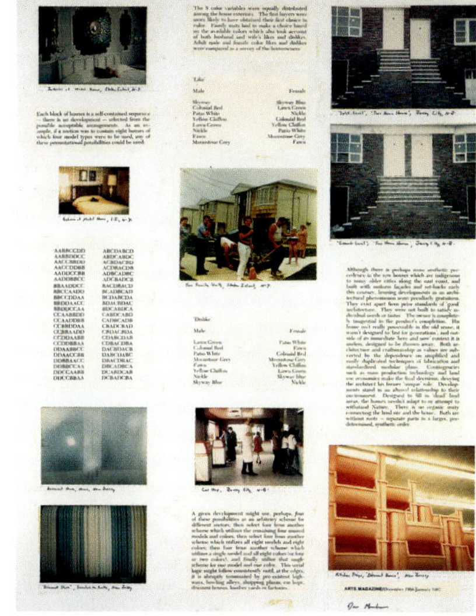

13

graphical design of a magazine article by giving equal treatment to blocks of text and pictures. The laconic work points beyond this to a central reason for the crisis in Modernism. For how can an essential subjectivism be upheld in art, how can art be credibly understood as an autonomous expression of artistic individuality, if in our modern consumer society subjectivity itself is reduced to the choice between mass-produced goods? The contradiction which becomes obvious in Graham's article between an increasingly de-individualized society and an aesthetic which makes subjective expression absolute, is perceived by many artists; in early Conceptual Art it was thematized time and again.

Against this background, Sigmar Polke, for example, puts an ironic gloss on the idea of "artistic inspiration" with his 1969 picture *Höhere Wesen befahlen: rechte obere Ecke schwarz malen!* (Higher beings commanded: paint the top right-hand corner black!). Mel Ramsden demystifies the mystical atmosphere that shrouded Abstract Expressionism with the monochrome *Secret Painting* (1967/68), which was accompanied by the following text: "The content of this painting is invisible; the character and dimension of the content are to be kept permanently secret, known only to the artist." The idea of the artist as a lonely creative genius was just as obsolete in the 1960s as in the classical genres of painting and sculpture.

It was obvious that the artistic practices of Fluxus, Minimal Art and Pop Art were no longer compatible with the normative aesthetic of Clement Greenberg, and were leading to a profound crisis in Modernism, which was also a crisis of a subject-centred philosophy and aesthetic. Suddenly the recognition of the conventional nature of art, concealed in the Duchamp ready-made, could no longer be swept under the table, and so a young generation of artists posed the old question anew: "What is art?" or rather: "What can art be?" Many of the answers formulated between 1966 and 1972 can be understood as what we today summarize under the term Conceptual Art.

Analyses and Language Games

While the West Coast of the United States saw artists like Ed Ruscha, John Baldessari and Bruce Nauman striking out for conceptual shores in, if anything, an intuitive manner, a group of artists associated with the gallery owner and promoter Seth Siegelaub in New York were working on a theoretically oriented re-underpinning of art. Robert Barry, Douglas Huebler, Joseph Kosuth and Lawrence Weiner each evolved their own concepts, in which the traditional art object evaporated, so to speak, in different ways.

1969 — Wim Beeren curates the exhibition "Op losse Schroeven: Situaties en cryptostructuren", Stedelijk Museum, Amsterdam, and Harald Szeemann curates "Live in Your Head. When Attitudes Become Form", Kunsthalle Bern

---

1969 MARCH 1969
SUN MON TUE WED THU FRI SAT
1
2 3 4 5 6 7 8
9 10 11 12 13 14 15
16 17 18 19 20 21 22
23/30 24/31 25 26 27 28 29

14

during the exhibition the gallery will be closed.

15

Until 1967 Lawrence Weiner had worked on pictures which related unambiguously to Minimal Art. He deliberately left the coloration and size to his buyers or clients, and sought in addition to eliminate the expressive element of painting as far as possible by the use of a standardized application of paint. The concept of the picture series already seemed more important than the individual results of their realization, and for this reason Weiner dispensed with signatures on his pictures. A little later he began to question on principle the point of actually executing his works at all, and in 1968 he drew up a programmatic statement, which was to accompany the publication of his works from then on. Theory and art at the same time, it states:

"1. The artist may construct the work.

2. The work may be fabricated.

3. The work need not be built.

Each being equal and consistent with the intent of the artist the decision as to condition rests with the receiver upon the occasion of receivership."

From then on, Weiner presented his works in the form of statements which made frequent use of past participles. Works such as *SIX TEN PENNY COMMON STEEL NAILS DRIVEN INTO THE FLOOR AT INDICATED TERMINAL POINTS* (1968), *A WALL STAINED BY WATER* (1969), and *AN OBJECT SECURED UPON A THRESHOLD* (1969) baldly describe in plain fashion actions, processes or states of materials and present these as facts. Although Weiner did go on "fabricating" some of his works right on into the 1970s, every fabrication, whether by himself or by others, was for him just one of infinitely many possibilities of equal worth. The declared equivalence of the different states of his "word sculptures" manifests not only a rejection of object-linked aesthetics, but also an ethical and political attitude, because his view of art, among other things, attacks the status of the work of art as simply a commodity available to the few. In an artist text of 1969, Weiner emphasized the libertarian and egalitarian aspect of his approach: "People, buying my stuff, can take it wherever they go and can rebuild it if they choose. If they keep it in their heads, that's fine too. They don't have to buy it to have it – they can have it just by knowing it… Art that imposes conditions – human or otherwise – on the receiver for its appreciation in my eyes constitutes aesthetic fascism."

In a line of development comparable with that of Weiner, in about 1968 Robert Barry and Douglas Huebler – who had undertaken investigations rooted in Minimal Art, in the fields of painting (Barry) and sculpture (Huebler) – reached a point at which occasionally the work of art literally dissolved into thin air. After Barry had experimented for a short time with the bracing of almost invisible

14.

<u>1969 March 1969</u>
1969, cover of the exhibition catalogue,
Seth Siegelaub Gallery, 17.8 x 21.6 cm
Private collection

15. ROBERT BARRY

<u>During the Exhibition the Gallery will be Closed</u>
1967, exhibition at the Art & Project Gallery, Amsterdam

16. JOSEPH KOSUTH

<u>Ruler</u>
1965, photograph, ruler and phototext,
120 x 125 cm
Berlin, Staatliche Museen zu Berlin – Preußischer
Kulturbesitz, Nationalgalerie, Marzona collection

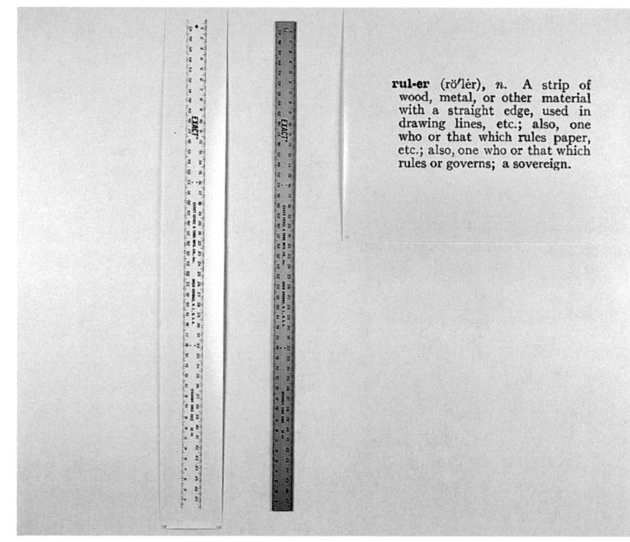

16

nylon threads, he began to work soon afterwards with totally invisible materials. For the – since famous – group exhibition "1969 March 1969", conceived by Seth Siegelaub essentially in the form of a catalogue, Barry's contribution consisted of the announcement that on the morning of 5 March he would release two cubic feet of helium into the atmosphere. Previously he had already exhibited works consisting of inaudible radio waves. But while these works were still based on actually present, albeit sensorily imperceptible physico-chemical phenomena, Barry soon extended his interest to the sphere of the human (sub)consciousness.

For the 1969 "Konzeption – Conception" exhibition in Leverkusen, Barry entered five verbal communications which related to unconscious processes. Works such as *SOMETHING WHICH IS UNKNOWN TO ME, BUT WHICH WORKS UPON ME* and *SOMETHING WHICH IS VERY NEAR IN PLACE AND TIME BUT NOT YET KNOWN TO ME* can no longer be unambiguously defined, and must on principle mean something different to every recipient. In their open linguistic form, these works by Barry resign themselves to the loss of concrete reference in order to set in motion mental processes in their recipients. Thus Barry's verbal communications are basically only the starting-points of works that embrace the totality of the mental activity they initiate on the part of the recipient.

"The world is full of objects, more or less interesting; I do not wish to add anymore. I prefer simply to state the existence of things in terms of time and/or place," wrote Douglas Huebler in 1969, shortly after he had started work on projects which could draw upon, as material, virtually at least, the totality of all documentable facts. Huebler's *Location* and *Duration Pieces* each follow rules laid down arbitrarily in advance, according to which events, spatial and/or temporal relationships are documented which are not accessible to direct perception. In the arrangement of text, cards and photographs, Huebler thus presents a record of reality that in his constructed system becomes recognizable as a function of space and time.

For the *Duration Piece #6*, for example, Huebler had a square measuring about 2 x 2 metres in the entrance zone of the Siegelaub Gallery strewn with sawdust. The young artist Adrian Piper was instructed to photograph the gradually dissolving square over a period of six hours at 30-minute intervals, and to stick the resulting polaroids to the gallery wall in non-chronological order. The photographs, and the description of what had been done, together constituted the work, so that it was left to the imagination of the beholder to understand the process as documented.

The artistic approaches of Barry, Weiner, and Huebler are in accord in two central points. They all relate to a reality, albeit one

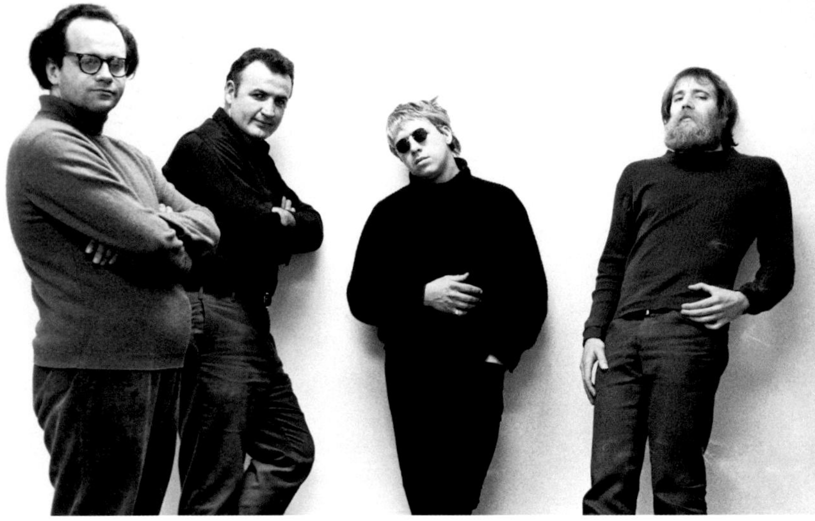

17.

<u>Robert Barry, Douglas Huebler, Joseph Kosuth, Lawrence Weiner</u>
The four artists took part in the "January 5–31" exhibition at the Seth Siegelaub Gallery, New York, in 1969.
Courtesy the Siegelaub Collection & Archives at the Stichting Egress Foundation Amsterdam

18. LAWRENCE WEINER

<u>A Primer</u>
1972, book cover
Private collection

19. DOUGLAS HUEBLER

<u>Variable Piece No. 98</u>
1973, photo-collage, 80 x 80 cm
Berlin, Staatliche Museen zu Berlin – Preußischer Kulturbesitz, Nationalgalerie, Marzona collection

not always accessible to the senses, and reject the presentation of objects, whose qualities are immediately accessible to sensory perception, in favour of the use of language. Thus they deny Greenberg's dictum that the experience of art is necessarily visual. In each conception a view of language is expressed, albeit drastically different in each case.

Weiner's project understands language as a transitory vehicle and as a material that can take on sculptural qualities when it is read. Barry by contrast understands the linguistic form of his works as a possibility of describing or triggering visually non-perceptible energetic processes, while Huebler, in the fusion of language and document, brings art closer to the everyday and at the same time noticeable extends its area of reach.

Joseph Kosuth, the fourth of the artists to be associated with Siegelaub at an early date, developed, from a particular interpretation of the ready-mades and the insights of positivist linguistic philosophy, a form of conceptual art which strictly rejects any relationship to reality. From his early works, which, like *One and Three Chairs* (1965/66), still presented a real object in association with its representation as a photographic image and dictionary definition, Kosuth quickly pressed forward to purely abstract concepts, whose dictionary definitions he enlarged, unchanged by the negative process, onto photo-

graphic paper. Works such as *Meaning* or *Universal* are part of an extended series, *First Investigation*, which, not for nothing, bears the superordinate title *Titled (Art as Idea as Idea)*. As Kosuth wanted at all costs to avoid any pictorial interpretation of his works, it was not long before he rejected the presentation of his investigations on photographic paper, and began to publish them in the advertising columns of magazines.

The central importance of Duchamp's ready-mades lay for Kosuth in their allegedly tautological structure. From his point of view, they say nothing more than: "This object is art because it is art." In his 1969 essay "Art after Philosophy", Kosuth transferred the idea of the tautological structure of the ready-made into art as such: "What art has in common with logic and mathematics is that it is a tautology; i. e. the 'art idea' (or 'work') and art are the same and can be appreciated as art without going outside the context of art for verification." Ironically, Kosuth, in spite of radically eliminating the aesthetic object, at first maintained the principle, in his project of a "pure" Conceptual Art, of art for art's sake, something that already Duchamp had wanted to consign to history.

In England in 1968, Terry Atkinson, David Bainbridge, Michael Baldwin and Harold Hurrell founded the joint project "Art & Language". At first integrated into an academic context, a year later they

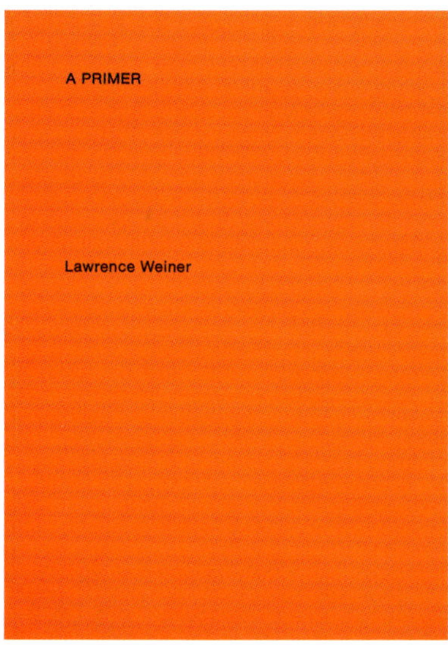

18

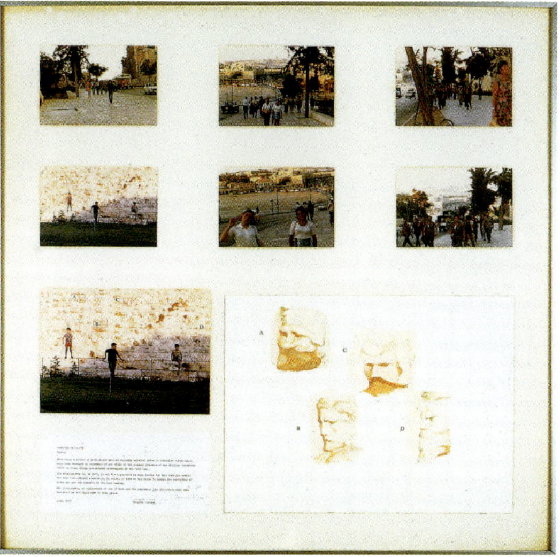

19

published the first number of the magazine "Art-Language". Starting out from the methods of linguistic philosophy, the group presented in various forms the results of their investigations and analyses, which at first addressed the logical contradictions of minimalist aesthetics, dissected different systems of the production of meaning, and later critically questioned the ideological conditions of the institutionalization of art. Conversations, classes, art criticism and philosophy were part of an open discourse, which was then itself viewed as art. Between 1969 and 1975, the configuration of the group changed a number of times, and new artists joined the collective, while some founding members distanced themselves because of political differences. As Conceptual Art established itself relatively quickly on the art market, from the mid-1970s the history of Conceptual Art itself became the focus of the theoretical reflections of Art & Language.

serial systems

Alongside the purely linguistically understood forms of Conceptual Art, at the same time there developed from Minimal Art conceptual approaches relating to mathematical-geometric, temporo-spatial, typological, and biographical systems. The conceptual component of Minimal Art became evident for the first time in the exhibition organized by Mel Bochner in 1966, entitled "Working Drawings and Other Visible Things on Paper Not Necessarily Meant to Be Viewed as Art".

In the School of Visual Arts, Bochner displayed four identical books, in which he photocopied sketches, drawings, blueprints, construction descriptions, and other material given to him by a few Minimal Artists, juxtaposed without further commentary. With its simple form of presentation, Bochner's project anticipated the unpretentious exhibition practice of later Conceptual Art, and at the same time raised the question of who was responsible, as "author" for the exhibition.

Not long afterwards, Bochner turned to projects that addressed the issue of the often contradictory relationship between visual and conceptual perception. In his *Measurement Rooms*, for example, he imposed an abstract system on the empty exhibition rooms by measuring them out exactly and noting the measurements of the individual zones on adhesive strips placed in the middle of the edges of the walls. In this way, Bochner contrasted the geometrically abstract and the actual existence of the exhibition rooms, which were now both accessible to the perception as a result of his intervention.

In 1967 Sol LeWitt, until then generally associated with Minimal Art, published his "Paragraphs on Conceptual Art". In accord with

1970 — Seminal Conceptual Art exhibition: "Conceptual Art and Conceptual Aspects" in the New York Cultural Center
1970 — "Conceptual art, arte povera, land art" in Turin

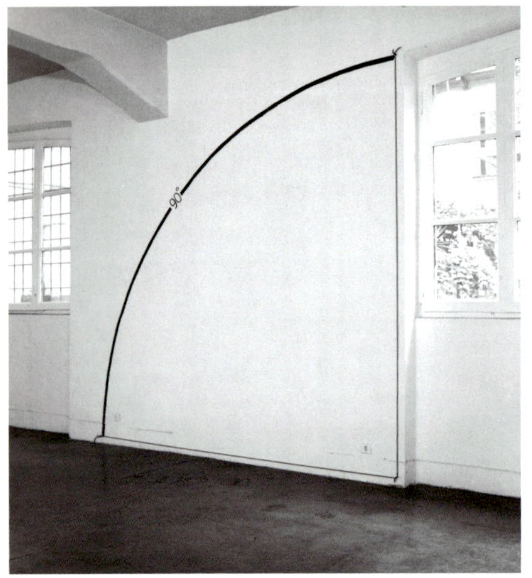

20

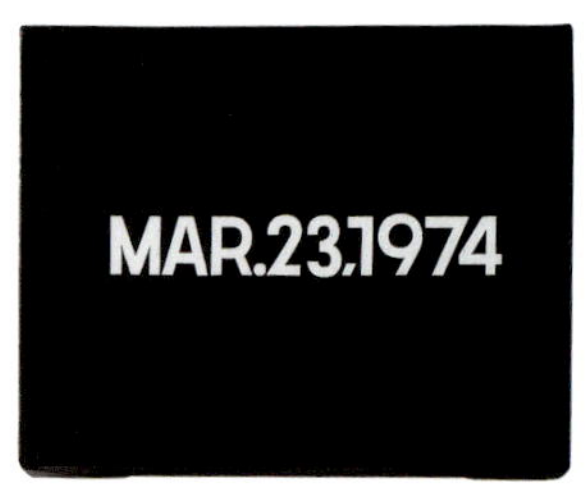

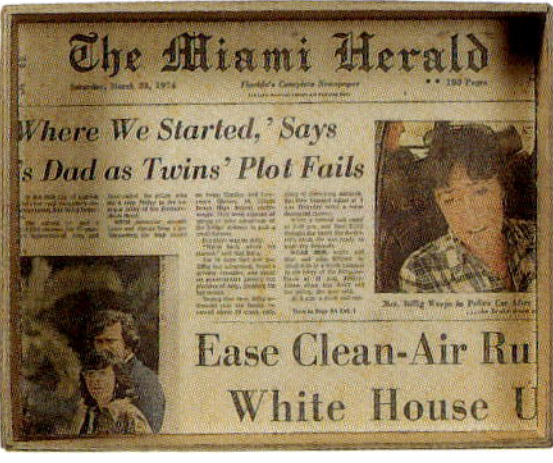

21

20. MEL BOCHNER

<u>Degrees (Quarter Circle)</u>
Installation at the Galleria Sperone, Turin
Photography: Berlin, Staatliche Museen zu Berlin –
Preußischer Kulturbesitz, Kunstbibliothek,
Marzona collection

21. ON KAWARA

<u>Mar. 23. 1974</u>
1974, acrylic on canvas, 20.3 x 25.4 cm,
from the *Today Series*, 1966 to date
Private collection

22. SOL LEWITT

<u>Wall Drawing #1, Drawing Series II 14 (A&B)</u>
1968, black pencil, variable dimensions
First wall drawing installed at Paula Cooper Gallery
in October 1968, installation view at San Francisco
Museum of Modern Art
Courtesy Paula Cooper Gallery, New York

many conceptual artists, LeWitt also accorded top priority to the idea or the concept, albeit clinging to the principle of its material realization. For LeWitt, Conceptual Art is neither the expression of philosophical ideas nor necessarily based on the rules of logic, but an "intuitive" and "irrational" undertaking. Starting from the simple geometric form of the cube, LeWitt began as early as 1966 to spell out the possible permutations of this shape in relatively simple, but in any case arbitrarily chosen, systems; during the process it soon became clear that even the simplest premises can lead to astonishingly complex structures when completely realized. Thus the *Serial Project No. 1 (ABCD)* on a 4 x 4 metre surface shows the visual complexity of "all relevant combinations" of open and closed cubes and squares, which for their part also contain open or closed cubes or squares.

In its consistency and obsessiveness, the artistic approach of Hanne Darboven is certainly comparable to that of LeWitt. Her first works, which are based on the mathematical abstraction of the calendrical system, appeared in 1968. In elaborate procedures, Darboven worked out the pictorialization of previously determined periods of time – sometimes a particular year, or maybe a whole century – in many-part series of drawings. From each date of the period in question, she drew the crossfoot (the sum of the digits) and frequently complicated the numerical results by subjecting them to further arith-metical operations. Each figure was inserted into a graphic grid, the result being complex diagrams in which the phenomenon of time is reflected in dual fashion. For Darboven's handwritten sequences of figures point not only to the continuity of the historical course of time that they represent, but are also in a sense a kind of index to the real time actually spent on their own creation. In the early 1970s, Darboven began to integrate language and later also pictorial material into her series of drawings.

Roman Opalka's and On Kawara's treatments of the phenomenon of time seem to be closely linked with their own biographies. For the conception of his series of *Infinity Paintings*, Opalka used the simple principle of progression. In 1965 he completed the first picture, which bore the title *1965/1 – ∞ (Detail 1 – 35327)*, which begins in the top left with the white figure 1 on a black background and by adding 1 in rows of numbers arranged one above the other, progresses to the number 35327. The second picture in the series follows on in the top left with the number 35328 and so on. All pictures in the series are the same size and executed using the same technique. In the early 1970s, the backgrounds then became grey, and Opalka increased the proportion of white paint from picture to picture by 1 %, which, in theory at least, could lead to the numbers becoming indistinguishable from the background when the latter becomes white

1970 — "Information" in the Museum of Modern Art, New York, establishes Conceptual Art as the major trend in the USA
1970 — "995.000" at the Vancouver Art Gallery with all the major exponents of Conceptual Art

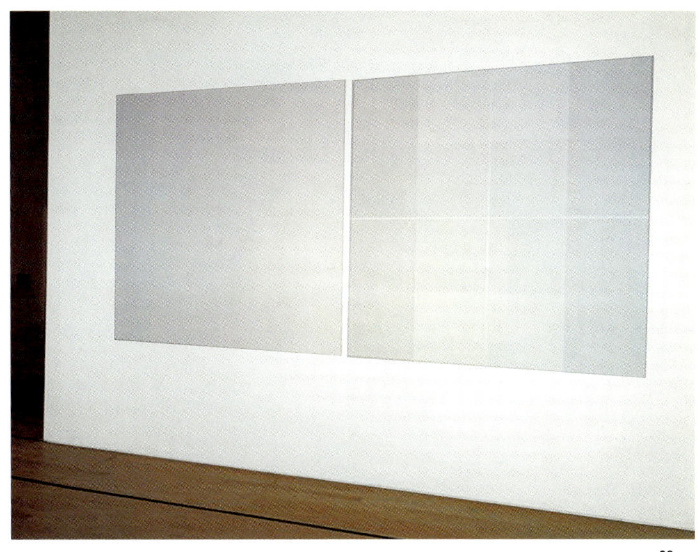

> **"your work isn't a high stakes, nail-biting professional challenge. it's a form of play. Lighten up and have fun with it."**
>
> Sol LeWitt

itself. For every picture, Opalka produced a sound recording, in which he is heard counting the numbers on the canvas, and having finished a picture, he also took a photographic self-portrait. Thus the progressive act of painting/counting – in other words the approach to infinity already hinted at in the title – and the progressive aging of the artist and the fact of his own mortality are contrasted with each other in the continuous activity.

Since 1966, the Japanese artist On Kawara has been painting pictures in which there is nothing to be seen apart from the date of the day in question painted in white on a monochrome background. The pictures are painted using a time-consuming technique and, if one is not finished by midnight, it is destroyed. The *Date Paintings*, which vary in size and colour, form part of the *Today Series, 1966 to the Present*, in which Kawara objectifies his own biography up to the present and in a sense transforms it into a real-time system that continues until his death. For the postcard series *I Got Up*, every day Kawara sent two postcards to friends or acquaintances, each marked with the exact time, date and place; in this way, he assured them of his continued existence. Between 1968 and 1979 he kept up this system of communication, in which with logical thoroughness, he aligned his consciousness (the moment of awakening) with the verifiable data of his existence (represented by the place and date).

In the 1960s many artists working in the conceptual field discovered the potential of seriality locked away in the reproduction media of film and photography. Thus as early as 1963 John Baldessari documented the happening of banal events in photo sequences, while Ed Ruscha, in artist books like *Twenty-six Gasoline Stations* or *Nine Swimming Pools,* presented a number, fixed in advance, of intentionally "art-less" photographs, which on his own admission he classed as ready-mades.

In Germany, Bernd and Hilla Becher, Hans-Peter Feldmann and Peter Roehr, among others, developed serial concepts of photography, albeit differing hugely one from another. In the late 1960s, Feldmann began to self-publish in small-format books, pictures he had either found or taken himself. He gave them such laconic titles as *6 Bilder* (6 pictures). In these and other works, such as *Alle Kleider einer Frau* (All Clothes of a Woman, 1974), the boundary dissolves between the picture as art work and the picture as everyday phenomenon.

By contrast, in the early 1960s Bernd and Hilla Becher took up an artistic position whose faith in the authenticity of the photographic image still seemed intact, and which in addition revealed a serious interest in the subject of the photographic depiction. In shots based on precisely determined parameters, the Bechers devoted themselves to the documentation of industrial architecture threatened with decay.

1971 — "Pier 18" at the Museum of Modern Art, New York

1971 — "Prospect 71 – Projection" at the Städtische Kunsthalle Düsseldorf

---

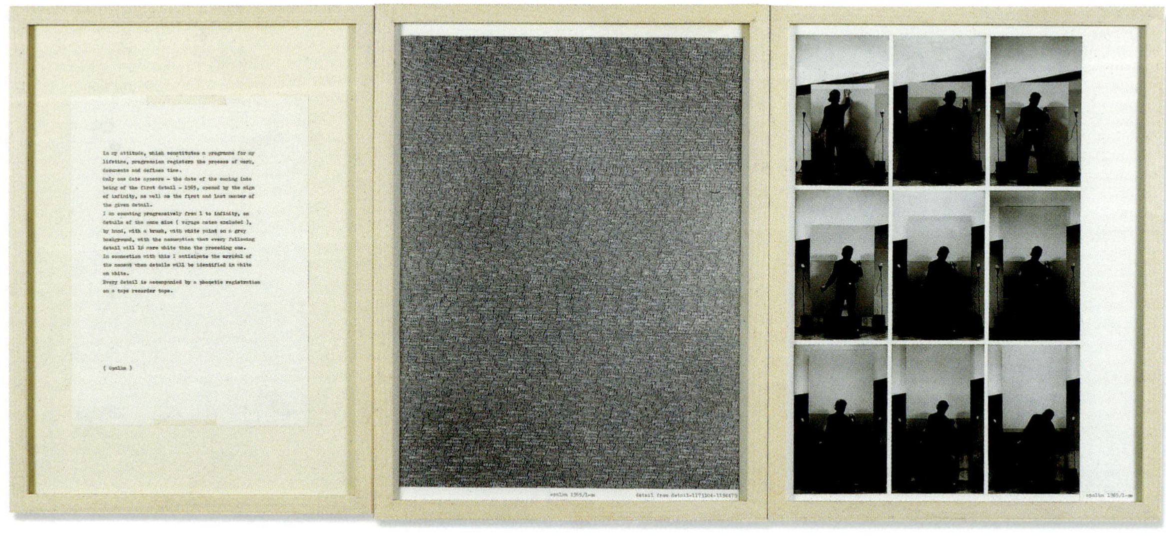

1969 saw the first publication of their photographs of cooling towers, with the title "Anonyme Skulpturen" (Anonymous Sculptures). Linking documentary and conservationist aspects, the Bechers presented their black-and-white photographs of water towers, blast furnaces, winding towers etc. mostly in typological tableaux of up to 30 individual pictures, which allow conclusions to be drawn about the evolution and variation within individual types of buildings.

Performance, intervention and critique of institutions

In the late 1960s, the political climate on both sides of the Atlantic had become increasingly polarized. In America hundreds of thousands protested against the madness of the war in Vietnam and in Europe student protest movements attracted large numbers. People took to the streets in masses, in order to demonstrate for a socialist society, and with ever-increasing frequency skirmishes with authorities took place in Paris and in Berlin in 1968 escalating into street battles that lasted for days and saw injuries and deaths on both sides. Art was not left unscathed by these events either, and artists started to work more and more often in openly political contexts. At the same time as the body was entering into art more and more conspicuously as a medium and as a bearer of experience, female artists in particular were taking up a feminist critique of social discrimination. Other conceptual approaches focused their interest on interventionist projects on the analysis and criticism of the institutional conditions in which art had to work.

For Bruce Nauman, art is everything an artist does in his studio. In accordance with this process-oriented view of art, in 1967 he began to capture on video everyday or absurd actions in his studio. In *Slow Angle Walk (Beckett Walk)* (1968) we see the artist parading a prescribed course up and down his studio for 60 minutes, using an uncomfortable gait. Alongside his video performances, in which he tried out the deployment of his own body as an artistic material at an early stage, at the same time he developed complex installations which also demanded a certain degree of physical effort from his public. His *Corridor Pieces* had to be walked through by exhibition-goers, whereby Nauman often complicated the experience of the work by the use of monitors and video cameras, which he linked up in closed-circuit systems. Unlike Nauman, who always avoided direct contact with the public, some artists continued the Fluxus tradition of happenings and performances, but with different methods and contents.

1971 — Formation of the Greenpeace environmental organization

1971 — Publication of the "Concept Art" survey by Klaus Honnef

1971 — On Kawara exhibits "One Million Years" at the Galerie Konrad Fischer, Düsseldorf

"one of the factors that still keeps me in the studio is that every so often ı have to more or less start all over."

Bruce Nauman

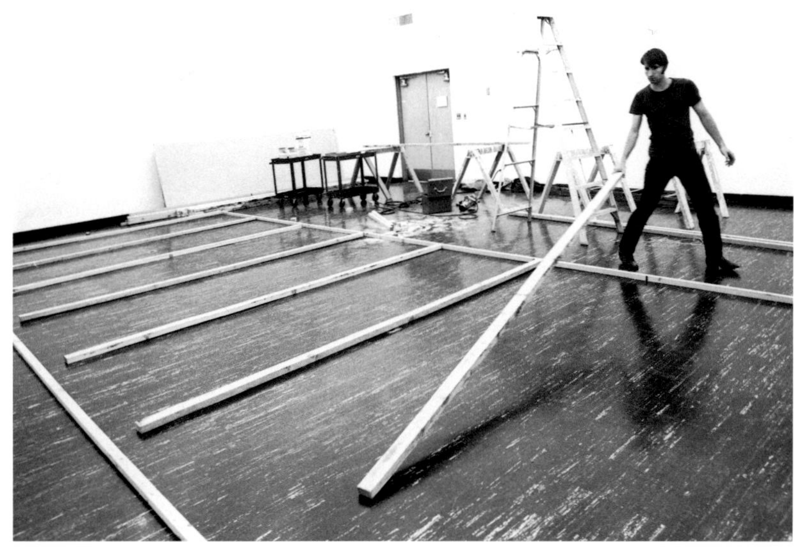

24

Vito Acconci worked in the late 1960s with a whole variety of forms of performance. For example, his *Following Piece* (1969) pursued the idea of totally subordinating his person to another's behaviour. Every day over a period of three weeks, Acconci followed someone selected at random until the person disappeared into a building not accessible to the public. He meticulously catalogued the daily course of events and documented them with photographs. In other performances, he got the public to witness body-related actions or interactions, which often reached the limits of what was physically or psychologically tolerable.

Since 1969, Mierle Laderman Ukeles has been using her Maintenance Art to attack gender-specific role-assignments and social marginalization; she does this by demonstrating as art, in her performances, the act of cleaning a public room, and thus inciting a re-evaluation of certain areas of activity that are traditionally associated with women.

Martha Rosler devotes herself more subtly to the same topic in her video performance *Semiotics of the Kitchen* (1975). The video shows the artist in an apron in the kitchen demonstrating the use of kitchen utensils in alphabetical order, until, obviously frustrated and bored, she starts waving a knife wildly in the air. The work not only criticizes the deadliness and stupidity of the cliché that a woman's place is in the home, and as it were the confirmation and duplication of this stereotype in film and on television, but seems on another level also to be ironically questioning the value of semiotics: that is to say, the analysis of the relationship between signifier and signified.

In the early 1970s Adrian Piper discovered her body, and its physical presence in the public space, as an artistic medium. In the performance pieces of the *Catalysis Series* (1970/71), Piper disturbs the usual course of anonymous encounters in public by, for example, boarding New York buses with a handkerchief hanging out of her mouth or going into shops with a T-shirt on which she has just painted the words "Wet Paint".

Even though early Conceptual Art as a whole was undoubtedly dominated by men, alongside the women already named, others such as Hannah Wilke, Ana Mendieta, Mary Kelly, Eleanor Antin and Laurie Anderson contributed to a major expansion of the reflective zone – whether by radically asserting their right to present their bodies, or by making people aware that our perception of the world and ourselves is not independent of gender identity.

While the conceptual approaches of women artists in the 1960s and early 1970s were, almost without exception, coupled with a political context, this was true on principle of conceptual art by either sex in South America. Not only in Brazil and Argentina did artists

---

1971 — Willoughby Sharp and Elizabeth Béar found the magazine "Avalanche"   **1972 — Harald Szeemann curates "documenta V"**
1972 — "The New Art", London: Anne Seymour curates an exhibition of British Conceptual Art

---

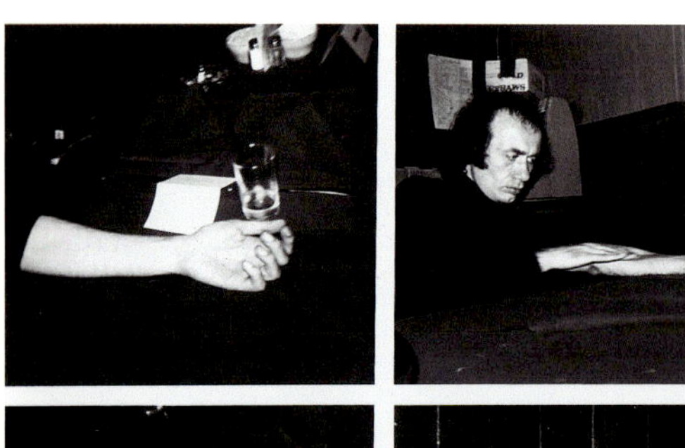

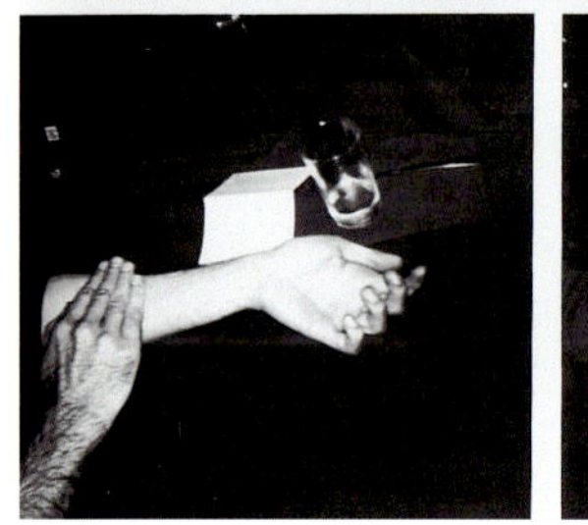

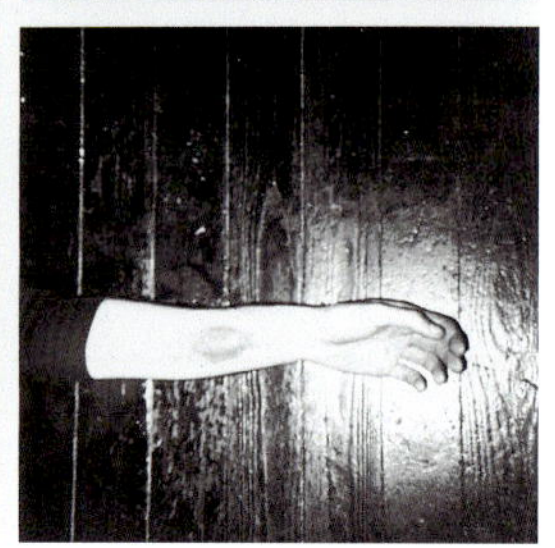

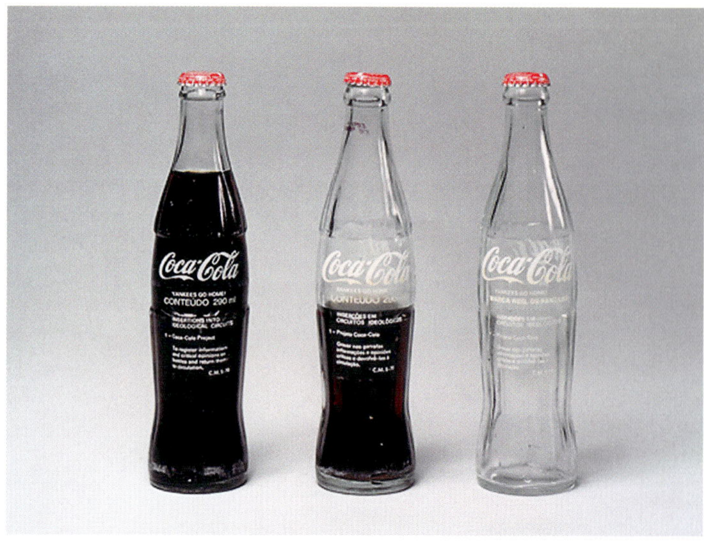

25

26

"it's the viewers which make the pictures."

Marcel Duchamp

see themselves confronted with the oppressive reality of dictatorial regimes, often seeing their work as a part of a comprehensive liberation and protest movement. Numerous artists, in their efforts to regain an oppressed public, developed participatory models, in which a large number of people could come together in collective formations.

Other projects latched onto existing distribution systems, in order to carry their protest into the public arena. Thus in 1970, for example, Cildo Meireles, in his *Insertions into Ideological Circuits* used dollar bills and Coca-Cola bottles, whose use-cycle he briefly interrupted in order to bring them back into circulation modified and equipped with political slogans.

Politically motivated in another way, by contrast, were the approaches of Daniel Buren, Hans Haacke and Marcel Broodthaers, who, each in his own way, confronted the socio-political and ideological implications of the institutionalization of art. They brought to light the now questionable framework conditions of art and the art world, and at the same time sought ways to change them.

conceptual ART – THEN and NOW

The forms of Conceptual Art tried out between 1966 and 1975 can hardly be interpreted as a uniform movement in respect of either medium or content. Even so, four areas can be made out, often not easily distinguishable from each other within which Conceptual Art has contributed to a comprehensive renewal of our understanding of art.

– Firstly, to separate the conception and material realization of the work of art, and to equate the one with the other, leads to a fundamental neglect of the artist's craft abilities and says goodbye, so to speak, to the idea of the work of art as a holistic aesthetic formation.

– Secondly, analytical strategies come up against the modernist dogma of the essentially visual nature of art, a dogma which soon loses its claim to universal validity in the face of artistic practices that radically negate the aesthetic content of art.

– Thirdly, the contextual conditions of art, its status as commodity and its circulation are thematized in artistic projects which, at least in the short term, will succeed in shaking the status quo of the distribution and presentation of art.

– Fourthly, the game with the possibilities of publicity and its functional analysis becomes the focus of different approaches in

25. VITO ACCONCI

<u>Rubbing Piece</u>
1970, Video, rubbing of arm and fingers, in Max's
Kansas City Restaurant, New York, duration: 1 hour
Photography: Berlin, Staatliche Museen zu Berlin –
Preußischer Kulturbesitz, Kunstbibliothek, Marzona
collection

26. CILDO MEIRELES

<u>Insertions into Ideological Circuits:
Coca-Cola Project</u>
1970, Coca-Cola bottles, transferred text,
height 18 cm
Courtesy Galerie Lelong, New York

27. ELEANOR ANTIN

<u>100 Boots Turn the Corner</u>
17 May 1971, 2 p.m., Solana Beach, California
Berlin, Staatliche Museen zu Berlin – Preußischer
Kulturbesitz, Kunstbibliothek, Marzona collection

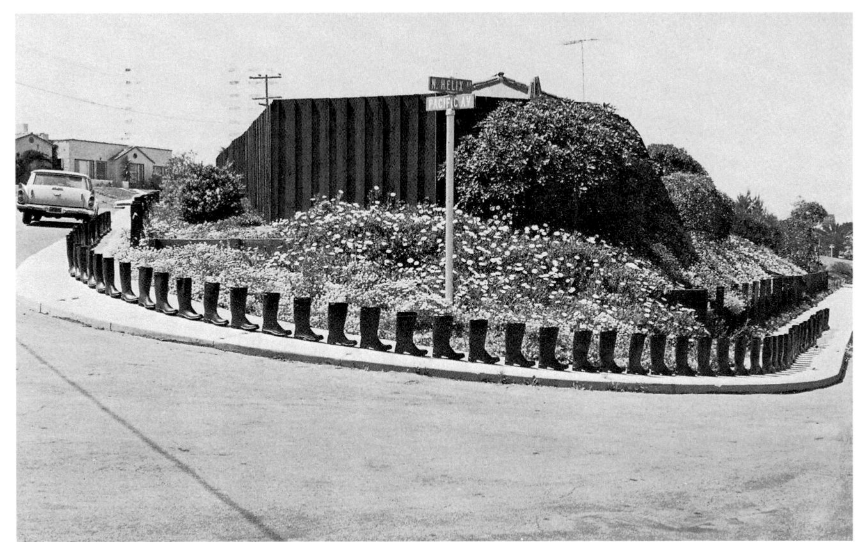

27

which art surrenders its autonomy and becomes anchored in a socio-political context.

Much of what in the early years of Conceptual Art manifested itself on uncertain ground and with a critical intention has come to be taken for granted in the last 35 years, so that the term now has a firm place in contemporary artistic vocabulary. The effects of Conceptual Art are far-reaching, and the work of artists such as Jenny Holzer, Sherrie Levine, Cindy Sherman, Louise Lawler, Richard Prince and others would be unthinkable without the creative confrontation with its Founding Fathers and Mothers. After the crucial opening up of the definition of art, the following decades saw a pluralistic differentiation of art, which, depending on point of view, was sometimes frenetically welcomed under the banner of Post-modernism, and sometimes condemned as a descent into self-indulgence. In any case, ever since it has been impossible to establish binding criteria for the assessment of art. However, this made little impression on either the art market or the institutions, for both grew to a previously unknown degree during the same period.

If we look at the present day, we can state that the seriousness and responsibility with which the early Conceptual Artists subjected the foundations of all aspects of art to critical revision has today given way to a largely ironically playful, detached and ideology-free art prac-tice, whether it is conceptual or not. In step with social reality, art has also changed, and maybe the integrity, utopian naivety and political claims of Conceptual Art can only be understood against the background of a period in which the radical change in art and society was still a real possibility for a young generation.

1973 — Lucy Lippard publishes the annotated collection of materials "Six Years: The Dematerialization of the Art Object"

1973 — The last American troops leave Vietnam   **1973 — Gregory Battcock publishes the critical anthology "Idea Art"**

The BOX in a valise

Cardboard box with miniature replicas, photographs and colour reproductions, 41 x 38 x 10 cm
Private collection

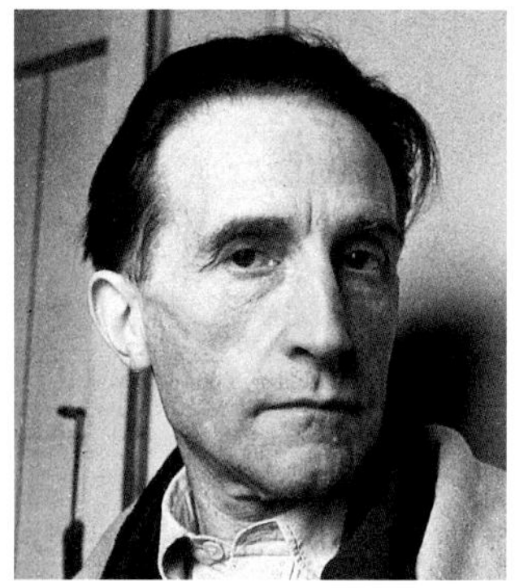

**b. 1887 in Blainville-Crevon,
d. 1968 in Neuilly-sur-Seine, France**

Alongside Pablo Picasso, the Franco-American artist Marcel Duchamp was indisputably the most influential innovative force in art in the 20th century. Irritated by the dogmatism of the Cubist avant-garde, Duchamp began as early as 1913 to doubt the meaning of an art that was oriented purely towards the visual. It was above all two strategies – the close association of linguistic and visual elements, and the ready-made – which Duchamp employed in his attack on the principle of art for art's sake of painterly abstraction, and which underpin his status as a pioneer of the conceptual view of art.

Perhaps even more noticeably than the re-literalization of art set in motion with the work known as *Large Glass* (1915–1923), Duchamp's strategy of the ready-made, often interpreted as an anti-art gesture, put the process of artistic creation on a totally different basis. For his first ready-made in 1914 Duchamp chose an ordinary commercially available bottle-rack in a Parisian department store to become the first ready-made. He added a sign, since lost, and without any further changes declared the bottle-rack to be an art work.

Seemingly totally independent of the craft abilities of the artist, the ready-made demands a reassessment of the conceptual component of art. At the same time, with the simple idea of interrupting the utilitarian cycle of everyday things, and in the choice and (re)naming of ubiquitous objects to give these new dimensions of meaning, Duchamp drastically expanded the field of art. Furthermore, the ready-made raises the question of where to draw the line between art and non-art, and clearly insists that this decision cannot be dependent on any aesthetic judgement however formulated, but rather rests on conventions. The insight, implicit in the strategy of the ready-mades, that these conventions are not immutable givens, but in artistic practice are subject to continual redefinition, was not to be without consequences for the art of the 1960s. So it may be no coincidence that Duchamp's many-layered work was not accorded its true significance until 1963 with a retrospective at the Pasadena Art Museum. Only then did the time appear to be definitively ripe for a recognition of Duchamp's creative redefinition of art and its attendant consequences.

In 1941 Duchamp published the first 20 de-luxe copies of his portable museum *From or by Marcel Duchamp or Rrose Sélavy (The Box in a Valise)*. Six further, differently furnished, versions were to follow before his death. For the first edition of the *Box in a Valise*, Duchamp had collected (for each box) a total of 71 greatly reduced reproductions of his early works, including numerous ready-mades and his showpiece *The Bride Stripped Bare by her Bachelors, even* or *The Large Glass* (1915–1923), in a small suitcase. The fold-out objects were in each case put together by hand in a demanding process. With his miniature museum, Duchamp not only brought about the paradoxical transformation of his industrially produced ready-mades into expensively reproduced multiples, but at the same time pointed to an internal coherence of his often cryptic works, which, in spite of intensive research, has still not been deciphered in all its aspects.

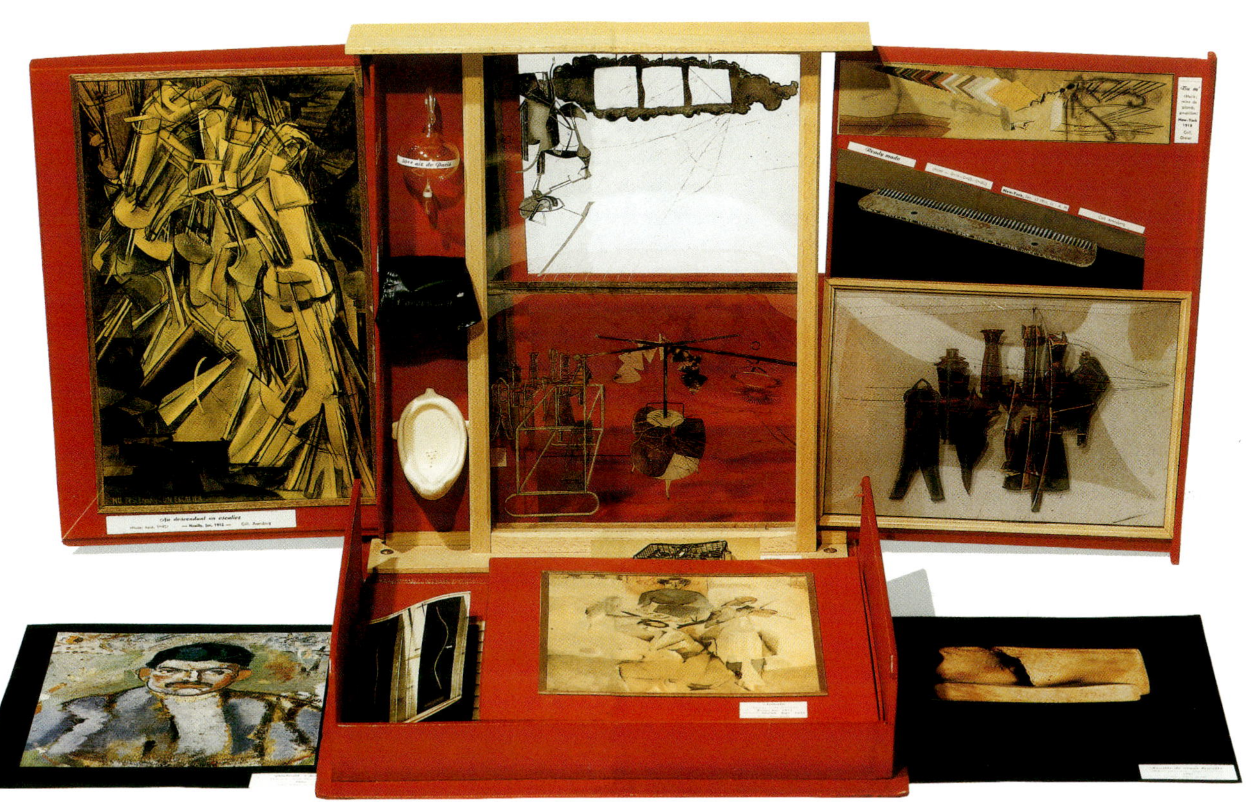

association Area

Video, duration: 1 hour
Photography: Berlin, Staatliche Museen zu Berlin – Preußischer Kulturbesitz, Kunstbibliothek, Marzona collection

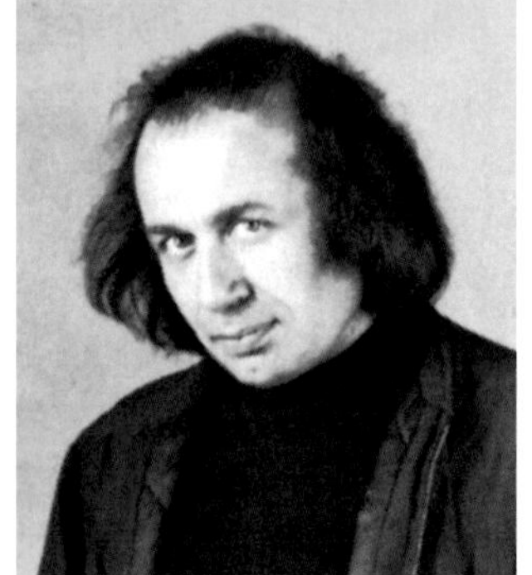

b. 1940 in New York (NY), USA

In the early 1960s, Vito Acconci was first a poet and writer, and regularly published his works, mostly poems or short prose texts, in literary magazines. By the end of the decade, he was beginning to take an increasing interest in the contemporary visual arts. Minimal Art fascinated him, as did the novel experiments in other artistic areas. And so, inspired by the lively climate of the New York art scene, he soon changed from only formulating his ideas in writing to trying them out in the context of performances, frequently in direct contact with the public. Thematically, Acconci's early works deal with a whole variety of aspects: subjective obsessions, reflections on the role of the artist in society, psychological mechanisms, the social construction of identity, and the relationship between the private and public spheres. These are just some of the topics that find their expression, mostly in a direct and confrontational fashion, in his performances and videos.

As his preferred medium, Acconci soon discovered his own body, and many of his early performances were based on body-related actions, which frequently reached the limit of what was physically tolerable. Thus he hammered so long against his reflection that the mirror shattered (*See Through*, 1970); he carried out physically strenuous activities for a fixed period of time in advance until he was totally exhausted, while keeping a record of his progress (*Step Piece*, 1970); he had a mountain of ice-cubes gradually melt on his chest; or in an act of symbolic sex-change singed his body hair with a candle (*Conversions, I–III*, 1973). His performance *Seedbed* (1972) is still notorious today. In the Ileana Sonnabend Gallery, hidden beneath a wooden construction that people could walk over, but easily audible for visitors, he would masturbate for a day at a time.

Acconci's performance *Association Area* is one of his *Instruction Pieces*, in which a certain number of participants tried to carry out actions according to rules clearly laid down in advance. *Association Area* involves two participants, who for the duration of the action are deprived of their senses of sight and hearing with earplugs and blindfolds. Each is instructed to imitate the movements of the other as exactly as possible. Before the performance begins, they are seriously disturbed in their spatial orientation by being turned on their axis a number of times. While the subjects seek to implement the instructions, useful hints boom out from loudspeakers offstage. These, however, can only be heard by the viewers of the video, who, for a period of an hour, are glued to the screen or else watch in frustration to see how and whether the two subjects manage to imitate each other's movements.

Since the mid-1970s, Acconci has stopped actively using his own body and began working on room installations, which, however, often demand a certain amount of physical activity from the public. Today, Acconci is concerned with interventionist architectural projects in urban settings.

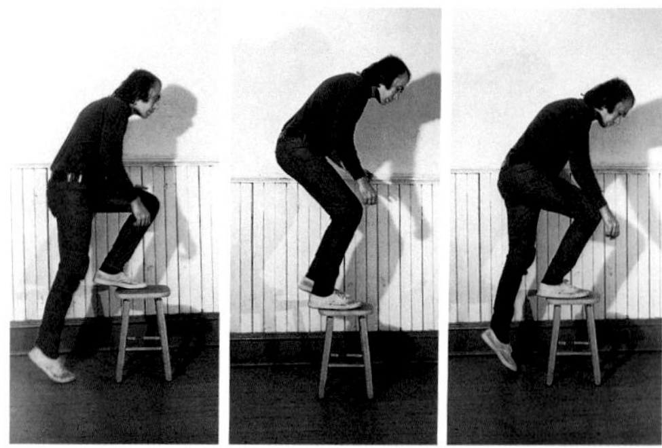

Step Piece, 1970

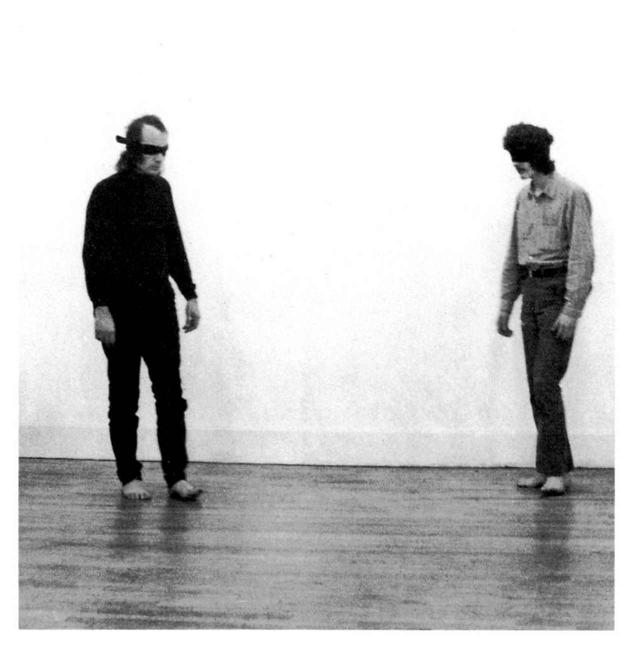
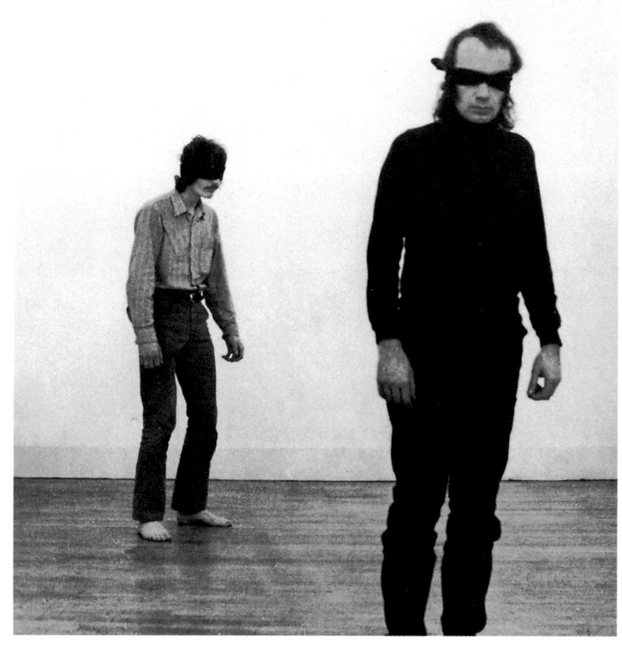
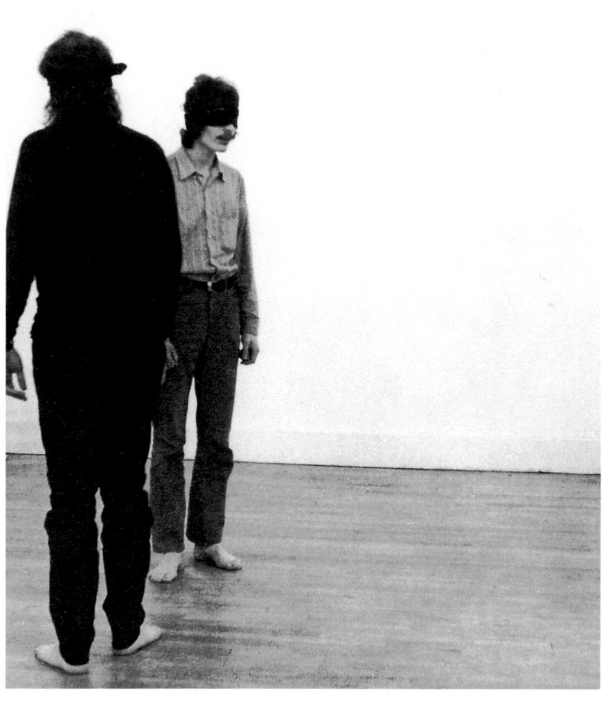
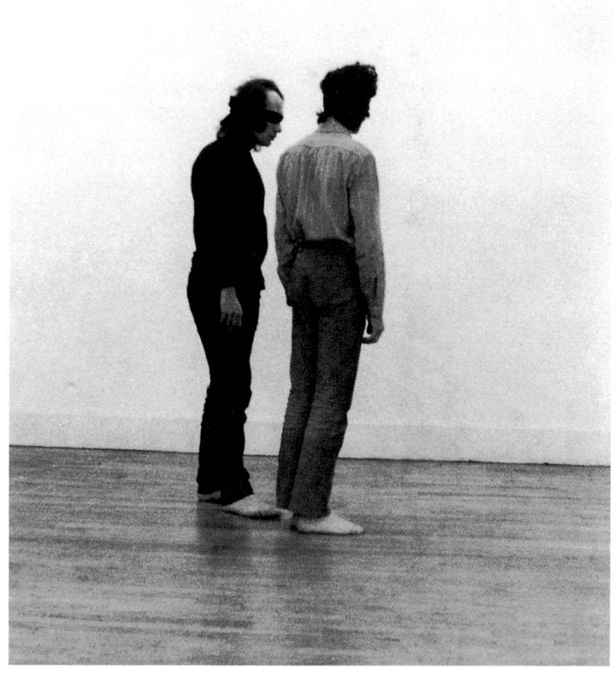

index 001

Text on paper, index-cards, file-cabinets, dimensions variable
Courtesy Lisson Gallery, London, and the artists

Terry Atkinson b. 1939; David Bainbridge b. 1941; Michael Baldwin b. 1945; Harold Hurrell b. 1940; all from England

The English artist group Art & Language has its origin in the co-operation between Terry Atkinson and Michael Baldwin, who got to know each other as students at the Coventry College of Art in 1966. Soon, further members joined the art collective, and in 1968 they founded the Art & Language Press in Cambridge, which a year later brought out their first publication, the magazine "Art-Language". Until the mid-1970s the group devoted themselves to extensive analyses of the conditions in which art operates, analyses characterized on the one hand by a Marxist discourse and on the other by the methods of Anglo-Saxon linguistic philosophy.

The declared aim of the formation is to use their investigations to contribute towards a demystification of art. Until the late 1970s, the artists largely refused to produce artworks in the traditional sense, and instead understood the discourse about art itself as a form of art. Teaching, panel discussions, and publications of their analyses, were all understood to be part of a comprehensive artistic process.

The self-referential and linguistic-analytical character of the work of Art & Language gave rise to affinities with the work of some other concept artists, such as Joseph Kosuth or Ian Wilson, who collaborated on various projects with the group. In the early 1970s, some of the founder-members left the group because of political differences, while other artists joined it. Thus Ian Burn (1939–1993) and Mel Ramsden (b. 1944), with their New York-based Society for Theoretical Art and Analyses, joined up with Art & Language in 1971.

At documenta V in 1972, Art & Language presented their hitherto most comprehensive project under the title *Index 001*. In a large room, two filing-cabinets were set up on each of four blocks. A total of 48 drawers contained the articles and fragments of articles hitherto published in "Art-Language", along with some as yet unpublished. The articles were sorted according to two criteria: at first they were placed in alphabetical order, and within this scheme, they were ordered by their degree of completeness. The large wall surfaces of the exhibition room were covered almost completely with sheets of paper on which Art & Language presented a complex system of indexing some 350 quotes. The system was based on three criteria: the quoted texts are characterized by the symbols +, − and T either as compatible, incompatible or lacking in any relational value. In this way, the results of the art-theoretical analyses by Art & Language are embedded in a many-branched system of reference.

There is hardly any other project in Conceptual Art which, in its scope and structure, makes the seriousness of the intellectual purpose so clear as does *Index 001* by Art & Language.

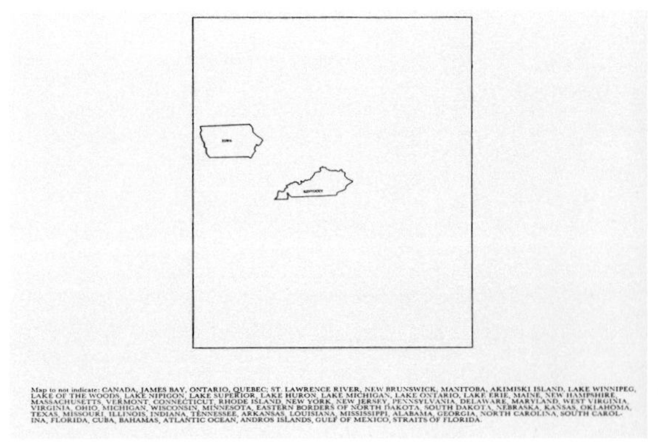

Map to Not Indicate…, 1967

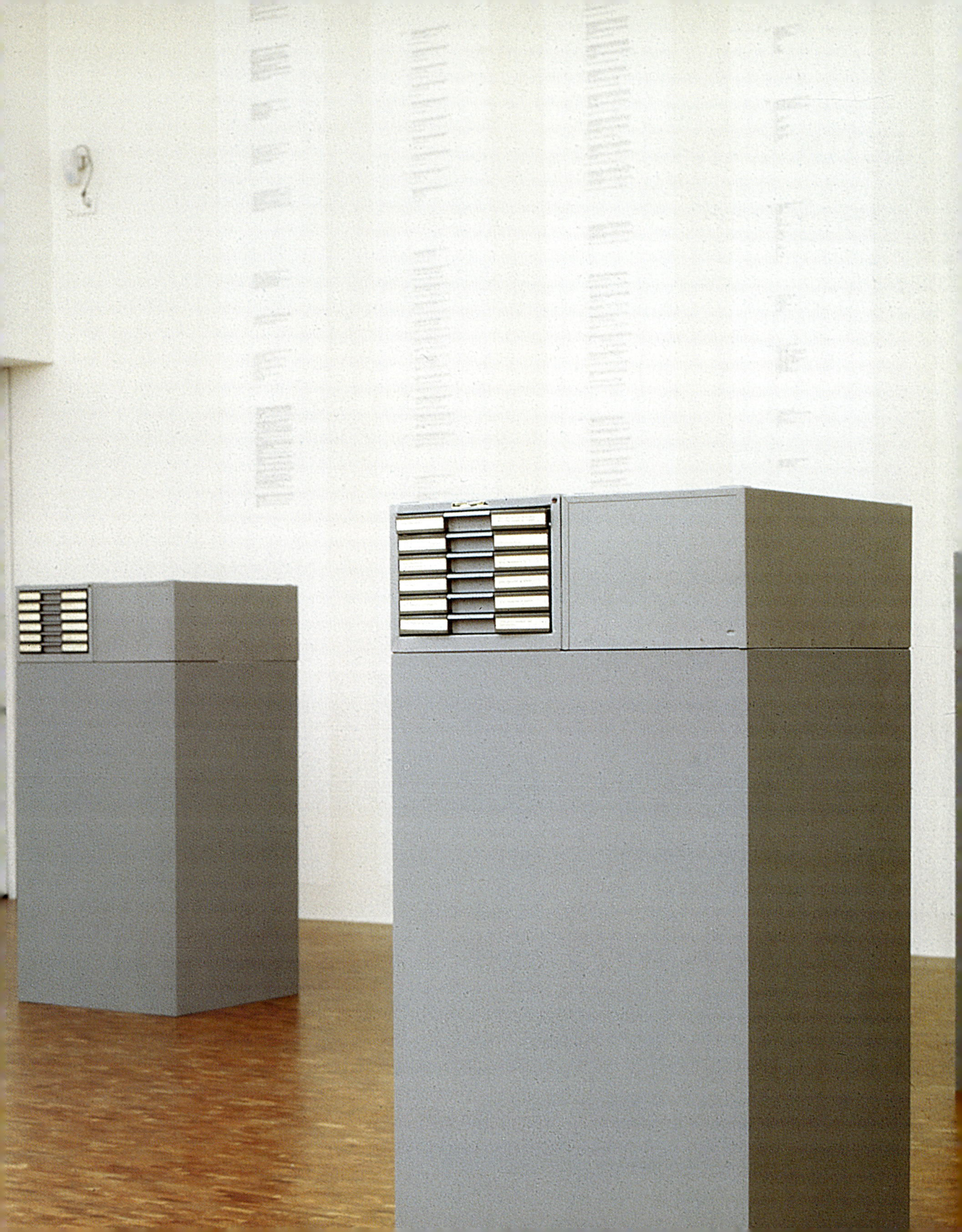

untitled

Project in the Galleria Franco Toselli, Milan
Photography: Berlin, Staatliche Museen zu Berlin – Preußischer Kulturbesitz, Kunstbibliothek, Marzona collection

b. 1943 in Los Angeles (CA), USA

Between 1967 and 1969, Michael Asher, who lives in Los Angeles, worked on projects which were in a contradictory relationship to what was then the dominant aesthetic. While Minimal Art was investigating the presence of objects and their relationship to both the room in which they were exhibited and its visitors, Asher was constructing sculptures in which he had air circulate using fans within closed exhibition rooms. In their conception these works were contextually based from the outset, and thus they deny any claim to autonomy on the part of art. After experimenting for a time with a wide variety of technical possibilities of generating air pressure in the garage next to his studio, in 1969 Asher publicly exhibited one of his *Airworks* for the first time at the group exhibition "The Appearing/Disappearing Image/Object". In the vicinity of the entrance zone a fan, not visible to the public, generated between the ceiling and the floor a constant flow of air, which could be transversed by visitors to the exhibition.

In the early 1970s Asher began to change the existing exhibition architecture directly, by adding or removing structural elements. Thus Asher deliberately dispensed with the production of (art) objects of whatever kind – an eccentric thing for an artist to do in that decade – and restricted himself largely to architectural interventions, which, by reason of their being tied to a specific location, remained largely inaccessible to the art market. By intervening in the architectural, historical and social context in which art is presented and displayed, and thus changing it, Asher was making public the conventions of the art business and implicitly subjecting it to criticism.

In 1973, in the Galleria Franco Toselli in Milan, Asher realized a project which allows an exemplary demonstration of how his work functions. Unlike earlier works, this exhibition had not been planned in any detail before Asher arrived in Milan. He decided on the spot to remove the white paint from all the walls and ceilings of the gallery with a sand-blaster. Beneath the many coats of white paint, the brown plaster eventually came to light, and with it the various alterations to the building that had been undertaken over the years. During the month-long exhibition, the rooms were illuminated only by natural daylight entering through the windows. Asher's work here fuses inseparably with the architecture of the exhibition rooms, whose classical function, namely the presentation of works of art, it frustrates at the same time.

In the brown of the plaster, the gallery rooms once more entered into a natural relationship with the neighbouring architecture, whose façades were coated with the same material, as a result of which visitors to the exhibition had the forceful impression of a constructed artificiality of the formerly white interior. Asher himself pointed to the central aspect of the work when he observed: "Traditionally, the white interior of a commercial gallery presented an artist's production within an architectural setting of false autonomy. If, through its absence, the viewer was reminded of the white paint, an interesting question was then raised: How does the white 'partition' of paint affect the context of art usually seen on that support surface?"

"I see myself as an author of situations, not of the elements involved in them."

Michael Asher

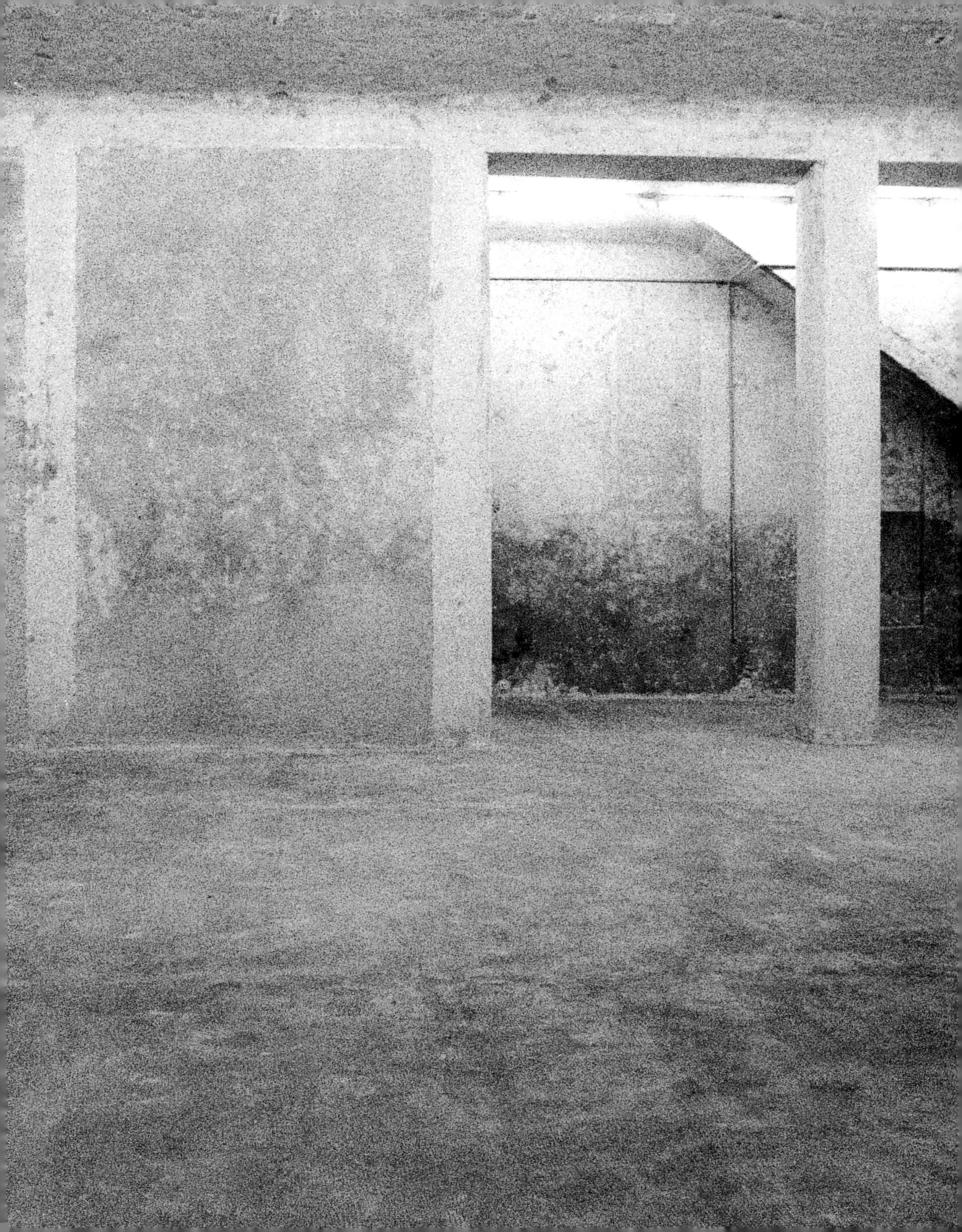

тrying to Photograph a ball so that it is in the center of the Picture

38 colour photographs, framed, 88.9 x 99 cm (detail)
Courtesy of the artist and Marian Goodman Gallery, New York

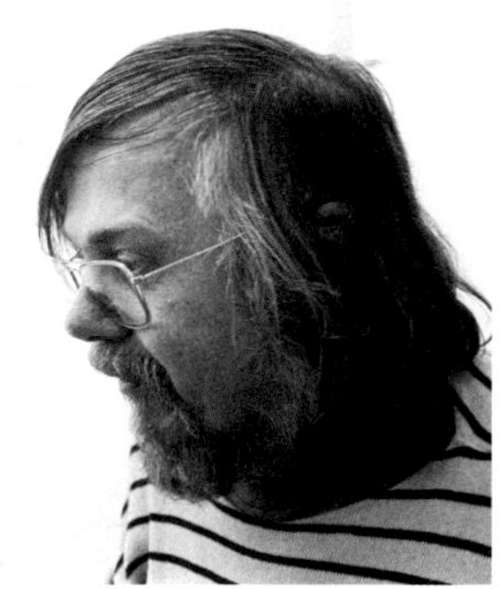

b. 1931 in National City (CA), USA

Before the Californian artist John Baldessari solemnly celebrated his definitive departure from painting in his *Cremation Project* in 1970, in which with few exceptions he burned all his early paintings, he had already cast doubt on the meaning of his painting by integrating text and photographs into it. In a series of pictures which he no longer painted himself, but had painted for him by professional sign-writers according to his instructions, for example, he quoted with obviously ironic intent famous art critics like Clement Greenberg or Barbara Rose, whose apophthegms were written out in black paint on monochrome canvases. In his so-called *Phototext Paintings*, which had also been appearing since the mid-1960s, Baldessari transferred banal snapshots he had taken himself on to canvas, using photo emulsion, and commented on the meaningless illustrations with hints taken from standard teach-yourself books on painting or photography.

By 1970 Baldessari had tired of his ironic project of negating painting as painting, and turned in the following years, with no less humour, to the media of photography and film, whose relationship to verbal information he analysed according to a wide variety of criteria. In 1971 he began to search for strategies with whose help he could escape the traditional rules of photographic composition. Thus for the group exhibition "Pier 18" he asked for a photograph of himself to be created that ignored all the conventions of composition. By asking the photographers to "capture" a ball bouncing up and down on a pier so that it was as close as possible to the centre of the picture, he created sufficient distraction to produce a portrait that, like a bad snapshot, shows Baldessari himself cut off by the left-hand edge of the picture.

He employed the same principle of photography according to rules laid down in advance in the work entitled *Trying to Photograph a Ball so that it is in the Center of the Picture*. In 38 small colour photographs, Baldessari, not without a certain comic touch, presented the results of the experimental set-up indicated in the title of the work. Only rarely was the orange ball even remotely near the centre of the picture; by contrast, in some pictures, palm trees, cut off by the edge of the picture, can be made out against the lightly overcast California sky. As a result of the goal, laid down in advance, of getting the ball as near to the centre of the picture as possible, Baldessari relieved himself of any further compositional decision and achieved pictures that no longer have anything to do with the problem of "that looks good alongside that". Like his painting before, his treatment of photography is no longer determined by craft skills or formal innovation, but by the strategic abandonment or deliberate disregard of conventional rules. In this way, Baldessari created images which even today have lost none of their ironic freshness and aesthetic attraction.

> **"Look at the subject as if you have never seen it before. Examine it from every side. Draw its outline with your hands, and saturate yourself with it."**
>
> John Baldessari

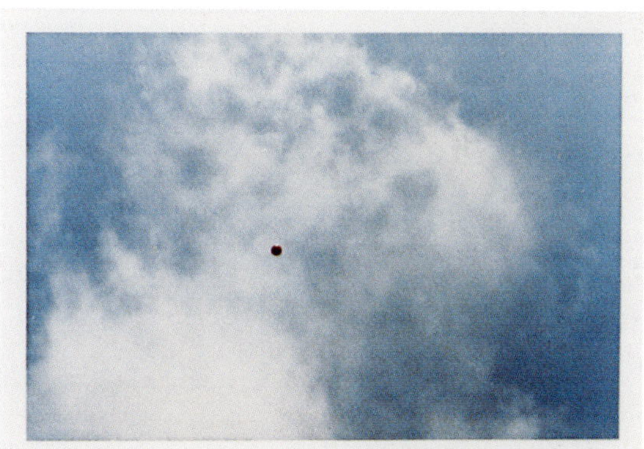

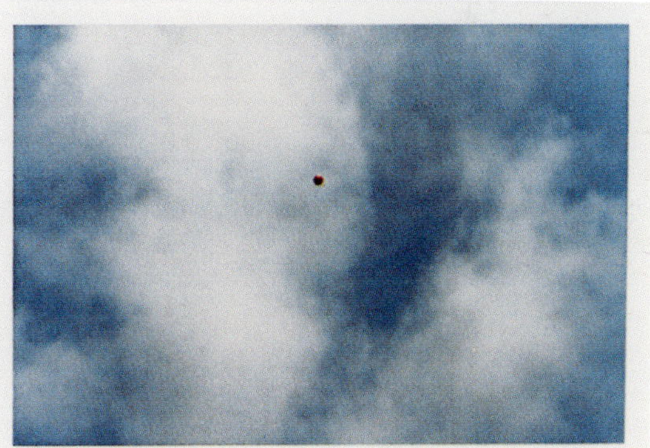

29 pieces as of June 7 1971

Typescript on paper, 5 pages, each 28 x 21.5 cm
Berlin, Staatliche Museen zu Berlin – Preußischer Kulturbesitz, Kupferstichkabinett, Marzona collection

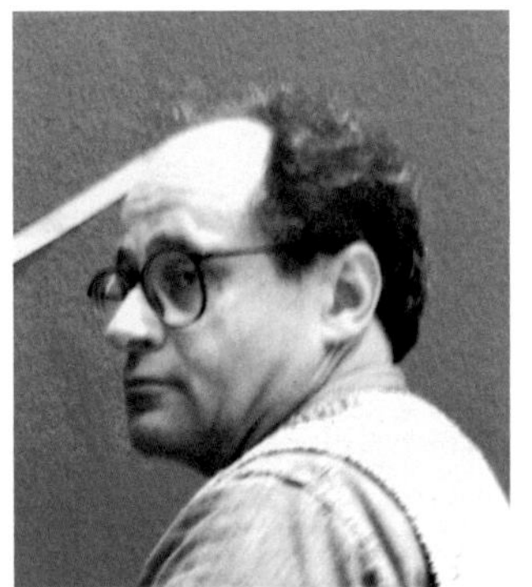

b. 1936 in New York (NY), USA

Until 1967 Robert Barry worked within what was then the widespread tendency in the USA towards reductionist painting, namely creating pictures which drew the attention of the beholder to the empty wall space between the monochrome canvases. Several works from this period consist of four small-format canvas squares, which, equally spaced, define the corners of a larger square and in this way incorporate the empty wall zone into the picture as an integral component thereof. In 1967 Barry finally abandoned painting and occupied himself for a short time with stretching transparent nylon threads, before turning a little while later to projects whose starting materials were totally inaccessible to visual perception. Thus in his *Inert Gas Series* he released various gases into the atmosphere, and for his *Radiation Pieces* experimented with radioactive rays, or else exhibited inaudible radio waves in the Siegelaub Gallery in New York. Although Barry's work at this time could stand up as prime examples of the dematerialization of art, we must nevertheless acknowledge that the works mentioned still related to a measurable physico-chemical reality, albeit a reality beyond the limits of human perception.

In 1968/69 came Barry's first purely linguistic works, which dispensed with any reference to the material aspects of reality and in their frank vagueness were not susceptible to any unambiguous definition. For the group exhibition "Prospect 69" in the Kunsthalle Düsseldorf, for example, Barry's contribution consisted of an interview that was published in the exhibition catalogue. The work consisted of the interview together with the thoughts raised in the mind of the reader.

In similarly drastic fashion, Barry undermined the conventions of the exhibition routine in a number of solo exhibitions held in 1969.

On the invitation cards and the doors of a number of galleries with which Barry worked, it said: "The Gallery will be closed during the exhibition", and indeed, the rooms were closed for the duration. In place of a concrete encounter with works of art in an exhibition room, Barry left it entirely to the imagination of the beholder to develop the meaning and form of the work.

Barry's *Telepathic Piece* for the 1969 "Simon Fraser Exhibition" in Burnaby likewise moves in a purely mental space. The exhibition catalogue contains the statement: "During the exhibition I will try to communicate telepathically a work of art, the nature of which is a series of thoughts that are not applicable to language or image."

As his *29 Pieces of June 7 1971* show, hardly any other conceptual artist has broadened the scope of art to such an extent and in the process freed himself so radically from conventions as Barry. In view of many of his projects, one must seriously ask where and precisely what the work of art is.

"I was interested in creating objects that involved other people, and I was really interested in different explorations of space and time and the way people interact and function in these mediums."

Robert Barry

ROBERT BARRY

SOMETHING WHICH IS VERY NEAR IN PLACE AND TIME, BUT NOT YET
KNOWN TO ME.   2 AUG. 1969.

SOMETHING WHICH IS VERY NEAR IN PLACE AND TIME, BUT NOT YET
KNOWN TO ME.   7 JULY 1970.

SOMETHING WHICH IS VERY NEAR IN PLACE AND TIME, BUT NOT YET
KNOWN TO ME.   27 SEPT. 1970.

SOMETHING WHICH IS VERY NEAR IN PLACE AND TIME, BUT NOT YET
KNOWN TO ME.   11 OCT. 1970.

SOMETHING WHICH IS VERY NEAR IN PLACE AND TIME, BUT NOT YET
KNOWN TO ME.   15 NOV. 1970.

2.

ROBERT BARRY

SOMETHING WHICH IS VERY NEAR IN PLACE AND TIME, BUT NOT YET
KNOWN TO ME.   9 JAN. 1971.

SOMETHING WHICH IS VERY NEAR IN PLACE AND TIME, BUT NOT YET
KNOWN TO ME.   24 JAN. 1971.

SOMETHING WHICH IS VERY NEAR IN PLACE AND TIME, BUT NOT YET
KNOWN TO ME.   6 FEB. 1971.

SOMETHING WHICH IS VERY NEAR IN PLACE AND TIME, BUT NOT YET
KNOWN TO ME.   11 FEB. 1971.

SOMETHING WHICH IS VERY NEAR IN PLACE AND TIME, BUT NOT YET
KNOWN TO ME.   13 FEB. 1971.

SOMETHING WHICH IS VERY NEAR IN PLACE AND TIME, BUT NOT YET
KNOWN TO ME.   19 FEB. 1971.

SOMETHING WHICH IS VERY NEAR IN PLACE AND TIME, BUT NOT YET
KNOWN TO ME.   19 FEB. 1971.

3.

ROBERT BARRY
SOMETHING WHICH IS VERY NEAR IN PLACE AND TIME, BUT NOT YET
KNOWN TO ME.   1 MAR. 1971.

SOMETHING WHICH IS VERY NEAR IN PLACE AND TIME, BUT NOT YET
KNOWN TO ME.   1 MAR. 1971.

SOMETHING WHICH IS VERY NEAR IN PLACE AND TIME, BUT NOT YET
KNOWN TO ME.   4 MAR. 1971.

SOMETHING WHICH IS VERY NEAR IN PLACE AND TIME, BUT NOT YET
KNOWN TO ME.   4 MAR. 1971.

SOMETHING WHICH IS VERY NEAR IN PLACE AND TIME, BUT NOT YET
KNOWN TO ME.   4 MAR. 1971.

SOMETHING WHICH IS VERY NEAR IN PLACE AND TIME, BUT NOT YET
KNOWN TO ME.   4 MAR. 1971.

SOMETHING WHICH IS VERY NEAR IN PLACE AND TIME, BUT NOT YET
KNOWN TO ME.   4 MAR. 1971.

4.

ROBERT BARRY
SOMETHING WHICH IS VERY NEAR IN PLACE AND TIME, BUT NOT YET
KNOWN TO ME.   4 MAR. 1971.

SOMETHING WHICH IS VERY NEAR IN PLACE AND TIME, BUT NOT YET
KNOWN TO ME.   4 MAR. 1971.

SOMETHING WHICH IS VERY NEAR IN PLACE AND TIME, BUT NOT YET
KNOWN TO ME.   4 MAR. 1971.

SOMETHING WHICH IS VERY NEAR IN PLACE AND TIME, BUT NOT YET
KNOWN TO ME.   31 MAR. 1971.

SOMETHING WHICH IS VERY NEAR IN PLACE AND TIME, BUT NOT YET
KNOWN TO ME.   27 APR. 1971.

SOMETHING WHICH IS VERY NEAR IN PLACE AND TIME, BUT NOT YET
KNOWN TO ME.   11 MAY 1971.

SOMETHING WHICH IS VERY NEAR IN PLACE AND TIME, BUT NOT YET
KNOWN TO ME.   17 MAY 1971.

SOMETHING WHICH IS VERY NEAR IN PLACE AND TIME, BUT NOT YET
KNOWN TO ME.   31 MAY 1971.

5.

ROBERT BARRY
SOMETHING WHICH IS VERY NEAR IN PLACE AND TIME, BUT NOT YET
KNOWN TO ME.   1 JUNE 1971.

SOMETHING WHICH IS VERY NEAR IN PLACE AND TIME, BUT NOT YET
KNOWN TO ME.   7 JUNE 1971.

winding towers

Black-and-white photographs, no dimensions given
From top left to bottom right: Gelsenkirchen, D 1974; Castrop-Rauxel, D 1975; Gelsenkirchen, 1967;
Unna, D 1966; Bochum, D 1965; Essen, D 1965; Bottrop, D 1982; Bottrop, D 1980; Gelsenkirchen, D 1966
Münster, Westfälisches Landesmuseum

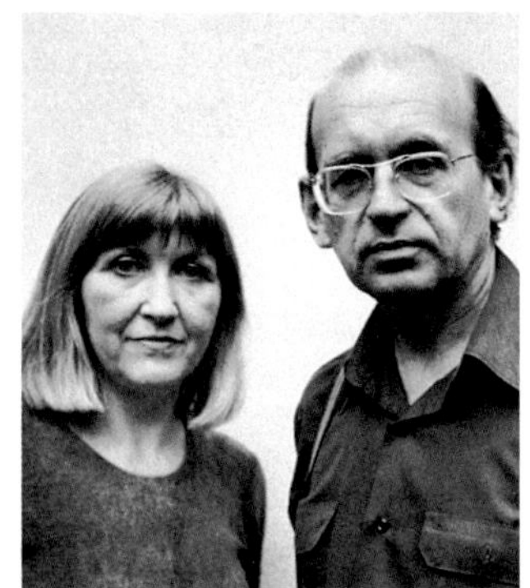

Bernd Becher b. 1931 in Siegen, Germany; Hilla Becher b. 1934 in Potsdam, Germany

Bernd and Hilla Becher began their collaboration in 1959, shortly after meeting at the Academy of Art in Düsseldorf. Since the early days, the Bechers have concentrated in their photographic project – which is still ongoing – on the subject of industrial architecture. At an early date they laid down particular parameters for their photographs, and they continue to respect them today. Thus in their exclusively black-and-white pictures, they almost always depict the motif austerely from the front, whereby the line of the horizon is usually low down and the lighting homogeneous and undramatic, as they prefer to work under overcast skies. Because of the relatively long exposure times, their photographs on principle contain no human figures.

The various shots of water towers, blast furnaces, cooling towers, winding towers etc. are presented arranged in typologies, within which typical characteristics and variations of a particular type of building can be clearly seen. Mostly nine shots of a particular type of building are included on one tableau, although the number of pictures thus collated can rise to 30. The Bechers' project was never limited to Germany, and on extended journeys throughout Europe and to the United States, they continue the photographic documentation of industrial architecture in decay.

1969 witnessed the first publication by Bernd and Hilla Becher, which bore the title "Anonyme Skulpturen: Eine Typologie technischer Bauten" (Anonymous Sculptures: a typology of technological buildings), and since then, their work has been discussed in connection with Conceptual Art time and again. Because of the logical consistency, the serial nature and the high degree of abstraction that characterizes their photographic concept, this association is not entirely misplaced, although the Bechers' work, as they themselves have emphasized on a number of occasions, consciously links up with the tradition of documentary photography, in particular the photography of the Neue Sachlichkeit movement. In their photographic work, the Bechers, like August Sander or Karl Blossfeldt, harbour no doubts about the capacity of photography to adequately depict reality and to contribute to objective knowledge of the objects depicted in the framework of an almost scientific systematization.

Indeed, the Bechers' photographs are of inestimable value for heritage conservation, which, in the case of some building types, now has access to an almost complete compendium of photographic documents, with whose help their history and development can be reconstructed.

Since the Bechers have from the outset oriented their work to an international perspective, their pictures additionally provide information on regional particularities in the design of industrial buildings. Thus a comparative look at the Bechers' photographs reveals that even in the design of functional architecture the famous dictum "form follows function" has only a limited validity. For although a French water-tower fulfils the same function as an American one, it looks completely different.

Alongside their artistic work, the Bechers were also extremely successful teachers. In 1976 Bernd Becher was appointed Professor of Photography at the Academy of Art in Düsseldorf, and in the course of more than 20 years trained some of the most important German art photographers, so that the "Becher class" has become a term of respect. Andreas Gursky, Candida Höfer, Thomas Ruff and Thomas Struth are just some of their former students.

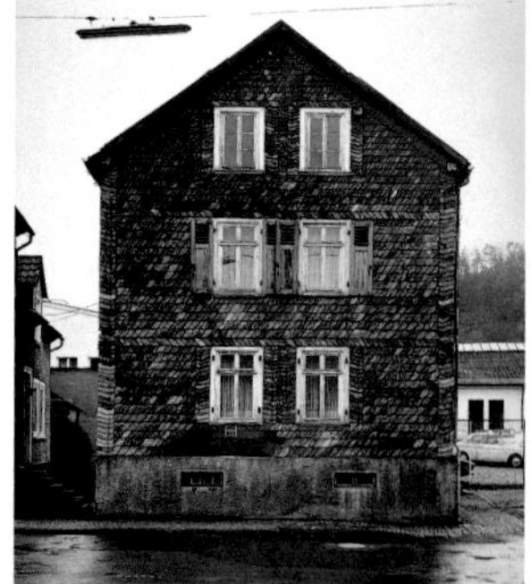

Schieferhaus, 1971

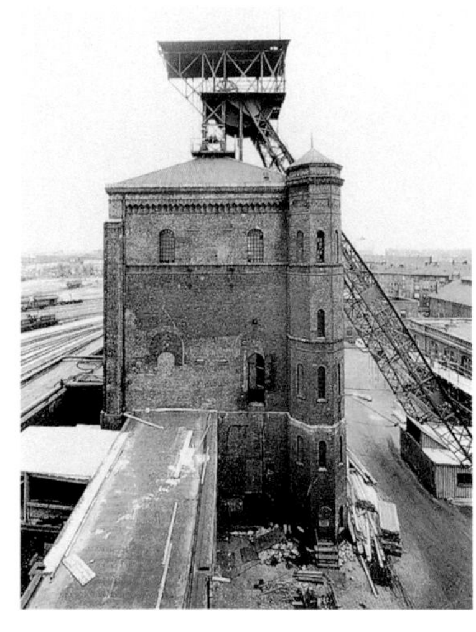
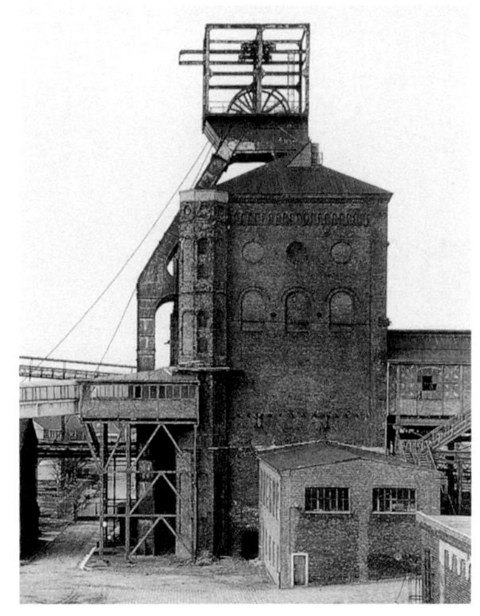
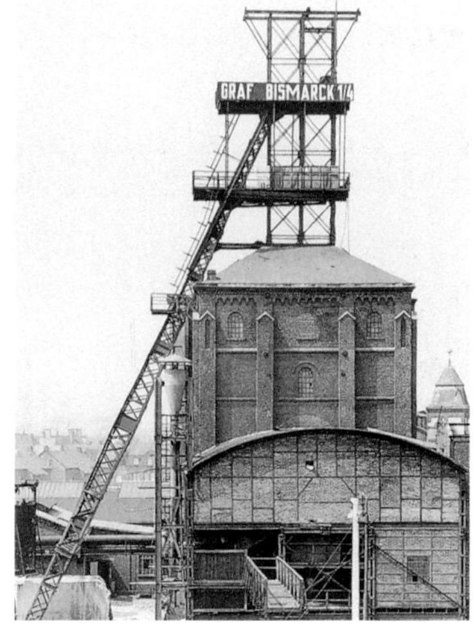
GRAF BISMARCK 1/4
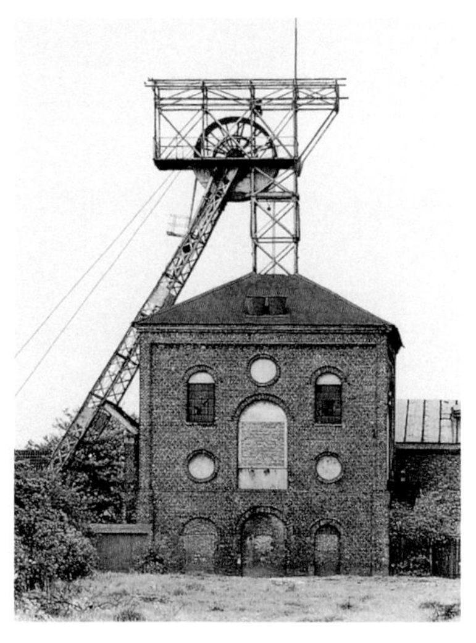
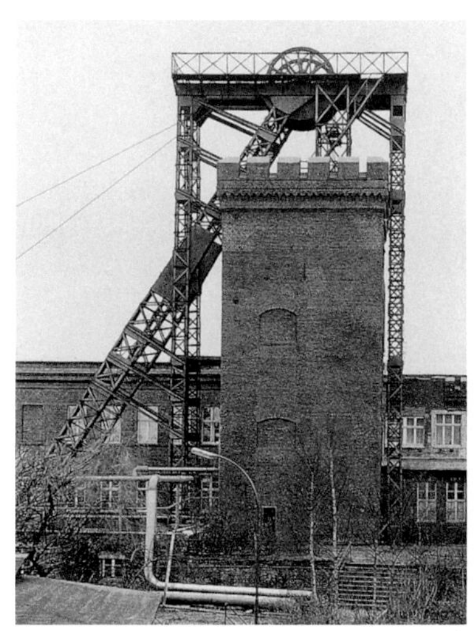
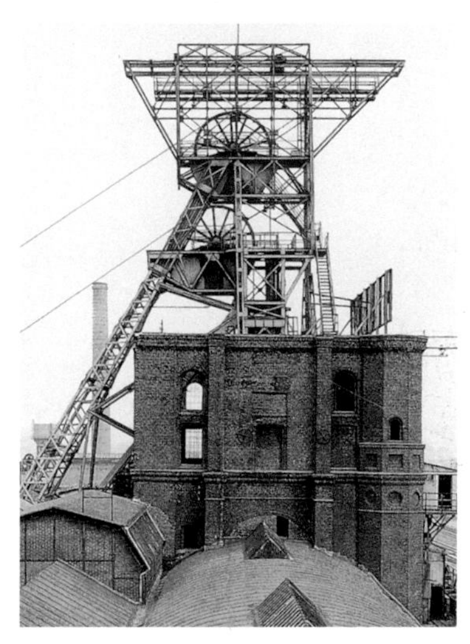
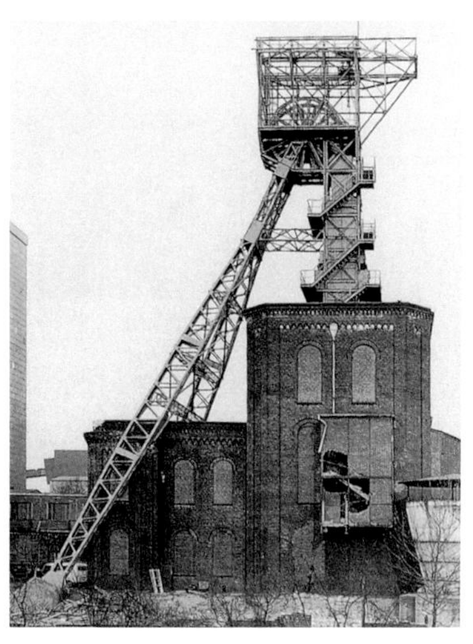
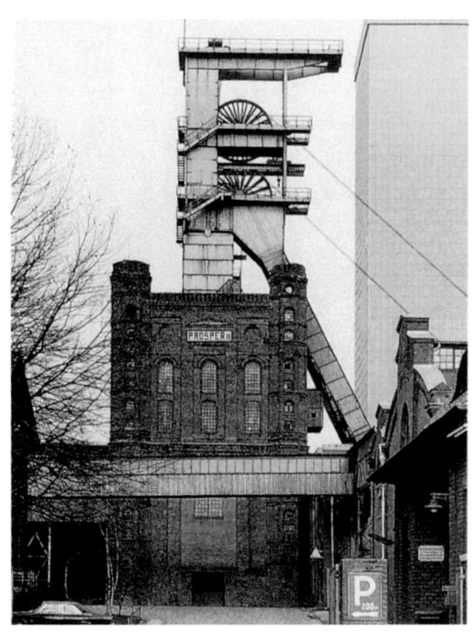
PROSPER III
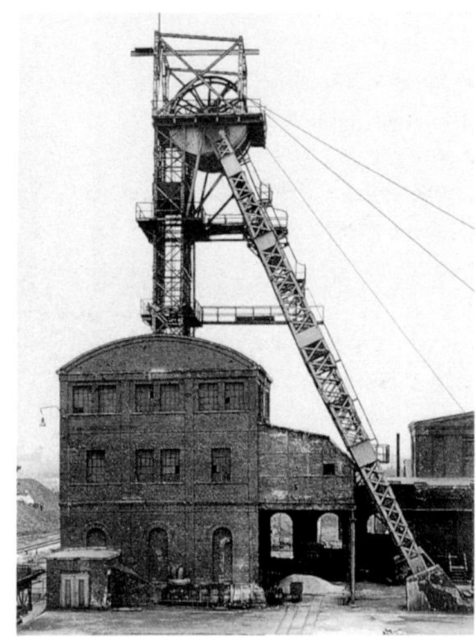

measurement room

Black adhesive tape and Letraset on wall, variable dimensions
Installation in a private apartment, Italy
Photography: Berlin, Staatliche Museen zu Berlin – Preußischer Kulturbesitz, Kunstbibliothek, Marzona collection

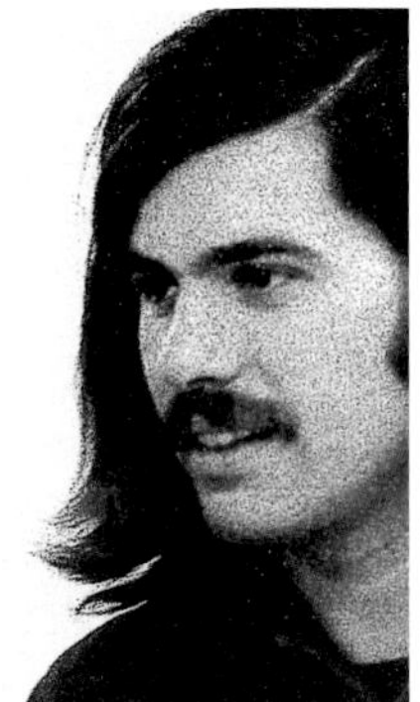

b. 1940 in Pittsburgh (PA), USA

Mel Bochner came to New York as a young artist in 1964, after he had spent a year travelling around Mexico and the USA. He had graduated from the Carnegie Institute of Technology in Pittsburgh in 1962. Having arrived in New York, he devoted himself to a wide variety of activities. For example he worked at first as a painter on assemblages and pictures which reveal a close critical investigation of the work of Robert Rauschenberg and Jasper Johns, and concern themselves with the nature of paintings as objects. In 1965 Bochner took up a teaching post at the School of Visual Arts and wrote regular columns as a critic for "Arts Magazine". As an artist, he was already working on Minimalist objects, and a little later, as a critic, was writing benevolently on the breakthrough of Minimal Art in New York, to which he soon responded, however, with a work that was structured more by thoughts and language.

1966 – in other words, in the year of the great Minimalist "Primary Structures" exhibition at the Jewish Museum – was also the year of the meanwhile hardly less famous exhibition "Working Drawings and Other Visible Things on Paper Not Necessarily Meant to Be Viewed as Art", to which Bochner contributed both as artist and curator, although he exhibited no works of his own. On display were four identical loose-leaf files on plinths, in which Bochner had collected copies of sketches, notes, and other material passed on to him by numerous Minimal Artists. Thus in the exhibition there were actually no complete art works to look at, but merely ideas about art, which is why "Working Drawings" is regarded by many art-historians as the first purely Conceptual exhibition. This project definitively pointed the way forward for Bochner, and in the years to follow, he practised an art that was often described as "thought made visible".

Following extensive experiments with photography and serial drawings, in which a systematic concern with the relationship between theory and practice, knowledge and experience, can already be discerned, in 1969 Bochner executed the first works in the series *Measurement Rooms*. For this group of works, Bochner exactly measured out the empty exhibition rooms and stuck the measurements of the individual elements of the rooms directly onto the walls with adhesive tape. In this way, for the beholder, the numerical facts of the measurements fuse indissolubly with the room as it was actually visible.

As in many projects by Michael Asher, here too the whole exhibition room became a work of art, thus losing its traditional function of "White Cube", or neutral venue for the presentation of art-works. Unlike Asher, however, Bochner seems, with his *Measurement Rooms*, to have been not so much criticizing the institutions as pointing out problems of perception, in that his interventions brought out the discrepancy between visual perception and abstract descriptive models by causing them to interpenetrate and making both visible at the same time. A year later, Bochner revealed his scepticism regarding the load-bearing capacity of abstract linguistic even more openly when, for a group exhibition at the Dwan Gallery, he wrote the words LANGUAGE IS NOT TRANSPARENT on the wall.

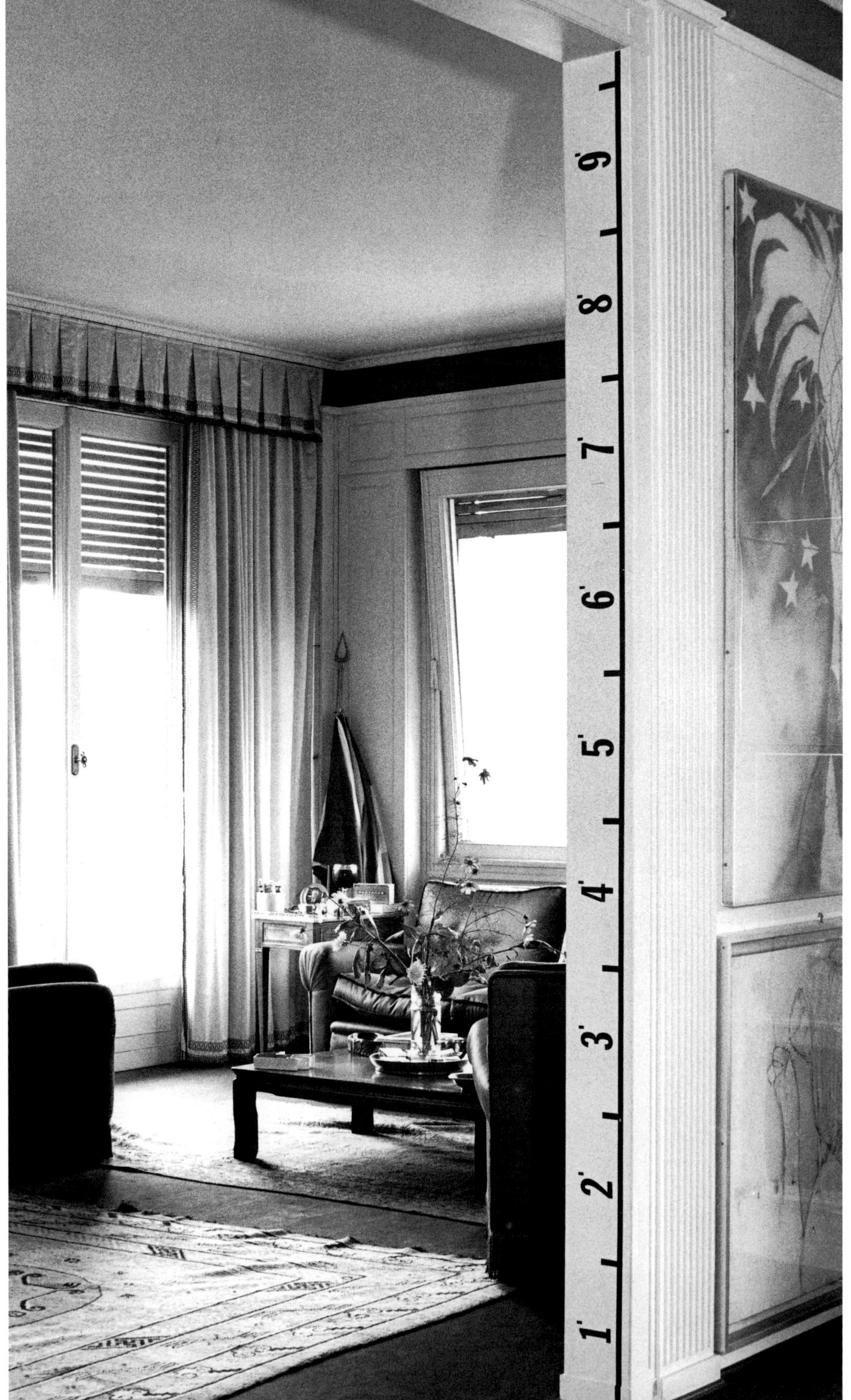

millenovecentosettanta

Wood relief, 49 x 49 cm

Berlin, Staatliche Museen zu Berlin – Preußischer Kulturbesitz, Nationalgalerie, Marzona collection

b. 1940 in Turin,
d. 1994 in Rome, Italy

Self-taught, Alighiero Boetti began his artistic career in the mid-1960s. In 1967 he first exhibited his works in the Christian Stein gallery in Turin. Since the start of his artistic activities, Boetti had taken an interest in dualist structures and in a wide variety of aspects of time. His 1966 *Lampada annuale*, for example, lights up just once a year for eleven seconds, in order to symbolize "the countless events that happen without our knowledge or involvement". In other works, such as the drawings from the *Lavori a biro* series or the embroidered maps, the phenomenon of time is incorporated into the duration of their production, and is thus an integral component of their conception. In 1971 Boetti first went to Afghanistan, and continued to spend lengthy periods there every year until the Russian invasion of 1979. Right up to his death in 1994, Boetti had numerous projects executed by Afghan carpet weavers, such as his *Mappe del mondo*.

For the *Lavori a biro*, executed as their name suggests with a ball-point pen, Boetti mostly commissioned students who, in a laborious and time-consuming process, made drawings on usually large-format sheets of paper in accordance with his instructions. Many of these drawings show in the top left the alphabet, and an arrangement of commas, hardly decipherable at first glance, which cover the entire expanse of the paper and as white holes stand out from the rest of the paper, which is completely covered in biro ink. Not only was the production of this work extremely time-consuming, but so is its perception. Not infrequently, the alleged chaos follows a complex logic. For the arrangement of the commas corresponds to a complex coding system, where they are each, by virtue of their position and the intervals between them, to be assigned to a particular letter of the alphabet. Only those who know the code can decipher Boetti's spoken message.

The dialectic of order and chaos, which the *Lavori a biro* symbolize in impressive fashion, and, in a sense, abolish, is reflected on another level in the game that Boetti has been playing with his name since 1968. In a simple act, Boetti anchored dualism as the creative principle in his own name, when he split his forename and surname, thenceforth calling himself Alighiero e Boetti. As if to symbolize the reconciliation of this inner polarity, the 1977 photomontage *Gemelli* showed two images of the artist walking hand-in-hand along an avenue.

One of the form-determining elements in many of Boetti's works is the squaring of texts or numerical progressions, first experimented with in 1970. The work *Millenovecentosettanta* (One thousand nine hundred and seventy), which has been executed in numerous versions, shows the written-out form of the calendar year in which it was created in horizontally ordered rows. The square, which encompasses 49 fields, thus encodes the simple information, i.e. the year, transferred from numerical to verbal form. Many of Boetti's later works use different, increasingly complex, systems of information coding, either by superimposing pictorial and verbal elements, or combining different models of description.

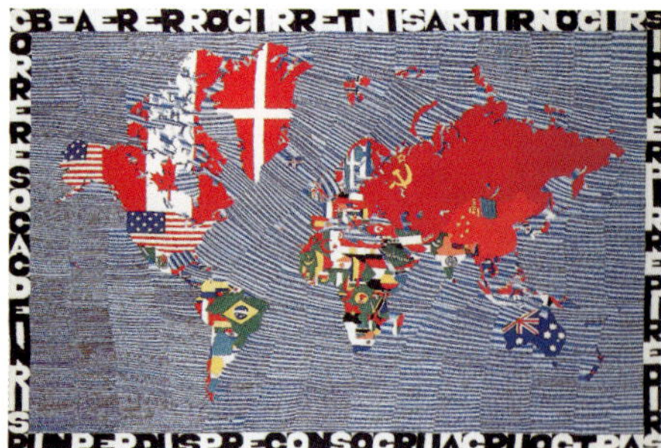

Mappa, 1971

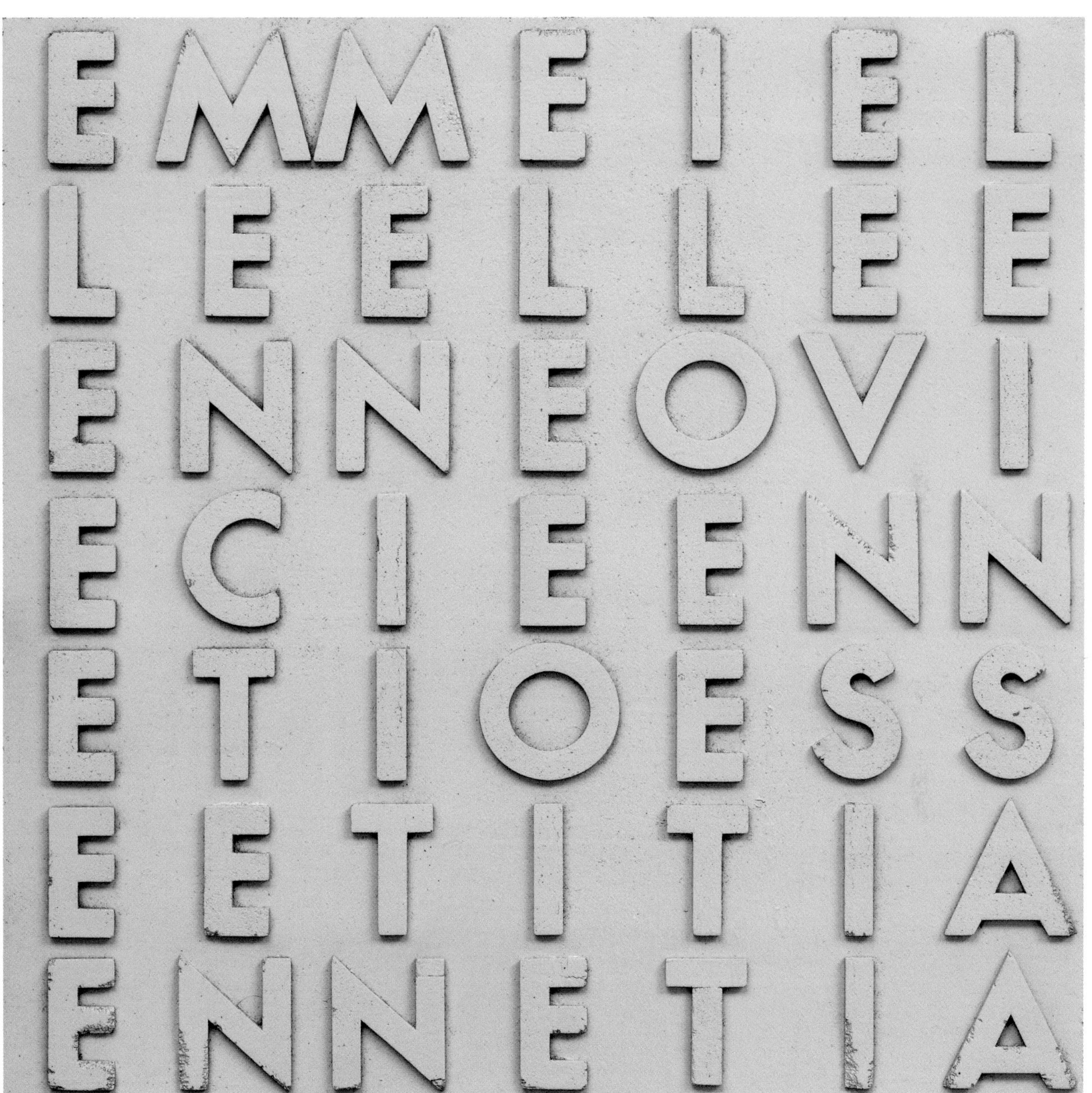
E M M E I E I E L
L E E L L E E L L E E
E N N E N N E O V I
E C I E E N N
E T I O E S S
E E T I T I A
E N N E T I A

Musée d'Art Moderne, Département des Aigles

Top: vacuum-formed plastic plate, 84.5 x 121.5 cm
Bottom: photomontage on card, 65 x 100 cm (framed)
Private collection

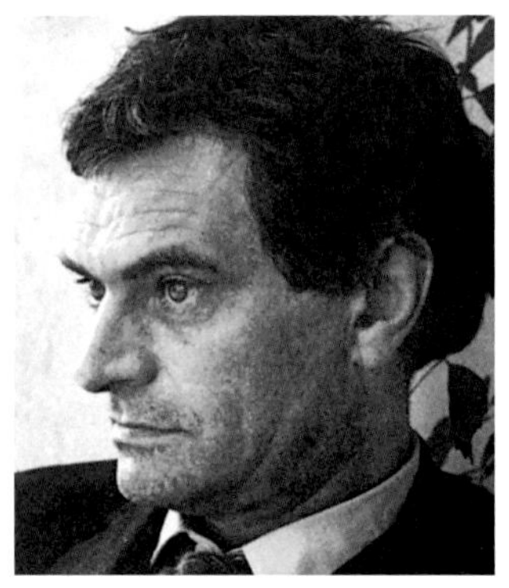

**b. 1924 in Brussels, Belgium,
d. 1976 in Cologne, Germany**

In the early 1950s, Marcel Broodthaers worked as a poet while at the same time earning his living as a bookseller. In 1963, in a symbolic act, he coated 50 unsold copies of "Pense-Bête", a collection of his poetry, with plaster-of-paris and thus created his first sculpture, which in a sense made his poetry impossible to read. The purported abandonment and literal silencing of literature thus went hand-in-hand with the start of a career as a visual artist, whereby the multiply ambiguous intermeshing of word and object or picture, which already characterized *Pense-Bête* (aide-mémoire), can be regarded as paradigmatic for Broodthaers' art. Basically, Broodthaers the artist was always a poet at heart, and his work is just as clearly in the tradition of the Belgian painter René Magritte as in that of the French poet Stéphane Mallarmé.

Always searching for the meaning and transfer of meaning in the relationship between signifier and signified, Broodthaers left an œuvre of extraordinary complexity, which reveals a high degree of moral intensity. Broodthaers strictly forbade himself to repeat anything, and neglected market considerations, indeed often deliberately boycotting the market altogether. Although Broodthaers always maintained a critical attitude to the fusion of art and politics, as evidenced by his dispute with Joseph Beuys, many works evince subtle criticism of a bourgeois view of art that saw contemporary art first and foremost in terms of its monetary value and the possibility of increasing the same. In late works, Broodthaers extended this critique to a general criticism of the contextual conditions of contemporary art production.

There is hardly a medium or a material that Broodthaers did not use in his twelve years as a visual artist, which ended with his early death in 1976: film, photography, sculpture, painting, assemblage, print, graphics and text all served as means of expression, whereby ideas always interested him more than their perfect concrete realization.

The *Musée d'Art Moderne, Département des Aigles*, set up in Broodthaers' apartment in 1968, soon expanded to become his most extensive artistic project. This virtual museum consisted at first only of a few empty packing cases and numerous art postcards, and was intended to serve as a forum for the cultural and political debates which in the wake of the Paris riots of May 1968 soon developed in Belgium too.

By the time Broodthaers displayed his *Musée d'Art Moderne, Département des Aigles* in the Kunsthalle Düsseldorf in 1972, it had grown considerably larger. In his capacity as curator, Broodthaers had assembled a huge number of objects, many of which were on loan from international museums. In order to caricature the normative and uplifting act of displaying objects in museums, Broodthaers provided many of his exhibits with labels which, in allusion to Magritte's famous picture *Ceci n'est pas une pipe*, contained the warning "This is not a work of art". By so doing, Broodthaers turned Duchamp's ready-mades gesture on its head, thus regaining some of the subversive strength that over the decades was showing visible signs of wear.

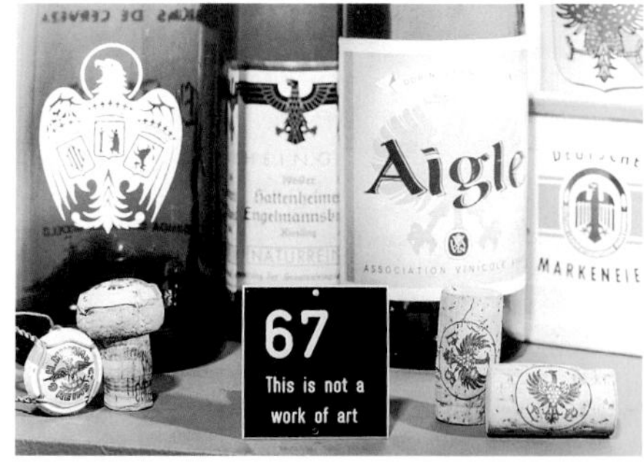

Musée d'Art Moderne, Département des
Aigles, Section des Figures (detail), 1968–1972

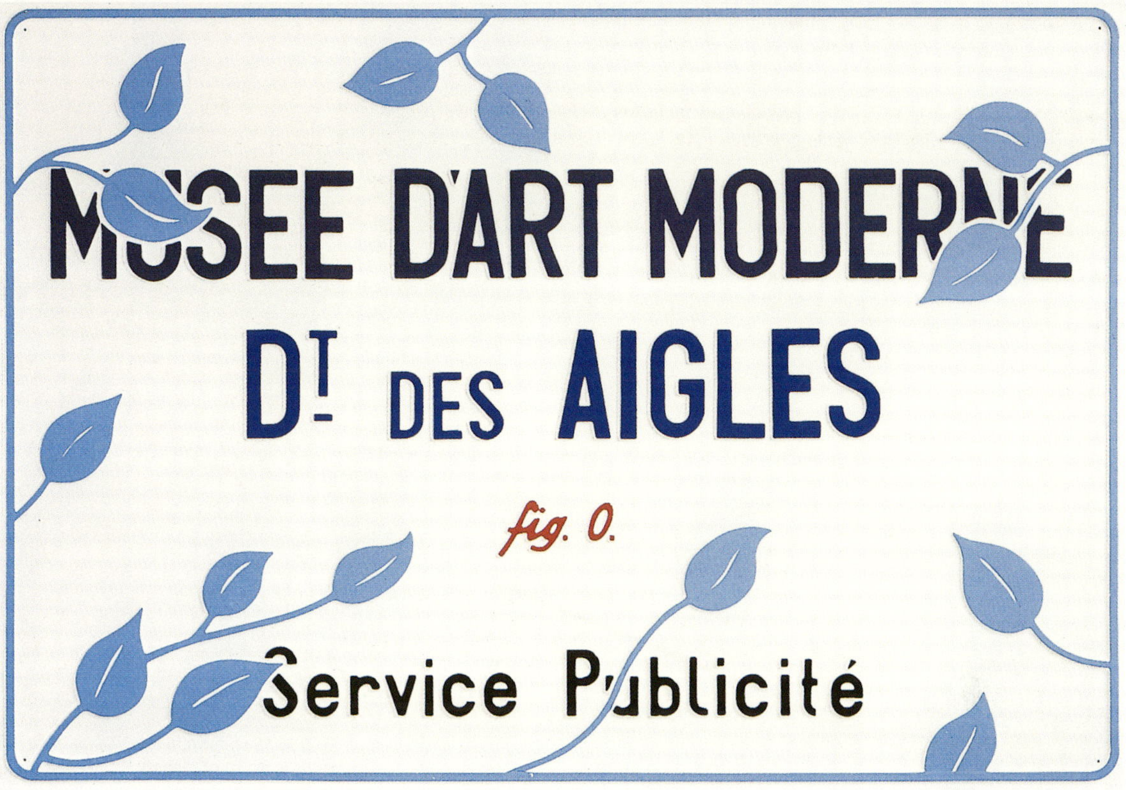

MUSEE D'ART MODERNE
Dt DES AIGLES
fig. 0.
Service Publicité

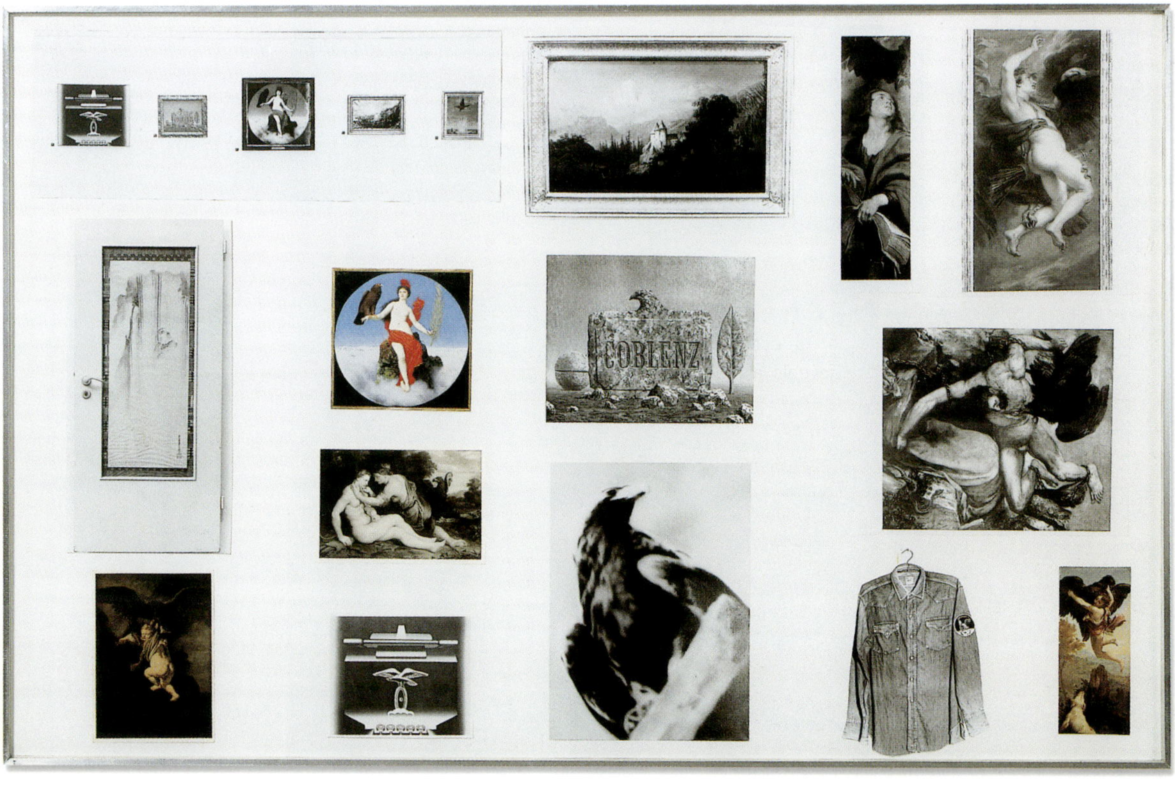

COBLENZ

1 step + 1 step

Aluminium plate on table, plate: 74.5 x 74.5 cm
Berlin, Staatliche Museen zu Berlin – Preußischer Kulturbesitz, Nationalgalerie, Marzona collection

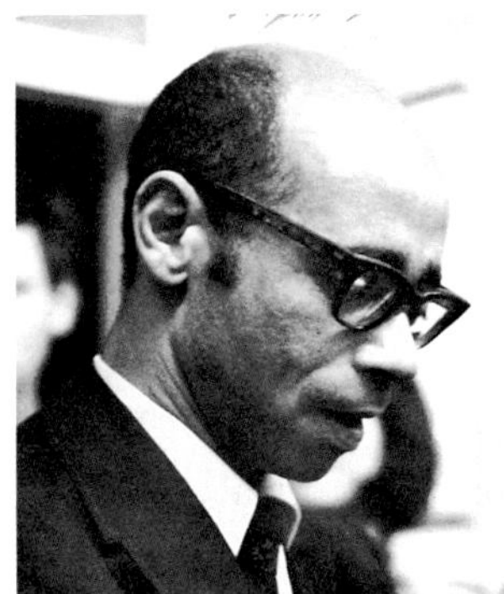

b. 1935 in Paramaribo, Surinam

In 1957 Stanley Brouwn moved to Amsterdam, where he began his career as an artist, at first on the fringes of the Fluxus movement. 1961 saw the appearance of the first works in the series *This Way Brouwn*, a concept to which the artist was to remain faithful for years. The concept is as follows: Brouwn asks passers-by at random to sketch the way to a particular place. Brouwn collects the sketches, stamps them with the title *This Way Brouwn*, frames them, and presents them at exhibitions as works of art. Another series of works dating from the early 1960s consists of large-format sheets of paper, which Brouwn lays out on the streets of Amsterdam to be walked over by passers-by. He them picks them up, complete with footprints, and exhibits them without further addition.

In later works, after 1970, Brouwn increasingly concentrated on researching his own steps and the path he had taken – whether real or fictitious – in relation to his biography and the metric system. The work *1 Step + 1 Step* is one of the actually rather rare sculptural manifestations of Brouwn's ongoing confrontation with measurement and distance. It shows in sober fashion a step in a square. While earlier works were not completely within his control, being dependent on the reactions of the passers-by involved, the post-1970 works are clearly defined and in their conception and execution no longer to be separated from the person of the artist.

Systematically, Brouwn from this point on examined a wide variety of aspects of the complex relationship between the step or the metre as a unit of measurement, and as the description of a distance. For his exhibition at the Stedelijk Museum in Amsterdam, for example, in the space of a month, Brouwn successively visited in 1971 a number of countries chosen in advance. The work entitled *Steps* consisted of Brouwn's steps in the respective countries, whose exact number he reported to the museum by telephone each day. This information was catalogued on index cards, which were added to the exhibition daily.

Like many Conceptual Artists, Brouwn often uses the artist-book medium as appropriate to the presentation of his ideas. If we look at Brouwn's books, for example *1–100,000 Steps*, in which precisely 100,000 steps are individually listed with a typewriter, it is clear that there is an affinity between his approach and that of Hanne Darboven and On Kawara. The three artists have in common that they pursue their concepts, once conceived, with great logical consistency and meticulousness, and thereby reveal a clearly recognizable system in the ongoing work. In this respect, they are following the dictum of Sol LeWitt that the "conceptual artist merely catalogues the consequences of his premisses". The fact that these premisses need not be abstract or rational, but may also be playful or concrete, is always evident in Brouwn's work.

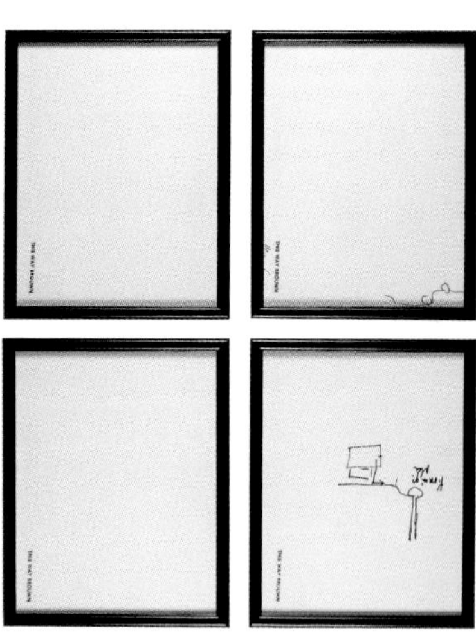

This Way Brouwn, 1964

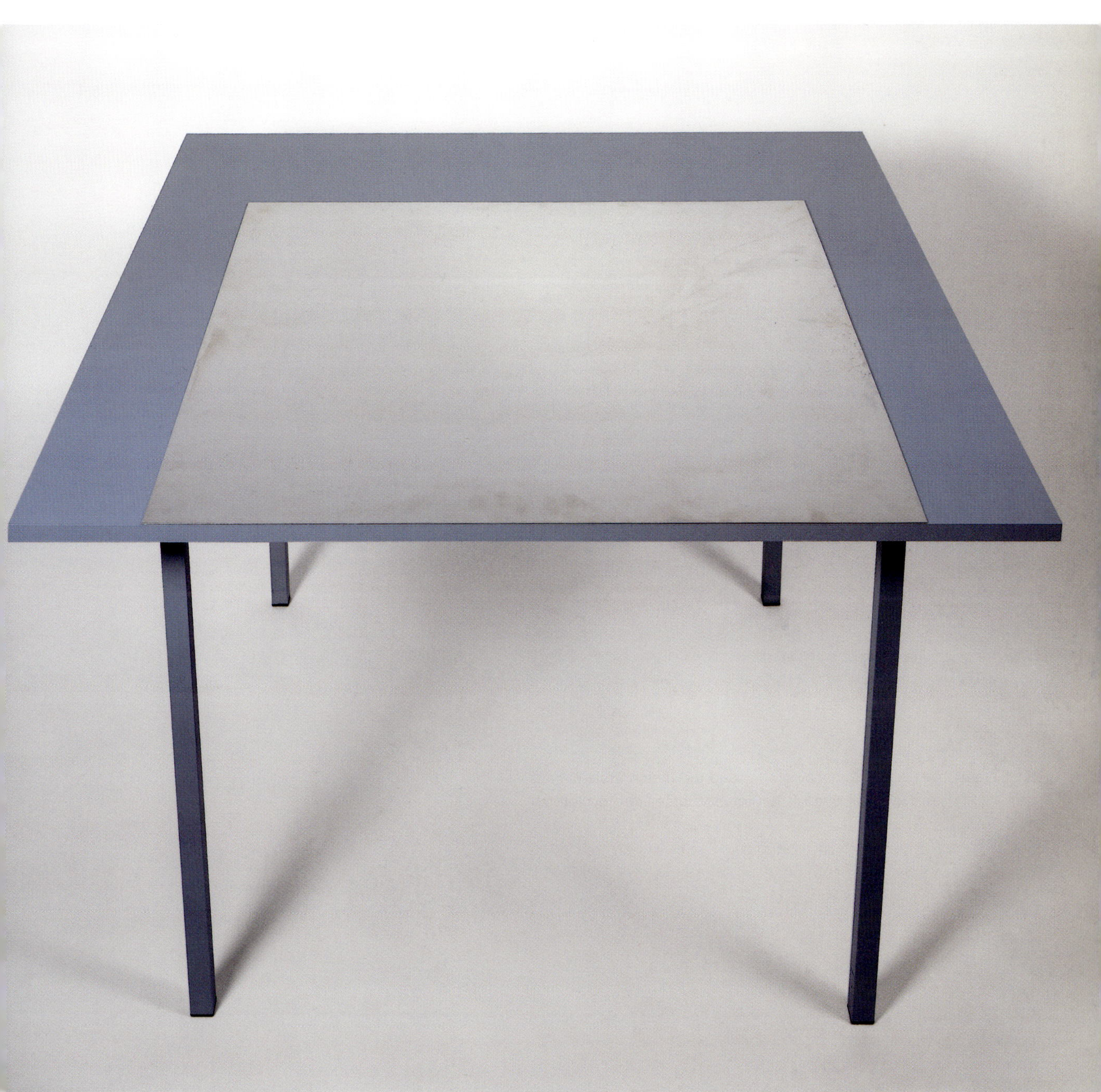

Pour

Painted cloth, 12 parts, each 320 x 140 cm, total dimensions variable
Berlin, Staatliche Museen zu Berlin – Preußischer Kulturbesitz, Nationalgalerie, Marzona collection

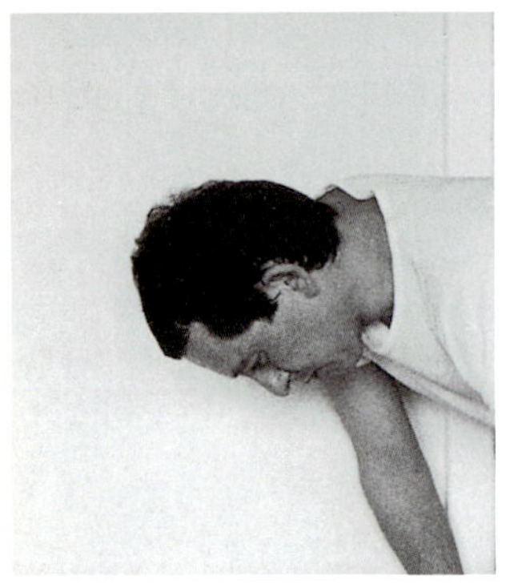

b. 1938 in Boulogne-Billancourt, France

In about 1965 the young artist Daniel Buren decided to liberate painting from all illusionist, representational and expressive qualities. Since then, his works have consisted of alternating white and coloured stripes always precisely 8.7 centimetres in breadth, vertically arranged, using different materials and different total dimensions. Buren himself regarded his project as "zero painting", and he wanted thereby to finally overcome traditional notions of art. As formal problems disappear when one confines oneself consistently to an identical motif, Buren succeeds in reinforcing the attention of beholders to the individual context in which his works appeared.

For a short time, Buren joined forces, loosely, with the painters Niele Toroni, Olivier Mosset and Michel Parmentier, who were likewise working in Paris, and who all worked in uniform formats. In 1967 they jointly exhibited their works for a day at the "Salon de la jeune peinture". During the opening, they confronted visitors via loudspeaker with the repeated message: "Buren, Mosset, Parmentier and Toroni advise you to become intelligent." A little later, the artists removed their works from the Salon and hung the room with banners that said: "Buren, Mosset, Parmentier and Toroni are not exhibiting." In a pamphlet accompanying the action, the four artists made clear their opposition to the ideological implications of traditional painting, and closed their manifesto with the words: "We are not painters."

In 1967 Buren began to work exclusively in situ, which meant that his projects were thenceforth directly related to the site in which they appeared. Because of his extremely critical attitude towards museums, which he described in the late 1960s as "dangerous weapons in the hands of the bourgeoisie", Buren decided at an early stage to by-pass the usual institutional art framework, and instead use public space more often for the presentation of his work. Thus in 1968 he pasted some 200 posters with green-and-white stripes around the streets all over Paris, publicizing a work that was not sponsored by an institution and for which no official permit had been granted. Buren remained totally anonymous as the perpetrator of this action. Many of his early works in an urban setting were temporary in nature, and today are only extant in the form of the photographs he took of his installations and published under the title *Photo/Souvenir.*

Like much of what was started with a critical intention in the 1960s, Buren's art has been – relatively painlessly – integrated into the institutional framework in the succeeding decades, as evidenced by numerous exhibitions and retrospectives in the world's leading venues. And yet the critical potential of his work is unbroken, in that it remains a constant pointer to the fact that "a thing never exists in itself".

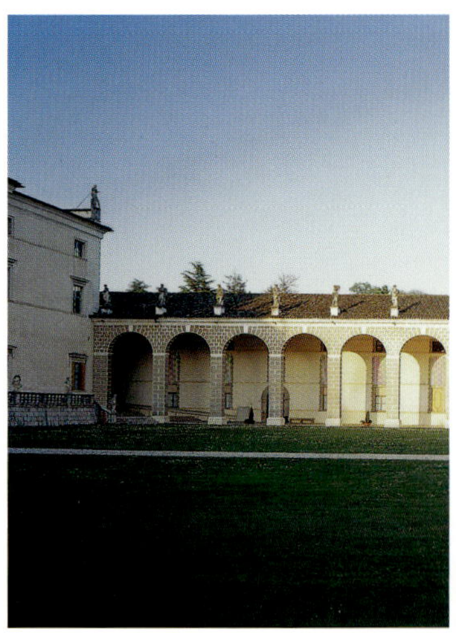

Pour (detail), 1973

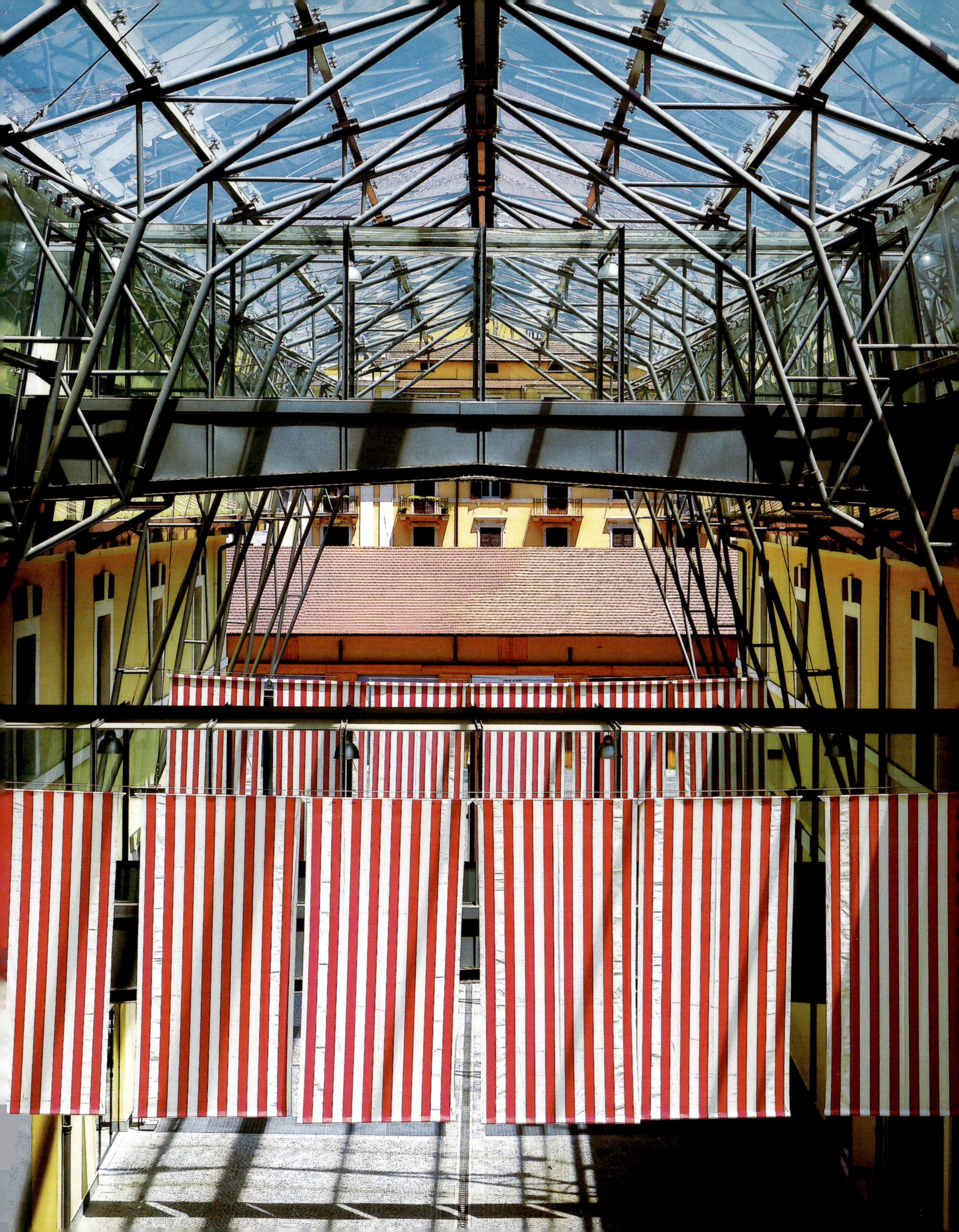

photath

Installation in the Fruitmarket Gallery, Edinburgh, 1985
Private collection

b. 1941 in Sheffield, England

Between 1965 and 1967 Victor Burgin attended, among other courses at Yale University, a seminar by Robert Morris, and so it is not surprising that in some early works the influence of his teacher is clearly apparent. Thus Burgin's *25 Feet Two Hours* (1967) integrates directly into the work the record of the process of its production, in the same way as Morris' *Box with the Sound of Its Own Making* (1962) or *Card File* (1962).

With *Photopath*, a work that Burgin executed in a number of versions between 1967 and 1969, he started to go his own way. Photographs of the floor on which the work was to be installed in the exhibition context were enlarged to the extent that they exactly matched the scale of the floor itself. These photographs were then laid out directly on the floor of the exhibition room, so that they covered the object that they simultaneously presented. In that Burgin's *Photopath* identified objective reality with its pictorial representation, the work raises general questions regarding the status of this pictorial representation. At the same time, Burgin's work interferes with the functionality of the object, which is now fused with its photographic representation, as it can no longer be walked on.

After using language as his exclusive artistic medium from 1969 for two years, from 1971 Burgin investigated the complex relationships between picture and text. From now on, his work evolved in an explicitly political context, as he was concerned first and foremost with uncovering hidden constructions of meaning and ideological motives in the everyday dissemination of picture and text.

Just as the English artists' group Art & Language, Burgin was concerned with decoding complex semiotic systems. But his work, in contrast to the purely theoretical focus of Art & Language, is directly involved in social reality, either by leaving the artistic context and taking place in the street, or by taking the advertising messages with which we are bombarded day by day and, by alienating them, revealing the many layers of meaning.

Thus in 1976 Burgin designed a poster for an exhibition project in Newcastle that contrasted an advertising photo he had found with quotations he had likewise picked up from "The Economist" magazine.

Above the picture of an embracing couple, the question "What does possession mean to you?" is posed, while beneath the picture we read the statistic "7% of our population own 84% of our wealth". Formally, Burgin's posters, which were pasted up all over the city, imitate the strategies of the advertisers, while at the same time the confusing combination of text and picture stimulates a critical reflection on social and economic conditions.

Alongside his innovative and politically significant work as an artist, in the last few decades Burgin has also contributed to the theory of photography. Some of his publications are still regarded as among the standard works of semiotically oriented photographic theory.

All Criteria, 1970

untitled

Indian ink on paper, 152 x 76 cm
Berlin, Staatliche Museen zu Berlin – Preußischer Kulturbesitz, Nationalgalerie, Marzona collection

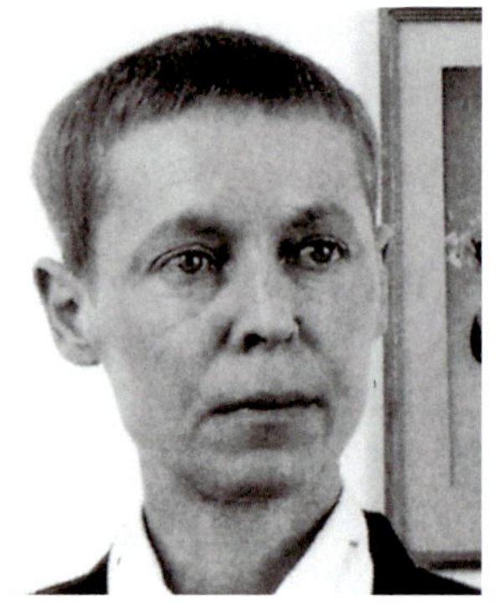

b. 1941 in Munich, Germany

Between 1962 and 1965 Hanne Darboven studied under various professors at the Hamburg Academy of Art. As she approached the end of her studies, she worked on abstract pictures and relief-like constructions, which related unambiguously to Constructivism. In 1966 the young artist decided to leave Germany for New York, without knowing what lay in wait for her there. During her stay in the city between 1966 and 1968, she got to know many of the representatives of American Minimal and Conceptual Art, such as Sol LeWitt and Carl Andre. During this time, her first *Konstruktionen* appeared, a series of drawings on square paper, based on the pictorialization of numerical relationships.

In 1968 Darboven returned to Hamburg for family reasons, and lives and works there still. Shortly after her return, she discovered a comprehensive system to govern her work when she changed to making calendar dates her starting point. Since then, in often complex processes, Darboven has been picturing historical periods in tabular drawings. Of the individual dates, she draws the respective crossfoot and, using a laborious technique, inserts the results into her drawings. In this way, we obtain visualizations of historical eras in which, as in an index, the time of their production is stored. Often a work is composed of hundreds of individual sheets, which represent the period of a year, a century or the lifetime of an historical figure. Each work is supplemented with an index, which provides information on the coding system used.

Darboven's drawings are often compared to musical scores. Indeed, the two systems of notation seem compatible, as Darboven made clear in 1974 when, for the two works *24 Gesänge – A Form* and *24 Gesänge B – Form*, she translated two numerical systems into scores. Both pieces exist not just on paper, but have been performed in public on several occasions.

Although the abstract representations of time are at the heart of Darboven's work, she nonetheless manages to integrate political, historical, literary and philosophical contexts into numerous more sizable works. Thus since about the mid-1970s she has included photographic material and texts by other people in her works. In 1978 with *Bismarckzeit* she produced her largest and most complex work thus far. In more than 900 drawings, into which she sometimes incorporated photographic material or else, for example, quotations from Bertolt Brecht or Willy Brandt, Darboven created a many-layered interpretation of the period (1850–1890) during which Otto von Bismarck was politically active, which, in impressive fashion, she related to the late 1970s when the work took shape. 1978, the year of its creation, was the centenary of Bismarck's anti-socialist laws.

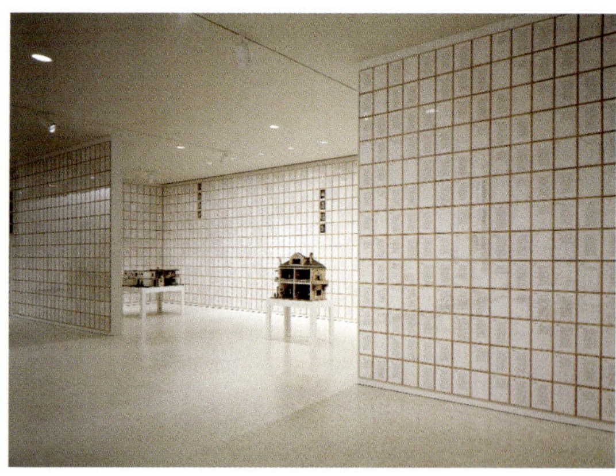

Leben, Leben/Life, Living, 1997/98

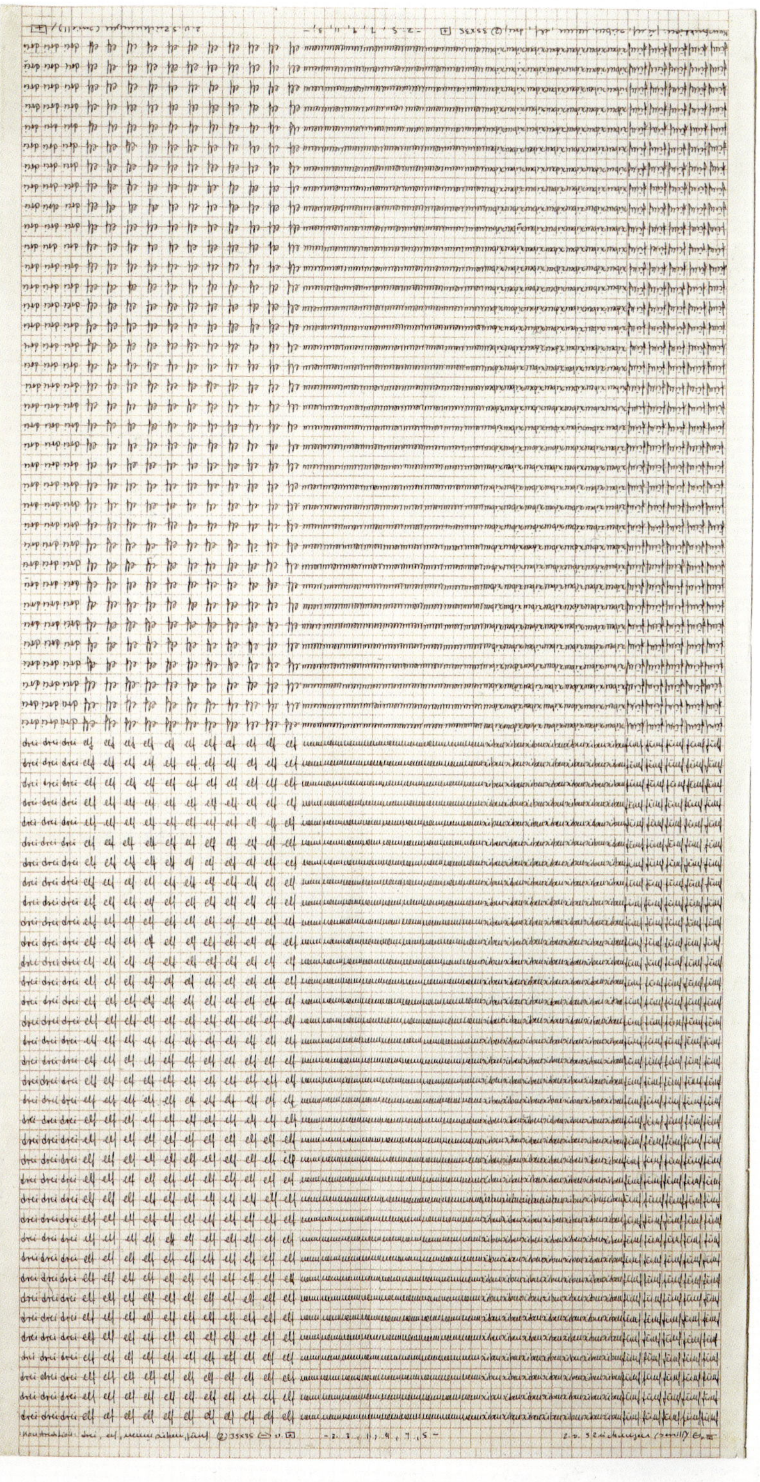

shortest Day at konrad Fischer's Gallery

Colour photographs on card, 175 x 180 cm
Private collection

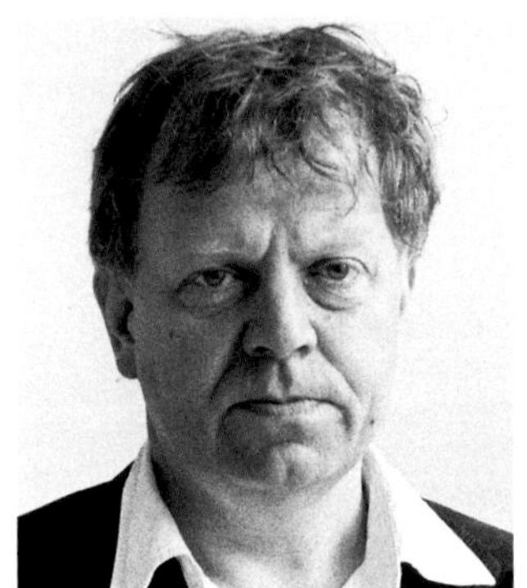

b. 1941 in Weert, The Netherlands

Hardly any other conceptual artist based his work, from the outset, so closely on the art-historical tradition as Jan Dibbets. He was well acquainted with the history and development of the perspective construction of three-dimensional space in the field of painting since the Renaissance, which became the starting point for a work that by way of photography was devoted to the sensitization of our perception. In contrast to many other conceptual artists, Dibbets sought to base the relationship between thought and vision in the picture itself and not in verbal-analytical form.

After he had been active for a few years as an abstract painter, while still a student at the St Martin's School of Art in London, in 1967 Dibbets began work on a series of photographic pictures with the title *Perspective Corrections*, in which he investigated the old problem of the relationship between two-dimensional plane and three-dimensional space but in a novel way. He integrated simple geometric shapes into a given spatial situation in such a way that in the photographic picture they seem to be not subject to the rules of perspective – at first with rope and string on lawns, and later, by drawing certain spatial elements in his studio. Like foreign bodies, the squares and rectangles float on the surface of these photographic pictures, and so Dibbets succeeds, using the simplest of means, illusionist doubling, to shake to the core the authenticity of the purportedly faithful depiction.

A little later there appeared works such as *The Shadows in my Studio* and *Shadows Taped off on a Wall, Museum Haus Lange, Krefeld* (both 1969), which document the change in the position of shadows. In one case, the position of the shadows is captured at intervals of time laid down in advance, using adhesive tape on the wall, while the other work records the course of the shadows photographically.

On the basis of these experiments, in about 1970 Dibbets evolved works that, utilizing the serial and sequential potential of photography with logical consistency, are devoted to the phenomenon of light. For the work *Shortest Day at Konrad Fischer's Gallery*, using always the same camera perspective, he photographed the same detail of the Galerie Fischer in changing light conditions, and mounted the individual photographs in chronological order on a large-format card. Thus integrated into a series of pictures, the individual photograph loses its fragmentary character, so that the ongoing flow of time becomes recognizable through the ebb and flow of the daylight.

As early as 1972, Dibbets drew attention to the difference between his work and the mostly verbally expressed forms of Conceptual Art, by noting: "In that concept there is quite simply nothing to see. I simply want to see something. For me their starting point is too literary."

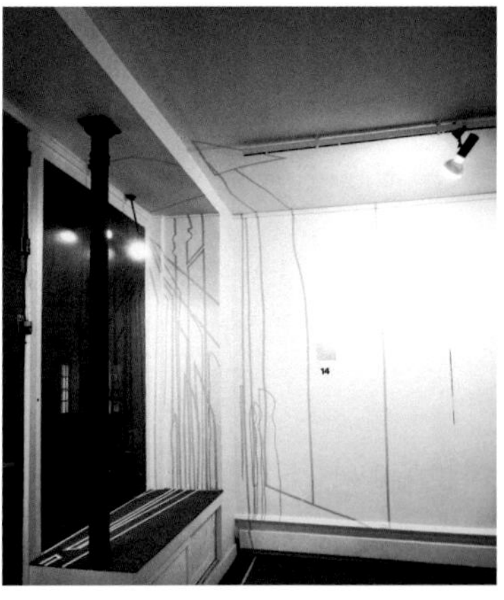

Shadow Piece (detail), 1970

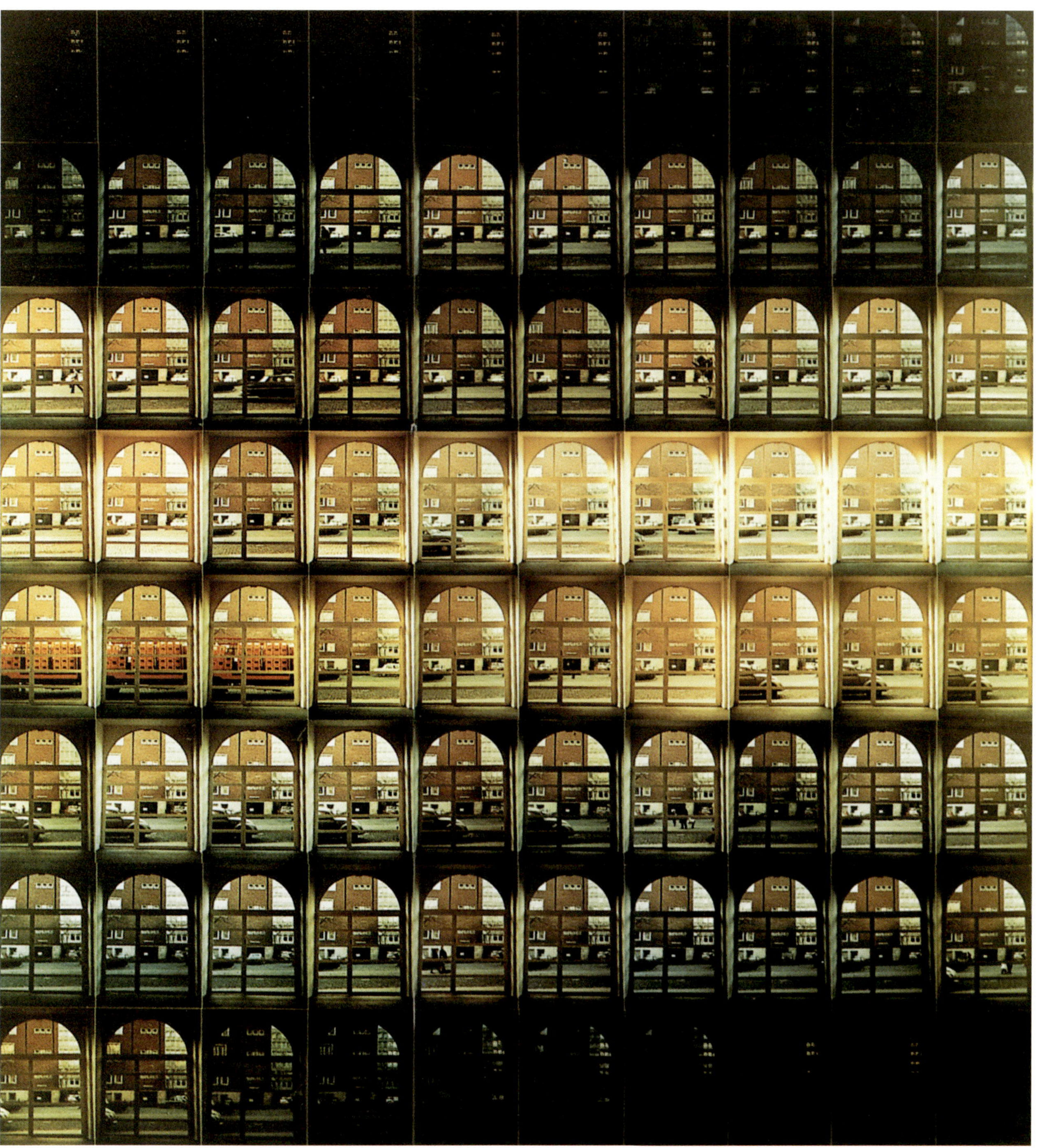

Alle kleider einer Frau

Black-and-white photographs on card, 72 parts, each 14.6 x 10.3 cm (detail)
Berlin, Staatliche Museen zu Berlin – Preußischer Kulturbesitz, Nationalgalerie, Marzona collection

b. 1941 in Düsseldorf, Germany

After working for some years on large-format pictures depicting over-life-size everyday objects, in 1968 Hans-Peter Feldmann began with the production and distribution of his "Hefte" (booklets), which made him into an early cult figure in German Conceptual Art. In small illustrated volumes with simple titles, Feldmann collected pictures of particular motifs which he had either found or taken himself, whose banality reflects the quality of the photographic reproductions amazingly well. Often bound in thin grey card, they had titles such as *8 Bilder* or *5 Bilder*, with the corresponding number of black-and-white photographs, in the first case depicting multiple ambulances and in the second unmade beds.

From a stock of usually 100 pictures of a particular motif, up to twelve were selected for a particular publication. Feldmann's "artist-books" were unsigned and printed in editions of 1,000 copies: i.e. cheaply produced mass goods, which in humorous fashion demonstrate the limited value of the application of Walter Benjamin's considerations on the loss of the aura of the work of art in the age of mechanical reproduction to the information culture of media ubiquity. For Feldmann's art was concerned from the outset with the omnipresent images that confront us every day, in order to use them for works that even conceptually exclude any idea of their being unique. In a certain sense, Feldmann's "booklets" can be understood as a publicly-made private appropriation of the world in pictures, making clear that production and consumption of media pictures without any verbal commentary or personal reference tend towards meaninglessness. Thus Feldmann's booklets literally hung in the air when he first exhibited them in 1977, dancing on threads suspended from the ceiling.

Later works, for which Feldmann hand-coloured found photographs of works by old masters and other pictorial material, as well as cheap copies of classical statues, show the reversal of Benjamin's dictum in even more drastic form. On the one hand, these works, through their use of the old technique of hand-colouring, give the reproductions the status of originals once more, as if to hint that it is no longer the uniqueness of the work of art that determines its charisma, but rather that, today, it is only through the ubiquity of its reproductions that the original acquires its aura.

Feldmann's predilection for everyday phenomena is also revealed by the 72-part work *Alle Kleider einer Frau* (All Clothes of a Woman), in which the apparently casually photographed garments are raised to the status of an art-work. The claim to completeness suggested by the title seems out of place in view of the substitutability and random nature of the motifs, so that the work as a whole can also be interpreted as a parody of the genre of conceptual documentary photography.

In 1980, with an exhibition in Ghent, Feldmann said goodbye for almost ten years to an art business which he had in any case regarded with scepticism from the outset. He destroyed all the works still in his possession, and applied himself for some time to the collection and distribution of tin toys.

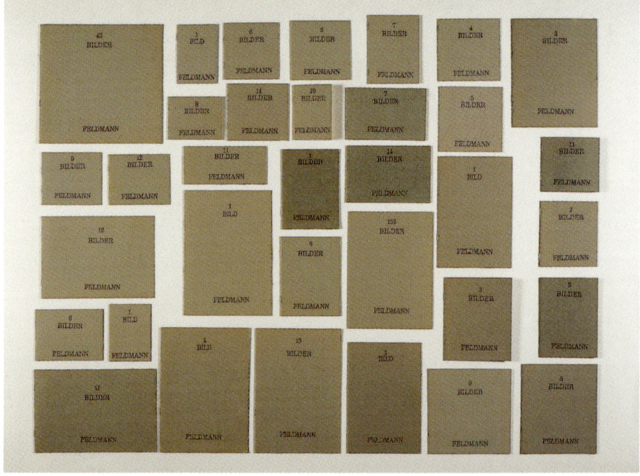

34 booklets, 1968–1974

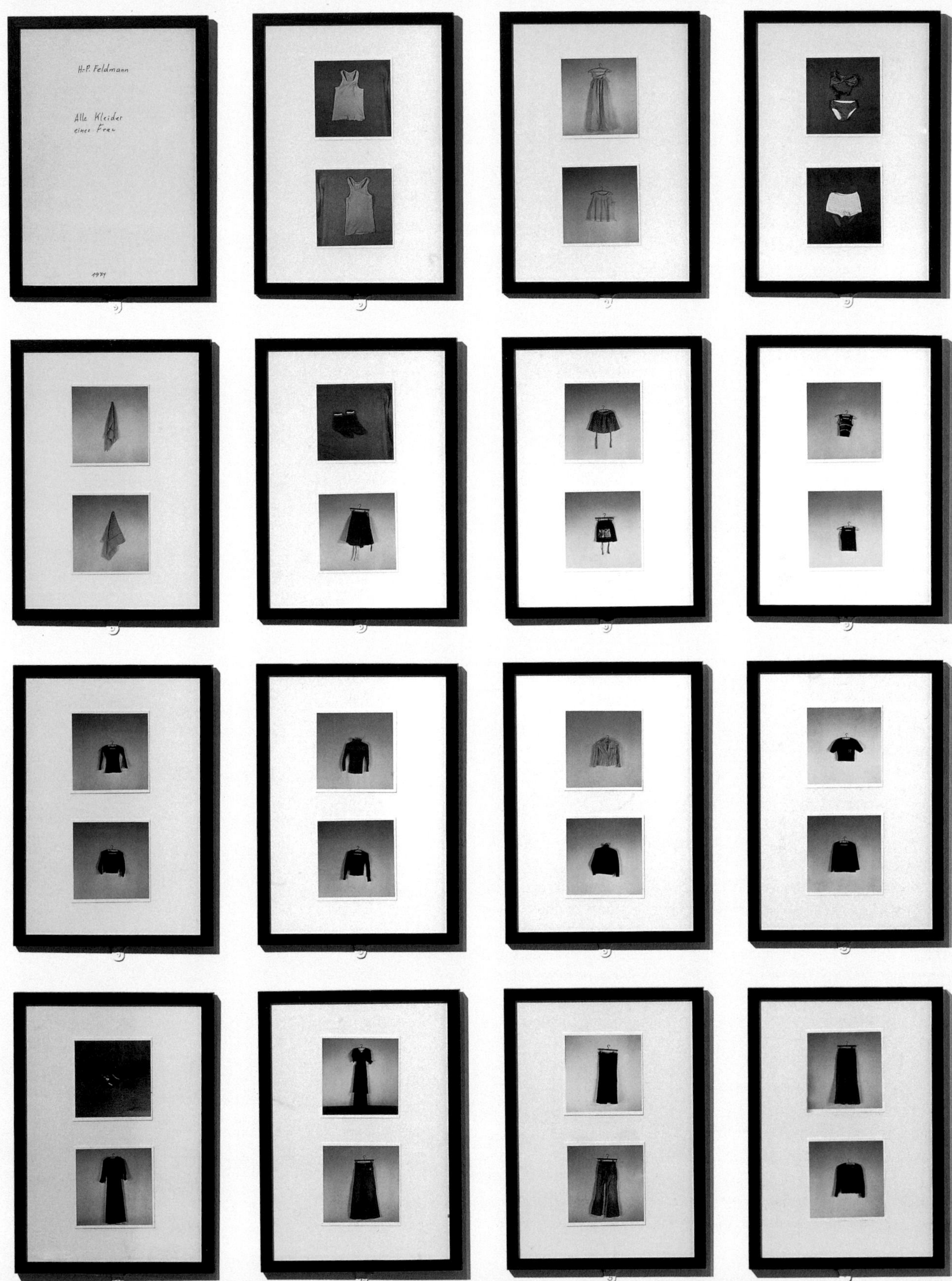

H.P. Feldmann
Alle Kleider
einer Frau
1974

singing sculptures

Performance
Courtesy Galleria L'Attico, Rome

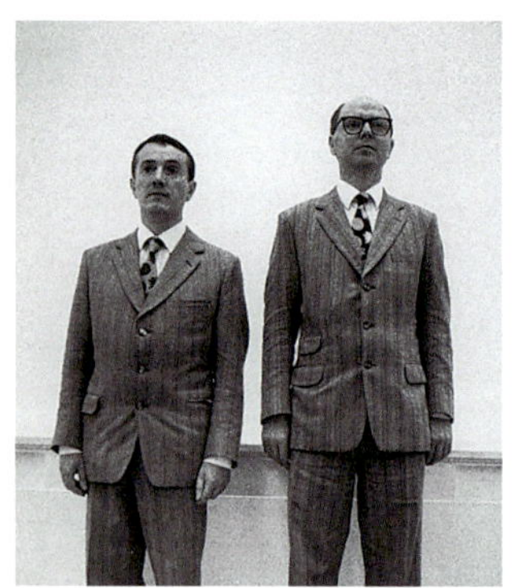

Gilbert Proesch b. 1943 in St. Martin, South Tyrol, Italy; George Passmore b. 1942 in Devon, England

The two artists Gilbert Proesch and George Passmore got to know each other as students at the St Martin's School of Art in London in the late 1960s. Since 1968 they have been working as an artist duo under the name of Gilbert & George. As Konrad Lueg and Gerhard Richter had already done in 1963 in their performance *Leben mit Pop. Eine Demonstration für den kapitalistischen Realismus* (Living with Pop. A Demonstration in Favour of Capitalist Realism), from 1969 Gilbert & George exhibited their own bodies as "living sculptures" in a variety of performances. Thus, in a relatively simple act, the two artists sought to solve the age-old problem of the gap between art and life. But what for Lueg and Richter was a one-off demonstration became a way of life for Gilbert & George. They understand not just their bodies as sculpture, but the totality of their artistic output, be it film, photography, performance, drawing or text, and thus they extend the concept of the genre to a degree that its traditional meaning totally evaporates. In 1969 the artists moved into a house in Spitalfields, a working-class district in London. Calling the house "Art for All", they thus emphasized the anti-elitist orientation of their artistic activities.

Artists and artworks at the same time, in 1969 Gilbert & George set themselves up for one of their first performances coated with metallic paint on the staircase of the Stedelijk Museum in Amsterdam, and remained there, motionless, for several hours. The same year witnessed the now famous performance *Singing Sculptures*, for which the two artists, in grey suits and with their faces and hands bronzed stood, on a table, dancing and singing silently to themselves, while beneath them a cassette recorder played "Underneath the

Arches" over and over without interruption. When the tape came to an end, the artists got down from the table, rewound it, exchanged their only props, a glove and a walking stick, to begin all over again without any further alterations.

Alongside their performances, since the 1970s Gilbert & George have been working intensively with photography and video. Thematically, many early works centre on the state of mental confusion caused by excessive consumption of alcohol. While video works such as *Gordon's Makes Us Drunk* or *A Portrait of the Artists as Young Men* (both 1972) show, in relatively conventional fashion, the two thirty-somethings posing as young men or getting themselves drunk on gin in the window of their flat, the photographic works are, formally and technically, altogether innovative.

Smashed (1972), for example, consists of ten originally identical photographs, which have been alienated through various manipulation techniques. Gilbert & George pinned the out-of-focus and in some cases doubly exposed pictures of themselves, standing at a bar, onto the wall in a chaotic pattern, so that simply the arrangement of the photos reflects the state of total drunkenness alluded to in the title.

In the early 1980s Gilbert & George began to make more use of the possibilities of colour-alienation in their photographic works, and to confront various aspects of city-living and sexuality.

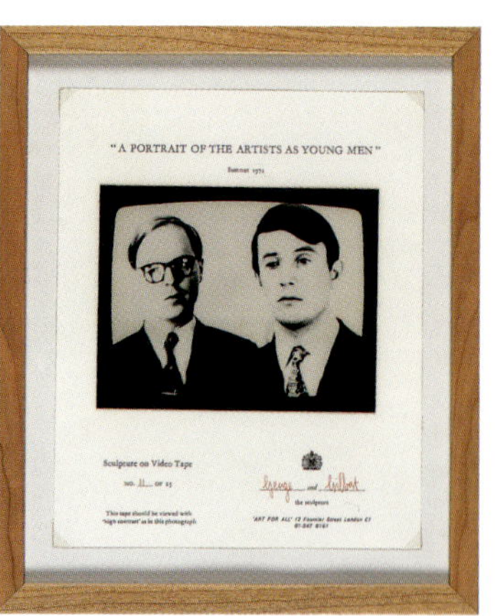

A Portrait of the Artists as Young Men, 1972

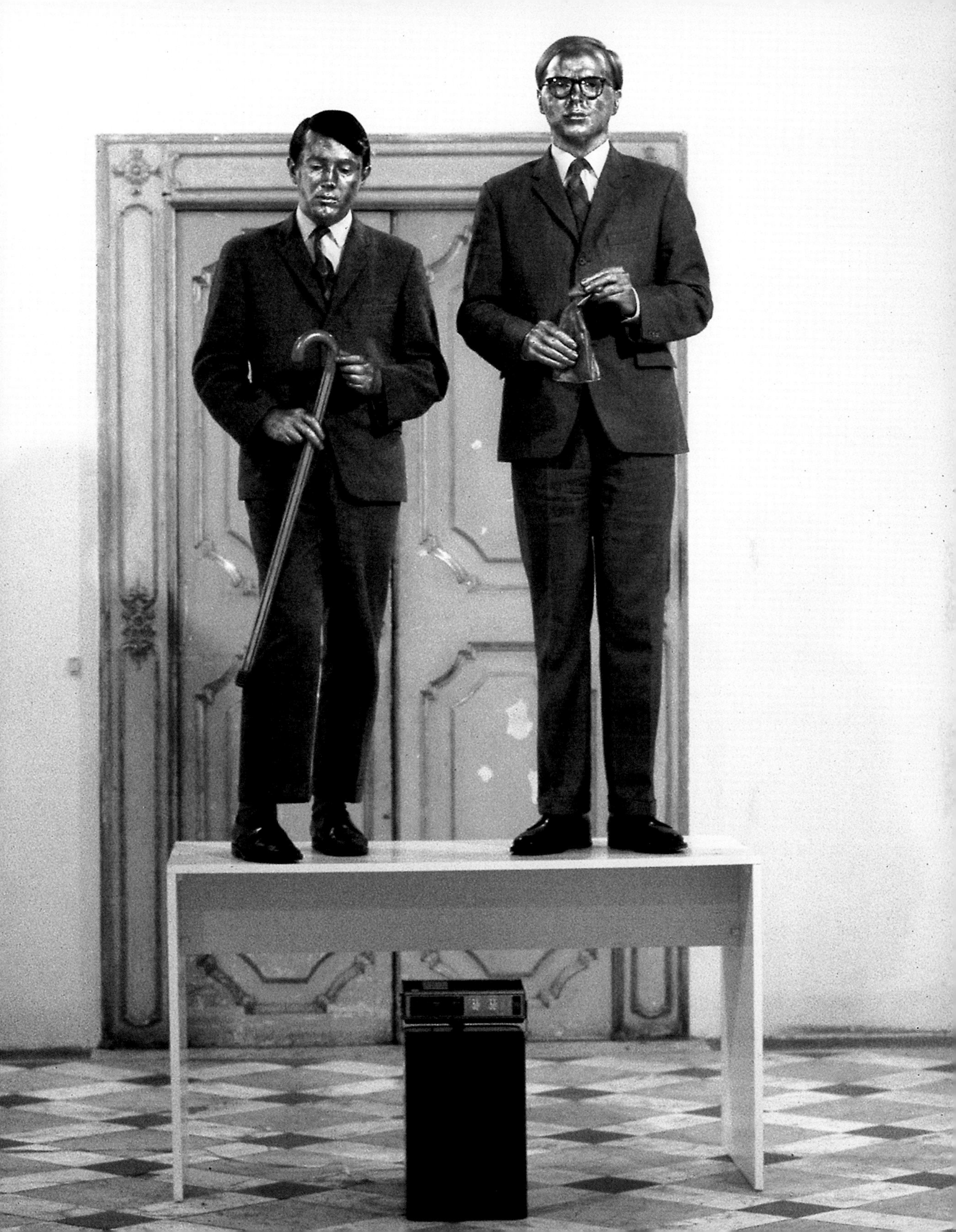

Figurative

Published in various contexts; illustration: "Harper's Bazaar", March 1965
Courtesy Marian Goodman Gallery, New York

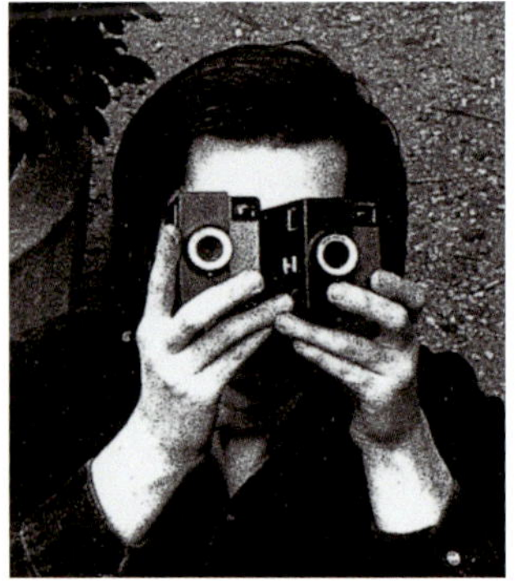

b. 1942 in Urbana (IL), USA

Before Dan Graham started using magazines as the forum for the publication of his works in 1965, he had been director and proprietor of the John Daniels Gallery in New York for two years. Although his gallery worked together with important artists and was one of the few places where avant-garde art was presented, Graham was forced by insolvency to close it in 1965. As he himself noted in retrospect, the strategies he tried out shortly after this failure were "a reaction against the gallery experience, but also as a response to contradictions I discerned in gallery artists".

Figurative was Graham's first work to deliberately appear before the public in a non-art context and in a new way. The, it must be said, poor reproduction of a simple till receipt (sales slip) with the additional text *Figurative by Dan Graham* appeared in 1965 in the magazine "Harper's Bazaar" between a small advertisement for tampons and a large-format one for a new kind of bra. Both the till receipt and the context of the advertisements point to the topic of consumerism and purchasability, whereby Graham's intervention in a strange way charges the banal character of the advertisements with significance and, so to speak, takes away their clarity.

While *Figurative* can be interpreted as a parody of the advertising genre, in that it uses the symbol of the till receipt to advertise the act of buying itself, Graham's work *Homes for America* (1966), published the following year, reveals itself as a caricature of a purportedly objective sociological article. In this essay, which was published in "Arts Magazine", Graham dryly describes important characteristics of American suburban architecture. The information is arranged in blocks of text that alternate with photographs Graham had taken himself. In ironic fashion, *Homes for America* draws attention not least to

how the reading of a text influences the interpretation of the pictures that illustrate it. For Graham's banal snapshots, in the context of his pseudo-scholarly text, take on the status of evidence in that they appear to give objective substance to the verbal statements.

In the late 1960s, Graham concentrated on performances and video works in which he self-referentially thematized their temporal and spatial structure and the act of seeing and filming. For *Two Correlated Rotations* (1969), a double film projection, two actors were required to move in spirals in opposite directions relative to each other, in order, during this process, to film each other as far as possible without interruption. In this way, the two subjects found themselves at the same time in the role both of the observer and of the observed. The pictures taken by each camera were projected at right angles to each other onto two walls of the gallery room, where they could be seen by visitors after a short time lapse.

In later works, Graham thematically confronts with a variety of aspects of urban living. Thus in recent decades he has realized numerous architectural projects in the public space, which in some cases have been integrated into functional contexts. In his so-called *Pavilions* — mostly room constructions reflected in complex fashion — the separation between the beholder and the object beheld is removed, at least in part, since sculpture, beholder and surroundings merge in ever-new reflections and can never be perceived in isolation from each other.

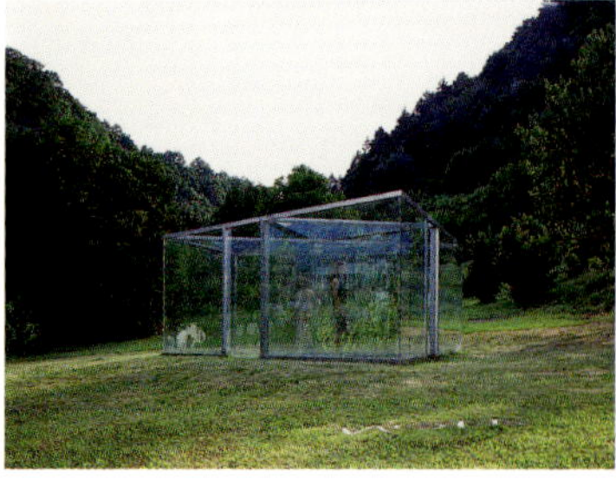

Bisected Two-way Mirror Triangle, 1998

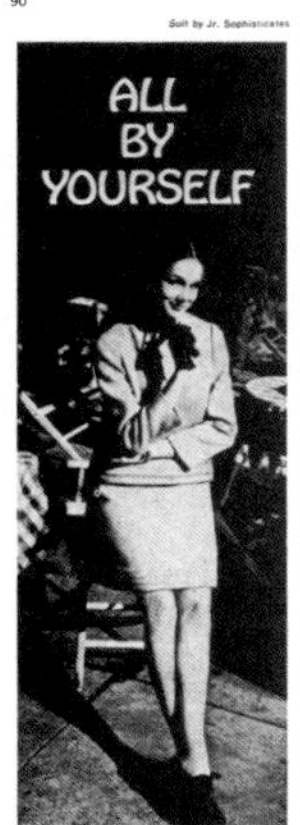

Perhaps you think 18-year-olds should vote, your curfew should be lifted and math be outlawed forever. But there's one thing on which you agree with millions of women in 106 countries — the modern internally worn sanitary protection — Tampax tampons.
Why does a girl with a mind of her own go along with women all over the world?
Tampax tampons give total comfort, total freedom. There are no belts, pins, pads. No odor. They can be worn in the tub or shower — even in swimming. There's nothing to show under the sleekest clothes. And Tampax tampons are so easy to dispose of, too — the container-applicator just flushes away, like the Tampax tampon.
If you haven't tried them already — get Tampax tampons today.

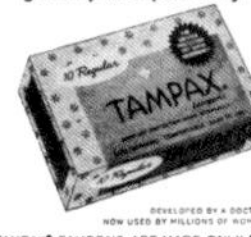

DEVELOPED BY A DOCTOR
NOW USED BY MILLIONS OF WOMEN
TAMPAX® TAMPONS ARE MADE ONLY BY
TAMPAX INCORPORATED, PALMER, MASS.

FIGURATIVE
BY
DAN
GRAHAM

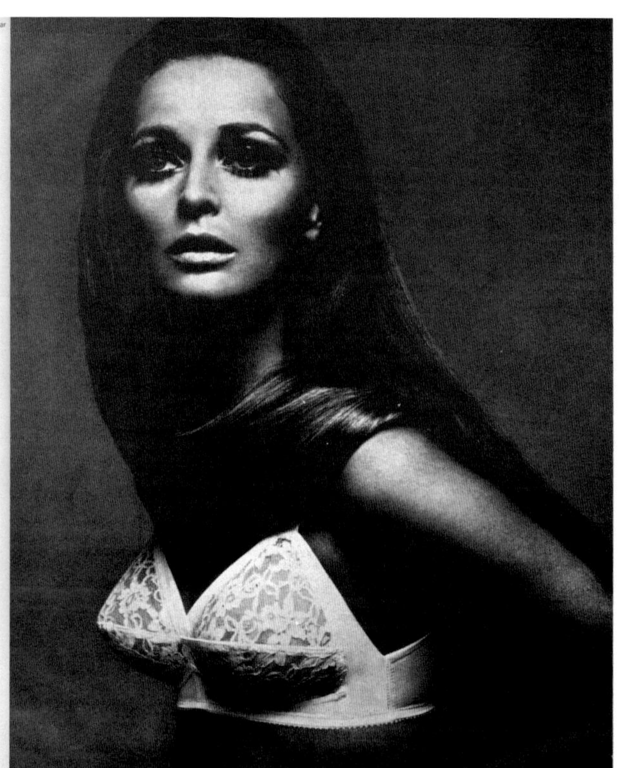

MOMA Poll

Text and two ballot boxes with counting device, each 102 x 51 x 24.5 cm
Installation at the exhibition "Information", The Museum of Modern Art, New York
Photography: Staatliche Museen zu Berlin – Preußischer Kulturbesitz, Kunstbibliothek, Marzona collection

b. 1936 in Cologne, Germany

In 1965 Hans Haacke moved from Cologne to New York, where he still lives and works. In his early works, he confronted the issue of the modus operandi of physical and biological systems. Thus Haacke's *Condensation Cubes* (water-filled Plexiglas cubes, with which he experimented between 1963 and 1965), which are formally in the vicinity of Minimal Art, can be understood as open physical processes. Depending on the temperature, the light conditions and the airflow in the room, the water enclosed in the cube starts to condense on the Plexiglas sides. In a simple construction Haacke succeeds in visualizing a physical process, a large part of whose charm lies in its ostensible never-ending quality.

In the late 1960s, Haacke's interest in biological-physical systems shifted towards an analysis of the social, economic and political conditions of the institutional context of art. In his early opinion-survey projects Haacke went about the task with almost scientific methods when he compiled empirically verifiable facts relating to the social background of the visitors to his exhibition and presented these data soberly and mostly without further comment.

For his project *MOMA Poll* in the context of the 1970 group exhibition "Information", Haacke questioned museum visitors about their political convictions and at the same time criticized, as it were, the political attitude of Nelson Rockefeller, who at the time was not only Governor of New York State but a member of the Board of Trustees of The Museum of Modern Art. At the entrance to the museum, visitors were given voting papers, which they could place in one of two Plexiglas boxes equipped with electronic counting devices. The following question was to be answered "yes" or "no": "Would the fact that Governor Rockefeller has not denounced President Nixon's Indochina policy be a reason for you not to vote for him in November?" Two months before the opening of the exhibition, President Nixon had ordered the bombing and American invasion of Cambodia, so that Haacke's action had to be seen as directly related to current political events. By the end of the exhibition, 68.7% of the visitors had voted "yes" and 31.3% "no".

In 1971 Haacke's work *Shapolsky et al. Manhattan Real Estate Holdings, a Real-time Social System, as of May, 1971*, which he wanted to present to the public for the first time on the occasion of his planned solo exhibition at the Guggenheim Museum, led to the cancellation of the exhibition and the resignation of the curator Edward Fry. The work, in which Haacke, using publicly accessible documents and photographs of the buildings in question, meticulously and accurately documented a real estate agency's speculations, was seen by the director of the Guggenheim Museum as not art-worthy and triggered the first scandal in connection with Haacke's artistic activities, but by no means the last. Not just Haacke's critical art practice itself, but also the widespread censorship to which his works were subjected in the institutional context, confirm the artist's view that "the social forces that have an effect on the art world naturally are the same forces that affect everything else in the country, and in the world".

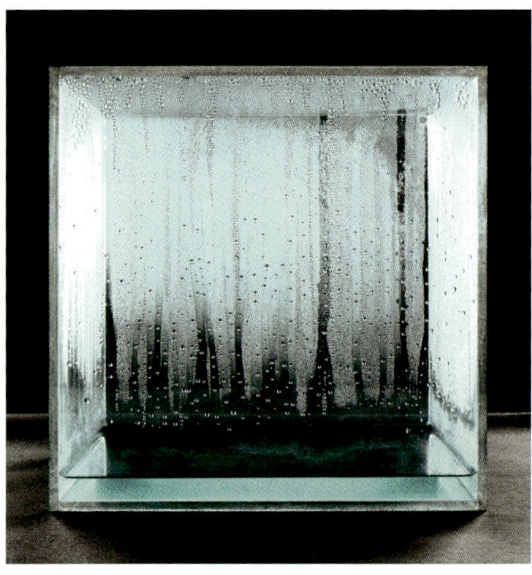

Condensation Cube, 1963–1965

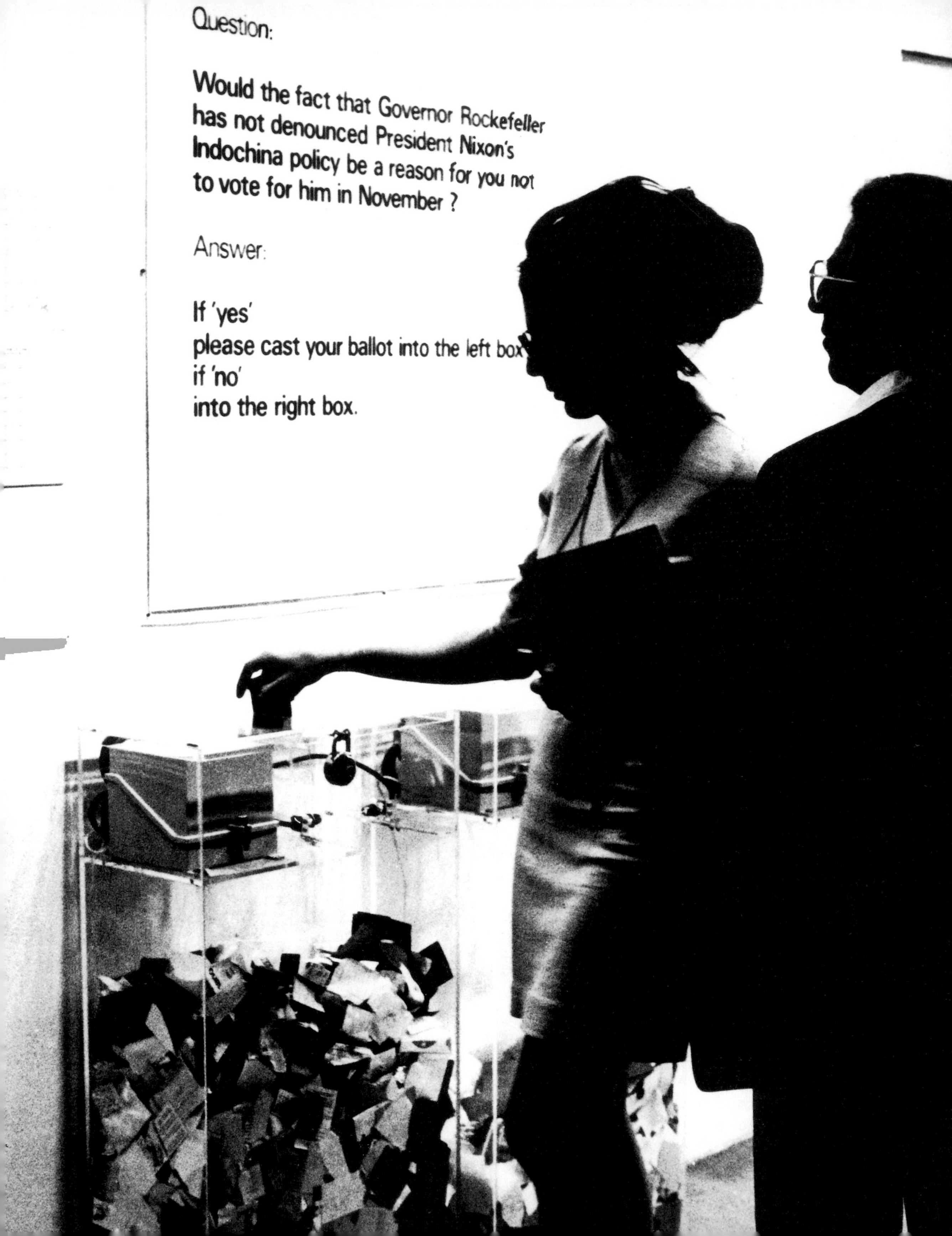

Question:

Would the fact that Governor Rockefeller
has not denounced President Nixon's
Indochina policy be a reason for you not
to vote for him in November?

Answer:

If 'yes'
please cast your ballot into the left box
if 'no'
into the right box.

Die Fast and Quiet…

Writing on aluminium, 38.7 x 45.7 cm
Berlin, Staatliche Museen zu Berlin – Preußischer Kulturbesitz, Nationalgalerie, Marzona collection

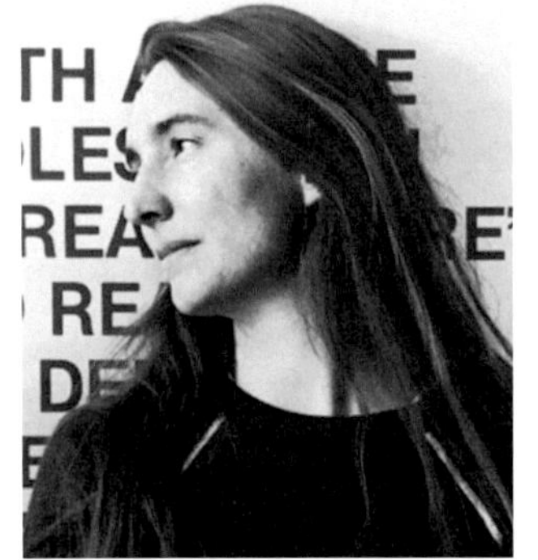

b. 1950 in Gallipolis (OH), USA

Between 1968 and 1975 Jenny Holzer studied at Duke University in Durham, then at the University of Chicago, and finally at Ohio University in Athens, where she graduated with a BFA in 1972. Two years later she attended graduate summer courses at the Rhode Island School of Design in Providence. Hitherto she had worked as an abstract painter, but here she began to incorporate verbal elements into her work and to take part in public art projects.

Since 1977 Holzer has been using language exclusively in order to gain the attention of a broad public, working in a variety of media and mostly in the public arena. The first attention-grabbing art actions took place between 1977 and 1979, when she displayed works from the *Truisms* series in New York City. Holzer had up to 40 such truisms, some with provocative content, printed on posters in alphabetical order, and pasted them up in large numbers in suitable places. Content-wise, the individual statements ranged from EVERYONE'S WORK IS EQUALLY IMPORTANT to ABUSE OF POWER COMES AS NO SURPRISE to such trivialities as BOREDOM MAKES YOU DO CRAZY THINGS.

Holzer herself describes her *Truisms* as "mock clichés", whose validity is left to the public to test. Indeed, the reactions of the public were remarkable. Numerous slogans were painted over or changed by passers-by, or else provided with value-judgement commentaries. Evidently Holzer's sometimes banal, sometimes philosophical statements challenge their recipients to confront them directly.

Holzer's declared intention of achieving an effect far beyond the art context is what connects her approach with the work of the politicized Dadaists in the Berlin of the 1920s and 1930s, and with the later interventions of the Situationists. Holzer's *Inflammatory Essays*, published between 1979 and 1982, relate quite openly to political conditions, and in some cases demand a drastic change in the existing situation. As with the *Truisms*, Holzer had her *Inflammatory Essays* printed on posters, albeit this time in colour, and pasted up in public, mostly on façades. Most of these "essays" comprise precisely 100 words. The following excerpt makes the radicalism of her utterances clear enough: "REJOICE! OUR TIMES ARE INTOLERABLE. TAKE COURAGE FOR THE WORST IS THE HARBINGER OF THE BEST. ONLY DIRE CIRCUMSTANCES CAN PRECIPITATE THE OVERTHROW OF THE OPPRESSORS. THE OLD AND CORRUPT MUST BE LAID TO WASTE BEFORE THE JUST CAN TRIUMPH."

In later works such as the *Living Series* (1980–1982) Holzer addressed more everyday phenomena and toned down the openly political character of her work in favour of a concentration on the more usual activities and concerns of everyday existence.

Over the last two decades Holzer has managed to get her work propagated via public information channels in an extraordinarily creative and effective fashion. Thus it has been seen in lights on Times Square as well as on baseball caps, walls, and buttons, in newspaper advertisements, on marble benches and T-shirts. Holzer's various messages, which we often encounter unexpectedly, have lost none of their irritating power to this day.

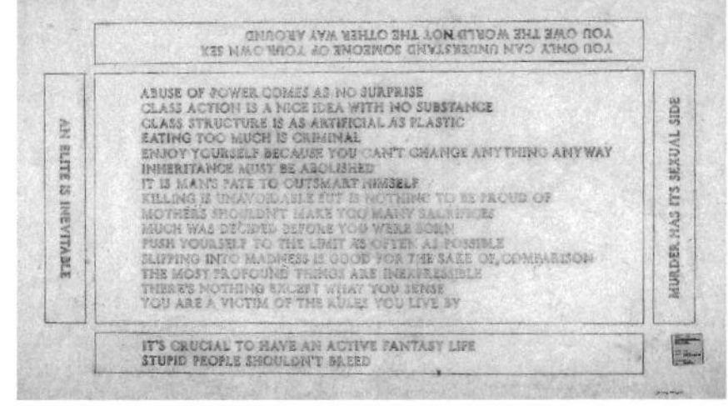

TRUISMS: ABUSE OF POWER COMES, 1977–1979

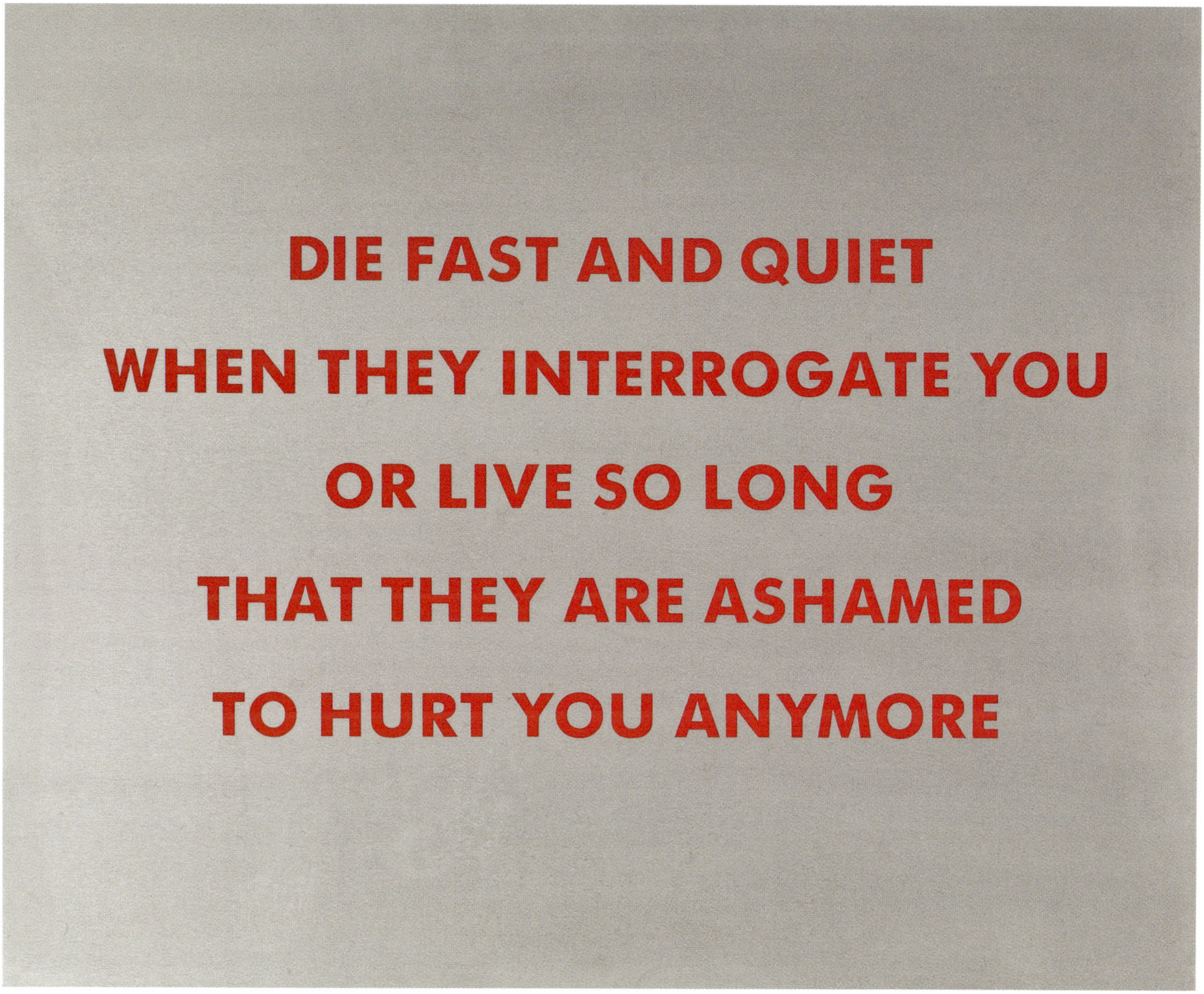

DIE FAST AND QUIET
WHEN THEY INTERROGATE YOU
OR LIVE SO LONG
THAT THEY ARE ASHAMED
TO HURT YOU ANYMORE

variable piece no. 70: 1971 (in process), global

Black-and-white photograph, contact print, typescript text, 68 x 59 cm
Grenoble, Musée de Grenoble

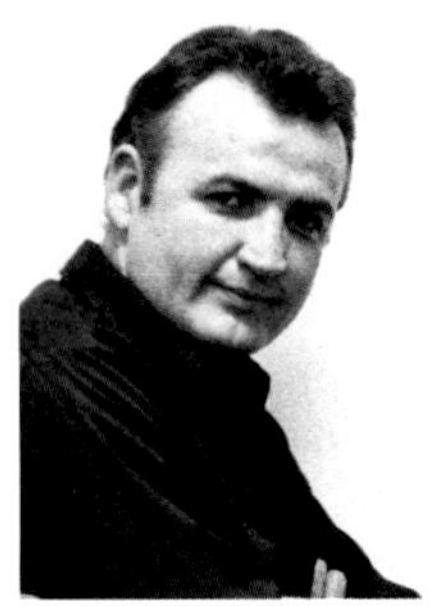

**b. 1924 in Ann Arbor (MI),
d. 1997 in Turo (MA), USA**

Before Douglas Huebler turned to a more conceptual approach to his work, he created Minimalist sculptures, which he displayed on numerous occasions at exhibitions that attracted considerable attention. Thus the curator Kynaston McShine invited him to take part in the first comprehensive museum exhibition of Minimal Art, "Primary Structures" at the Jewish Museum in New York in 1966. Two years later, in 1968, Huebler finally stopped working in three dimensions, and evolved his *Location*, *Duration* and *Variable Pieces*, which he first exhibited that same year at the Siegelaub Gallery, and to which he remained loyal throughout the 1970s, before once again radically changing direction. In his *Location* and *Duration Pieces* Huebler documents real systems of time and space in the arrangement of photographs, text and cartographic material: systems which, whose complexity excludes any direct perception.

For Harald Szeemann's major survey exhibition "Live in Your Head. When Attitudes Become Form", held in Bern in 1969, Huebler entered a work which gives an insight into essential characteristics of his approach. *Duration Piece No. 9* consists of a transparent Plexiglas box, a map on which a straight line is drawn between the east and west coasts of the USA, and a short text, which explains the documented process. Huebler handed the box to the post office with a fictitious address, and it was of course returned to sender as undeliverable. The sender did the same thing with a different fictitious address, and so on and so forth. In this way, the object covered a distance of some 10,000 miles. The six-week to-and-fro process between the east and west coasts was now preserved in an unassuming Plexiglas box and could be grasped within a very short time by the beholder. Thus the work superimposes temporal and spa-tial aspects of a real happening, that normally would be perceived separately.

While much of Huebler's work describes temporal and/or spatial processes in a dry documentary fashion, *Variable Piece No. 70: 1971 (in Process), Global* is more utopian and at the same time bears witness to the profoundly democratic character of his view of art. Between 1971 and his death in 1997, he took countless photos of people he happened to meet in the street or whom he knew personally. In the text, which, alongside the picture, constitutes the work, and which accompanies all presentations of the work, Huebler writes: "Throughout the remainder of the artist's lifetime he will photographically document, to the extent of his capacity, the existence of everyone alive in order to produce the most authentic and inclusive representation of the human species that may be assembled in that manner. Editions of the work will be periodically issued in a variety of topical modes: '100,000 people', '1,000,000 people', '10,000,000 people', 'people personally known by the artist', 'look alikes', 'overlaps', etc."

"more specifically, the work concerns itself with things whose interrelationship is beyond direct perceptual experience."

Douglas Huebler

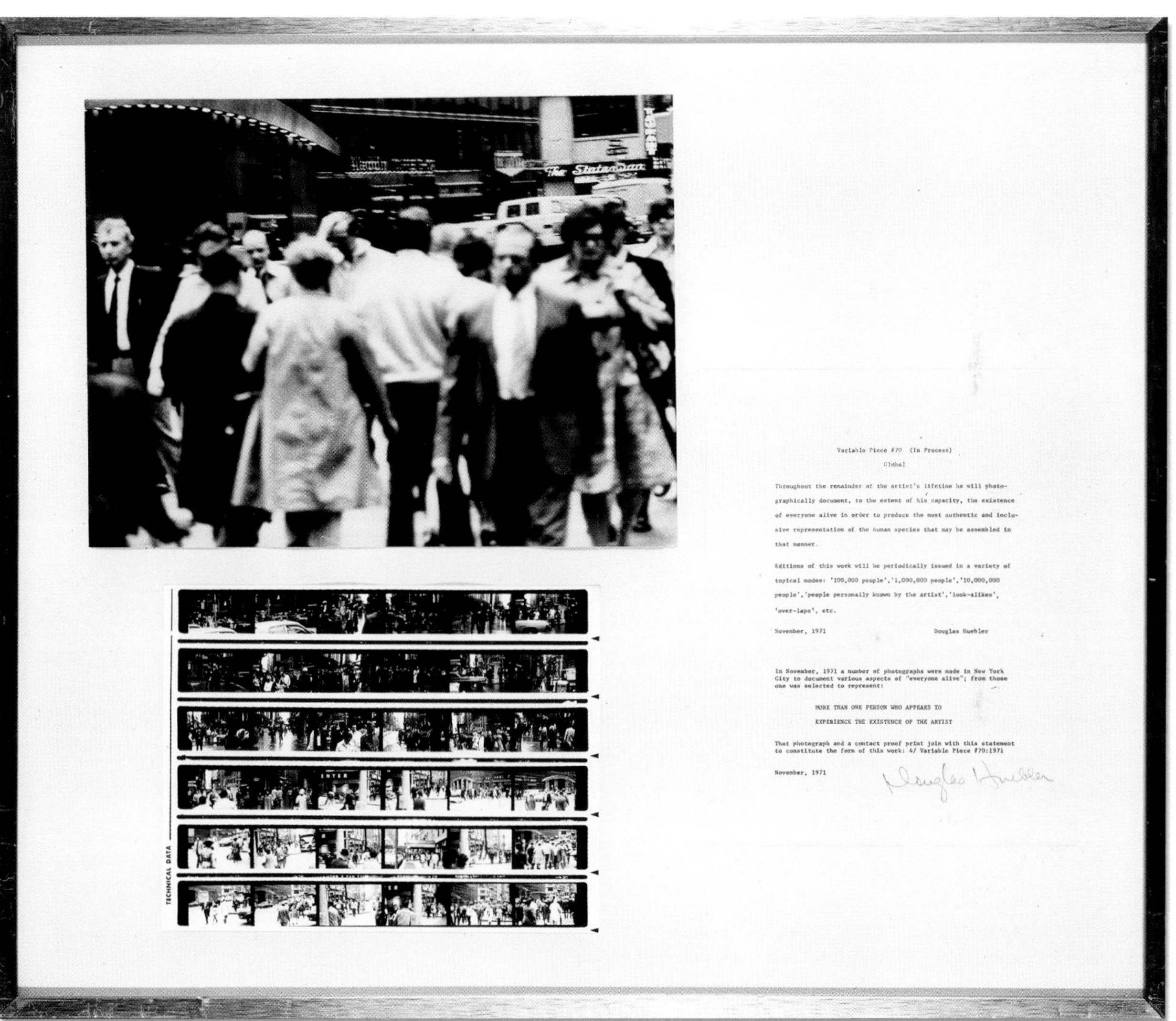

Variable Piece #70 (In Process)

Global

Throughout the remainder of the artist's lifetime he will photographically document, to the extent of his capacity, the existence
of everyone alive in order to produce the most authentic and inclusive representation of the human species that may be assembled in
that manner.

Editions of this work will be periodically issued in a variety of
topical modes: '100,000 people','1,000,000 people','10,000,000
people','people personally known by the artist','look-alikes',
'over-laps', etc.

November, 1971   Douglas Huebler

In November, 1971 a number of photographs were made in New York
City to document various aspects of "everyone alive"; from those
one was selected to represent:

MORE THAN ONE PERSON WHO APPEARS TO

EXPERIENCE THE EXISTENCE OF THE ARTIST

That photograph and a contact proof print join with this statement
to constitute the form of this work: 4/ Variable Piece #70:1971

November, 1971

TECHNICAL DATA

ART WORKS

Cast iron, 13.5 x 21 cm
Berlin, Staatliche Museen zu Berlin – Preußischer Kulturbesitz, Nationalgalerie, Marzona collection

b. 1940 in Battle Creek (MI), USA

Like Bruce Nauman, Stephen Kaltenbach must also be seen, by dint of the variety of his artistic approaches, as an unorthodox representative of North American Concept Art. During his time as a student at the University of California in Davis between 1966 and 1967, he worked on "walk through" room constructions – geometrically simple structures which, while showing a relationship in the formal respect with Minimal Art, nonetheless were set up with the declared aim of having a lasting and disconcerting effect on those who passed through them.

In the middle of 1967, Kaltenbach moved to New York, where until 1970 he always sought to undermine traditional views of art. While they are structurally fundamentally different, Kaltenbach's projects have at least one thing in common: namely that they circumvent the institutional context of art by addressing the public in unconventional ways.

In November 1968 Kaltenbach placed his first ad in the magazine "Artforum": it took the form of his statement *ART WORKS*, and appeared without any indication of authorship between various announcements of exhibitions. In later ads, the relationship of his anonymous communications to art increasingly evaporated when he started placing brief instructions such as *Build a Reputation* or suggestive messages like *You Are Me*. At the same time Kaltenbach, over the space of a decade, sent to fellow artists and people he knew from the art world his *Time Capsules* – welded metal tubes, in which he had instructions to the respective recipient engraved. Thus on the *Time Capsule for Bruce Nauman* there is the message "Retain possession of this capsule. Do not open it until notified.", while the capsule addressed to the art critic Barbara Rose bore the message "Please open this capsule when, in your opinion, I have attained (national) prominence as an artist." In the collection of the Museum of Modern Art there is a capsule with the instruction to open it after his death.

The *Time Capsules* project reveals two telling characteristics of Kaltenbach's total art production. On the one hand, even conceptually they are impossible for the art market to make any money out of, and on the other they contain, at least virtually, the negation of their status as artwork, which they would lose at the moment of their opening because this would deprive them of their concealment function. In comparable fashion, nearly all of Kaltenbach's projects of the late 1960s move in a grey area between art and the everyday.

With his 1968 *Sidewalk Plaque Series* Kaltenbach literally took his art onto the street by having bronze plaques made, which were intended to be set in the concrete of New York's sidewalks. The six anonymous plaques, sited in New York's public space, bearing the inscriptions "Art Works", "Air", "Blood", "Bone", "Fire" and "Water" bear witness to Kaltenbach's radical view of art: he deliberately dispensed with any claim to authorship or with saleability, in order to be able to test the functional value of art in changed contexts.

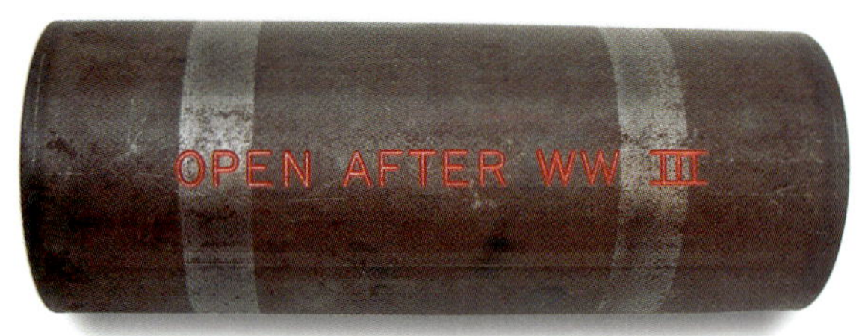

Time Capsule – Open After WW III (2), n. d.

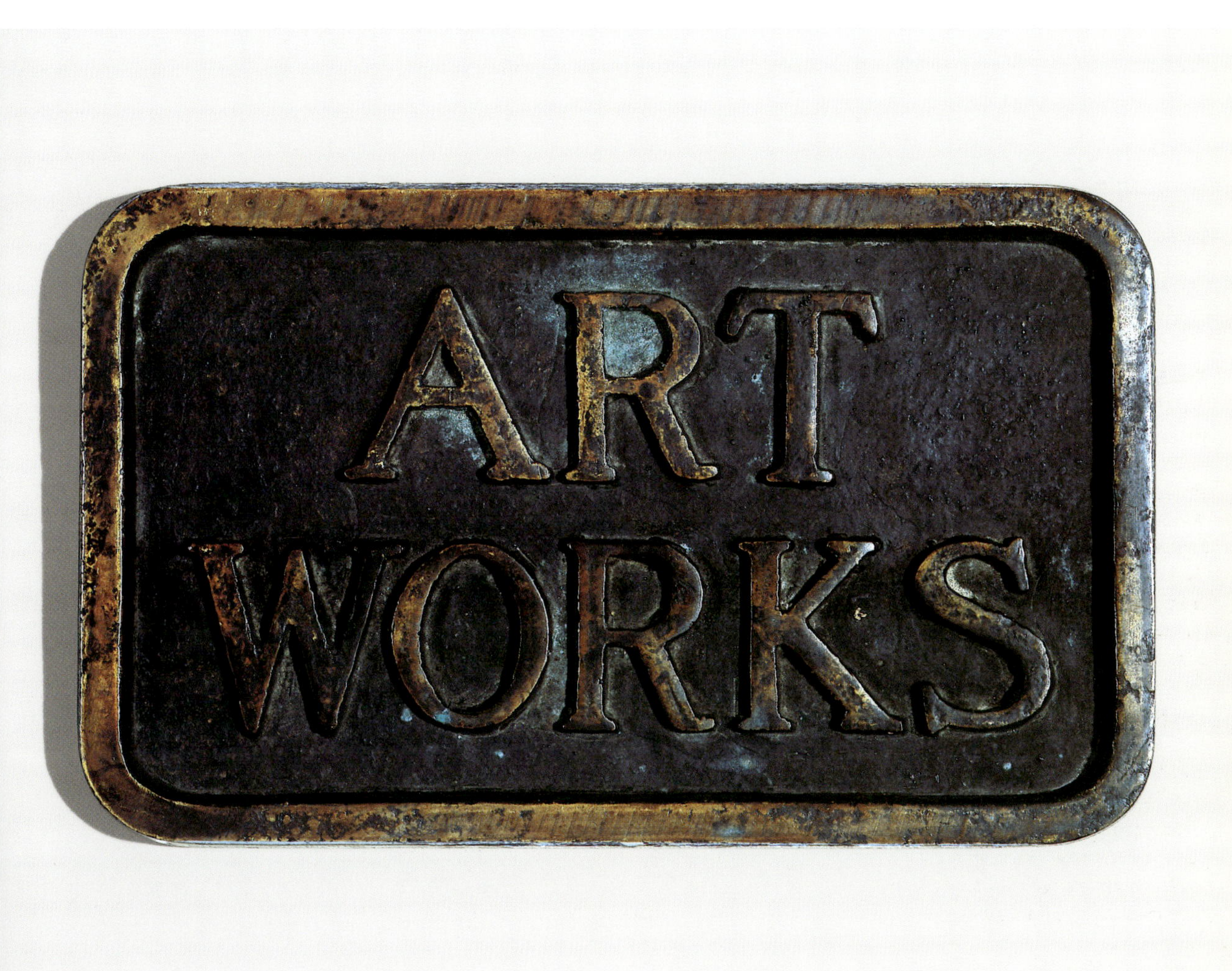
ART
WORKS

I Got Up

Post cards with rubber stamp, 21 parts, each 8.9 x 14 cm
Berlin, Staatliche Museen zu Berlin – Preußischer Kulturbesitz, Nationalgalerie, Marzona collection

b. 1933 in Kariya, Japan

After On Kawara had visited far-flung parts of the world on extended journeys, he settled in New York in 1965. While his early paintings were still figurative, in the mid-1960s he developed an artistic concept that, while still in principle belonging to the painting genre, liberates it from any expressiveness, and instead concretizes the abstract and immaterial phenomenon of time through the medium of painting.

In January 1966 the first painting in the *Today Series, 1966 to the Present*, appeared, which the artist from the outset understood as a connected work, which would only be consummated with his death. On the pictures, which in principle have not changed to this day, there is nothing to be seen but the date of the day on which Kawara produced it. This date is immaculately painted with perfect craftsmanship on a monochrome ground. As for his *Date Paintings*, depending on the format, up to three pictures can be painted on one day. If a work is not completed by midnight on the day in question, however, Kawara destroys it.

The way the pictures are produced is time-consuming and labour-intensive. First, the canvases are primed with up to five coats of paint. For the dates, which are painted by hand, Kawara then needs up to seven layers of white paint. In the early years of work on the *Today Series* in particular, Kawara stuck newspaper cuttings from the day in question on the back of the picture. For every picture, he also made a cardboard box, lined on the inside with newspaper.

Alongside the *Today Series*, a short time later Kawara started other sequences of works, some of which involve the regular dispatch of postcards. For the project *I Got Up*, started in 1968, he sent two postcards every day to friends or acquaintances. On the backs of the cards there is a rubber stamp with the message "I Got Up" and beside the date, the exact time and place that he did so. In this way, Kawara transfers the transitory moment of getting up, of awakening thought, to the focus of an eccentric communication system.

The actual centre of Kawara's art seems to be to convey an idea of a duration filled with consciousness. While his *Today Series* preserves the past as the present in the picture, his works *One Million*

Years – Past (1969) and *One Million Years – Future* (1981), presented in book form, give us the opportunity to place the duration of temporal perception (both of the individual and of the entire human species) in a superordinate perspective. *One Million Years – Past* lists, in ten books and more than 20,000 pages, the numerical designations of a million years. The year 1969 forms the start of a sequence of dates going back into the past. *One Million Years – Future* goes forward on the same principle from the year 1980. The duration of an average human life is represented by a few lines of a page of a book, and the whole of human history takes up just a few pages in one of the ten books. Kawara dedicated these works respectively to "all those who have lived and died" and to "the last one".

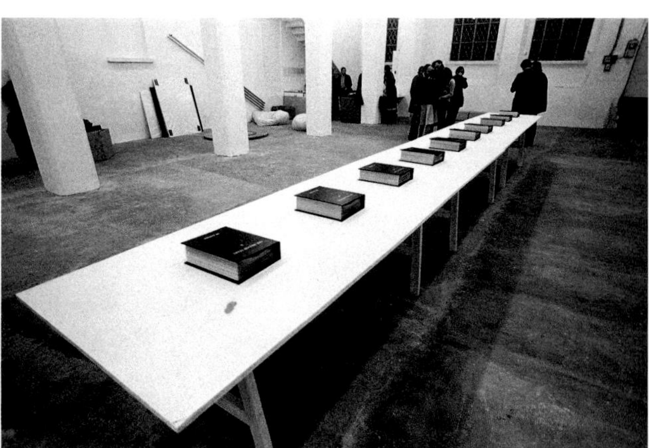

One Million Years – Past, 1971

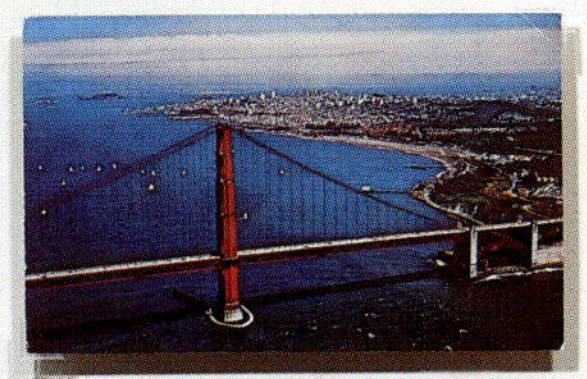 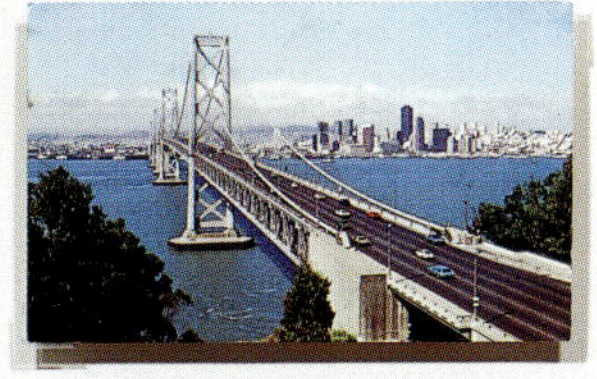 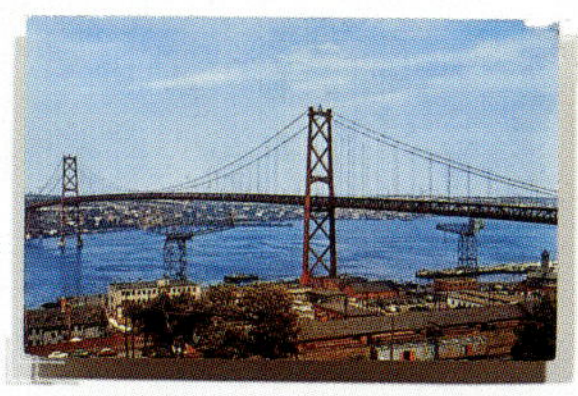

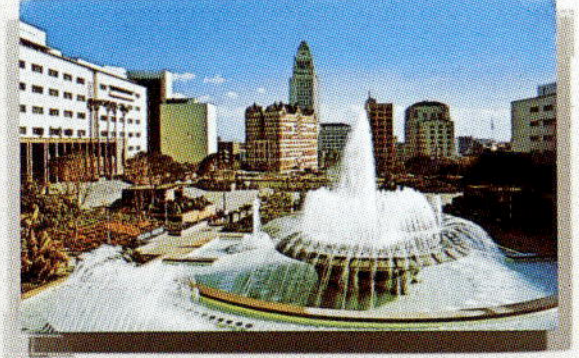 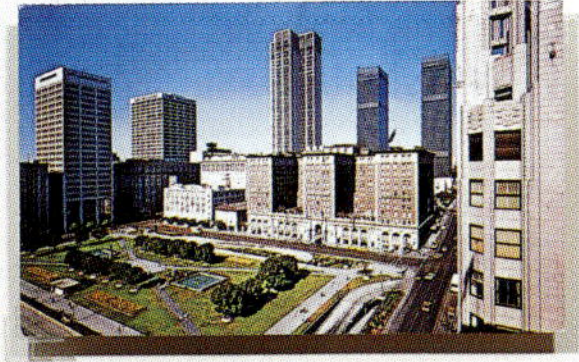 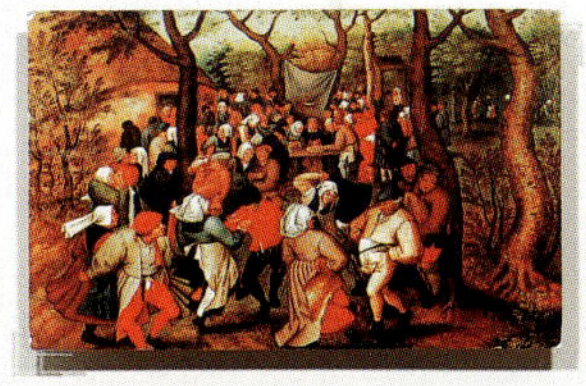

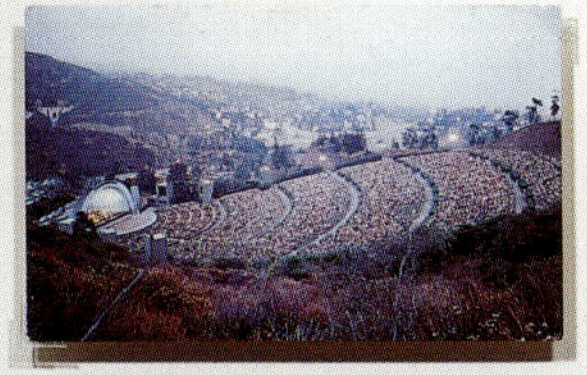 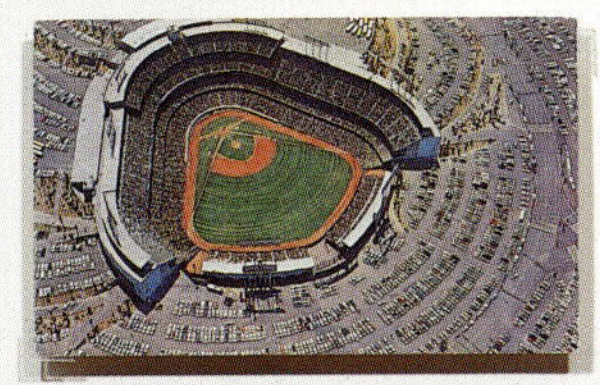 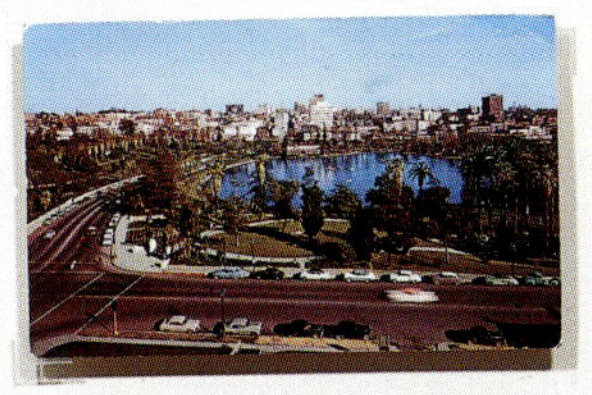

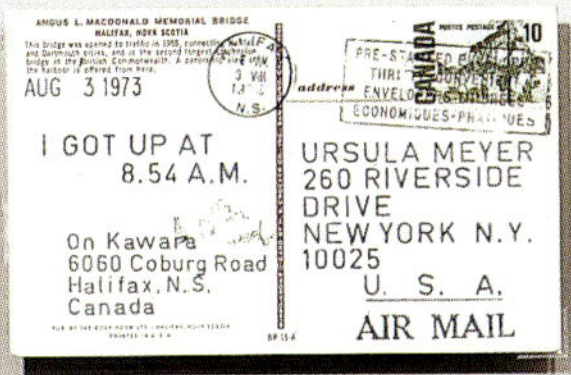
AUG 3 1973
I GOT UP AT
8.54 A.M.
On Kawara
6060 Coburg Road
Halifax, N.S.
Canada
URSULA MEYER
260 RIVERSIDE
DRIVE
NEW YORK N.Y.
10025
U.S.A.
AIR MAIL
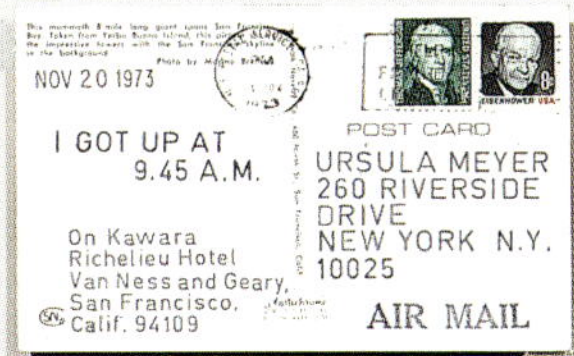
NOV 20 1973
I GOT UP AT
9.45 A.M.
On Kawara
Richelieu Hotel
Van Ness and Geary,
San Francisco,
Calif. 94109
POST CARD
URSULA MEYER
260 RIVERSIDE
DRIVE
NEW YORK N.Y.
10025
AIR MAIL
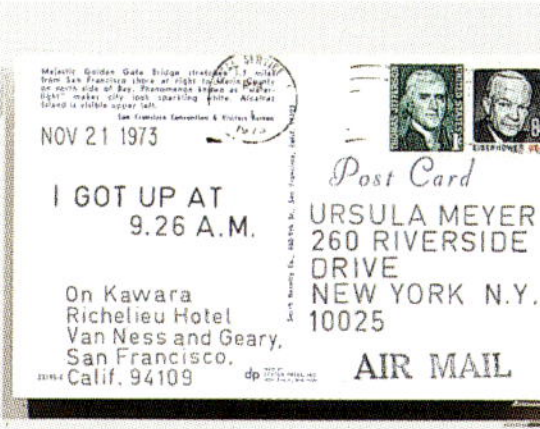
NOV 21 1973
I GOT UP AT
9.26 A.M.
On Kawara
Richelieu Hotel
Van Ness and Geary,
San Francisco,
Calif. 94109
Post Card
URSULA MEYER
260 RIVERSIDE
DRIVE
NEW YORK N.Y.
10025
AIR MAIL

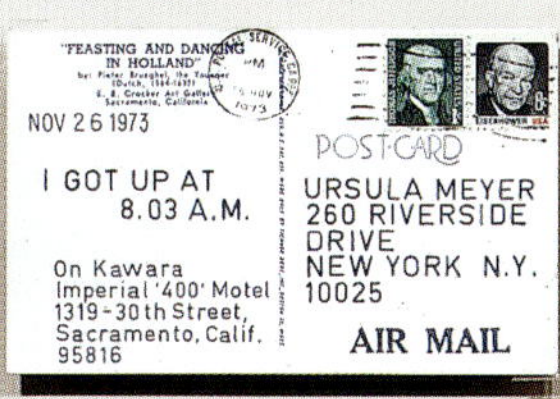
NOV 26 1973
I GOT UP AT
8.03 A.M.
On Kawara
Imperial '400' Motel
1319-30th Street,
Sacramento, Calif.
95816
URSULA MEYER
260 RIVERSIDE
DRIVE
NEW YORK N.Y.
10025
AIR MAIL

NOV 27 1973
I GOT UP AT
9.12 A.M.
On Kawara
Holiday Lodge
1631 West Third Street,
Los Angeles, Calif.
90017
POST CARD
URSULA MEYER
260 RIVERSIDE
DRIVE
NEW YORK N.Y.
10025
AIR MAIL

NOV 28 1973
I GOT UP AT
10.02 A.M.
On Kawara
Nutel Motel
1906 West Third Street,
Los Angeles, Calif.
90057
POST CARD
URSULA MEYER
260 RIVERSIDE
DRIVE
NEW YORK N.Y.
10025
AIR MAIL

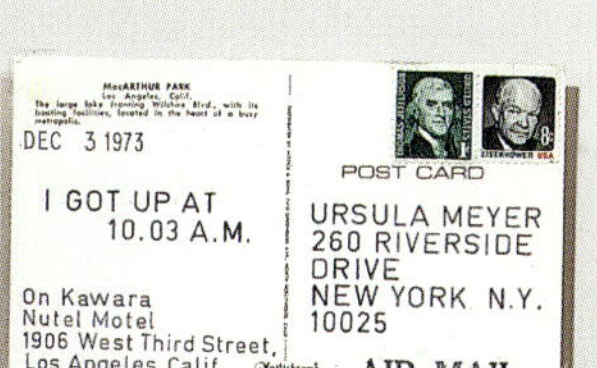
DEC 3 1973
I GOT UP AT
10.03 A.M.
On Kawara
Nutel Motel
1906 West Third Street,
Los Angeles, Calif.
90057
POST CARD
URSULA MEYER
260 RIVERSIDE
DRIVE
NEW YORK N.Y.
10025
AIR MAIL

DEC 4 1973
I GOT UP AT
10.48 A.M.
On Kawara
Nutel Motel
1906 West Third Street,
Los Angeles, Calif.
90057
POST CARD
URSULA MEYER
260 RIVERSIDE
DRIVE
NEW YORK N.Y.
10025
AIR MAIL

DEC 5 1973
I GOT UP AT
11.34 A.M.
On Kawara
Nutel Motel
1906 West Third Street,
Los Angeles, Calif.
90057
POST CARD
URSULA MEYER
260 RIVERSIDE
DRIVE
NEW YORK N.Y.
10025
AIR MAIL

A Four color sentence

Neon, 136 x 7.3 x 6.4 cm
Berlin, Staatliche Museen zu Berlin – Preußischer Kulturbesitz, Nationalgalerie, Marzona collection

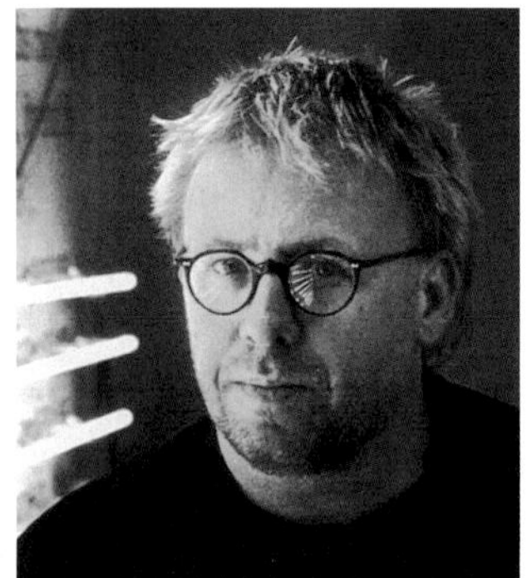

b. 1945 in Toledo (OH), USA

The early work of Joseph Kosuth is regarded by many as a prime example of the Conceptual Art practice of the 1960s, but has also been criticized, vehemently in some cases, for a variety of reasons. As early as 1965, Kosuth came to a novel view of art, which programmatically advocated a strict separation of aesthetics and art. For Kosuth, the task of art consists in constantly questioning its own essence and, in extended analyses, to contribute to the clarification of the question of what art is. Art works are understood by Kosuth in the framework of his conception as analytical proposals, which, by reason of their tautological structure, cannot contain any statements about facts external to art.

1965 saw the appearance of the first works, such as *One And Three Chairs*, which show real objects together with their photographic and lexicographical representations. At the same time, Kosuth was working on neon pieces, which like *A Four Color Sentence* represent as an object precisely what the verbal information says. A little later, Kosuth raised the degree of abstraction in his works once more, when, in 1966, in connection with his *First Investigation*, he started to enlarge the dictionary definition of abstract terms such as "meaning" or "nothing" on photographic paper. All the works in this series bear the title *Art as Idea as Idea*, whereby Kosuth on the one hand stresses the tautological character of art as such, and on the other makes clear that not the actual photographic plates, but the ideas to which they give expression, are what is to be understood as art. Purely verbal definitions here replace the formerly pictorial content of art, which is now no longer to be judged in aesthetic categories.

Since Kosuth seeks to avoid conventional interpretations of his works as pictures or art objects at all costs, in his *Second Investigation* between 1968 and 1969, he dispensed with any presentation of objects, by publishing categories from the thesaurus anonymously in magazines and other public media. Although they have obviously left the traditional art context, Kosuth understands these works too as "comment on art".

In 1969 Kosuth published in the magazine "Studio International" his essay "Art after Philosophy", in which he laid out in detail the theoretical foundations of his work, seeking to distinguish it from other forms of Conceptual Art. Thus he categorically rejected the application of the term "Conceptual Art" to the artistic approaches of Lawrence Weiner, Douglas Huebler or John Baldessari, since their work still related to a reality external to art. From Kosuth's point of view, "Pure Concept Art" had to abandon any reference to traditional materials and techniques and present itself exclusively in conceptual form.

One sentence in "Art after Philosophy" summarizes Kosuth's attitude: "The 'purest' definition of conceptual art would be that it is an inquiry into the foundations of the concept 'art', as it has come to mean." Only in later, post-1970, works did Kosuth extend the fundamental question of meaning into philosophical, literary and psychoanalytical contexts.

"Art's only claim is for art. Art is the definition of art."

Joseph Kosuth

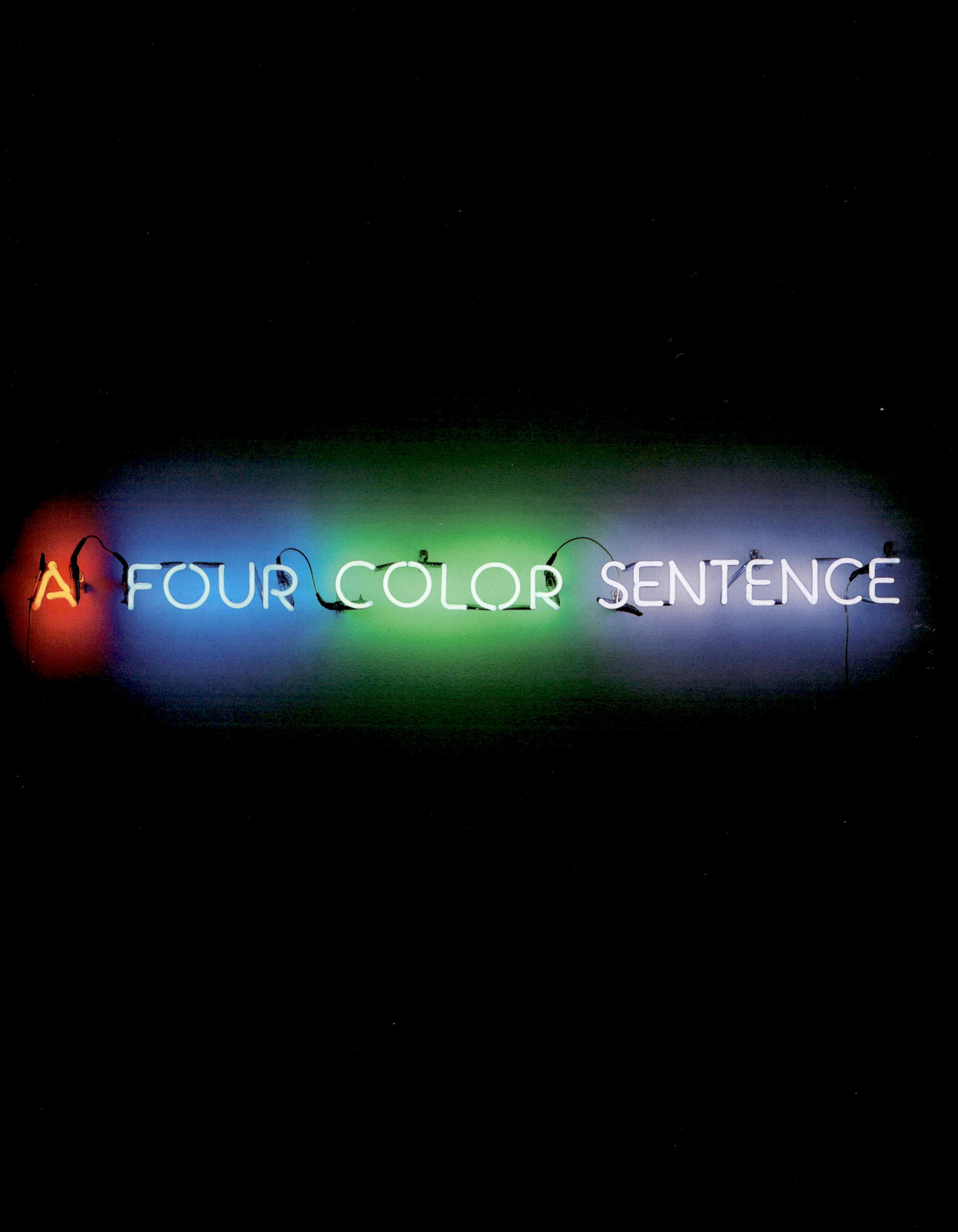

A FOUR COLOR SENTENCE

HOW many pictures

C-Print, 122 x 157 cm
Courtesy Metro Pictures, New York

b. 1947 in Bronxville (NY), USA

Alongside Allan McCollum, Richard Prince, Jenny Holzer and Sherrie Levine, Louise Lawler is one of the most important artists to carry on the legacy of Conceptual Art in the United States in the different conditions prevailing in the 1980s. After the 1960s and 1970s, which had seen the definitive abandonment of formal-aesthetic restrictions of artistic practice in the context of Conceptual Art, Process Art, Land Art, and other boundary-crossing tendencies, the interest of a younger generation of artists working in the Conceptual field was concentrated increasingly on a fundamental critique of the institutional and socio-economic conditions of art, which even since the 1960s had seen drastic and lasting changes.

As one of the most important representatives of the so-called institutional critique, Lawler had, since the late 1970s, critically confronted the context in which art was created. Her work focused on the question of how contexts originally external to art changed or produced the meaning of art. What happens to art, after it has left the artist's studio?

As possible answers to these questions, Lawler's photographs focus attention on art works in museums, galleries and private collections, during the setting-up and taking-down of exhibitions, in stores, auction houses etc., whereby we are quite evidently less concerned with the response to, or the re-interpretation of, the photographed works than with the visualization of the institutional, social and economic structures, within which art is shown and perceived. Time and again it is polished floors, elegant furniture, labels, signatures, cabinets, or similar accessories, that Lawler's photographs depict as equal-status elements alongside the actual artworks. Thus her works draw our attention to the fact that it is precisely these (in some cases) totally unassuming objects or additions that construct an atmosphere of the valuation and added value of art. At the same time it becomes clear that an authentic or direct experience of art outside the ordinary presentation conventions is scarcely possible any longer.

For this reason, the mid-format Cibachrome *How Many Pictures* does not show the work of art – a painting by the American artist Frank Stella – but its reflection in the polished wood floor, which takes up the top quarter of the photograph. By depicting the abstract painting as indissolubly bound up with its surroundings, its alleged autonomy seems to have been busted and revealed as a chimera. In a certain respect, the calm and diagnostic view of *How Many Pictures* can be seen as typical of Lawler's artistic attitude. For while her photographs implicitly criticize the often unnoticed influence that contextual factors have on the perception and significance of art, they do this without false pathos, and always in the awareness that one's own work, too, is circulating within the parameters one is criticizing.

"my pictures present information about the 'reception' of artworks."

Louise Lawler

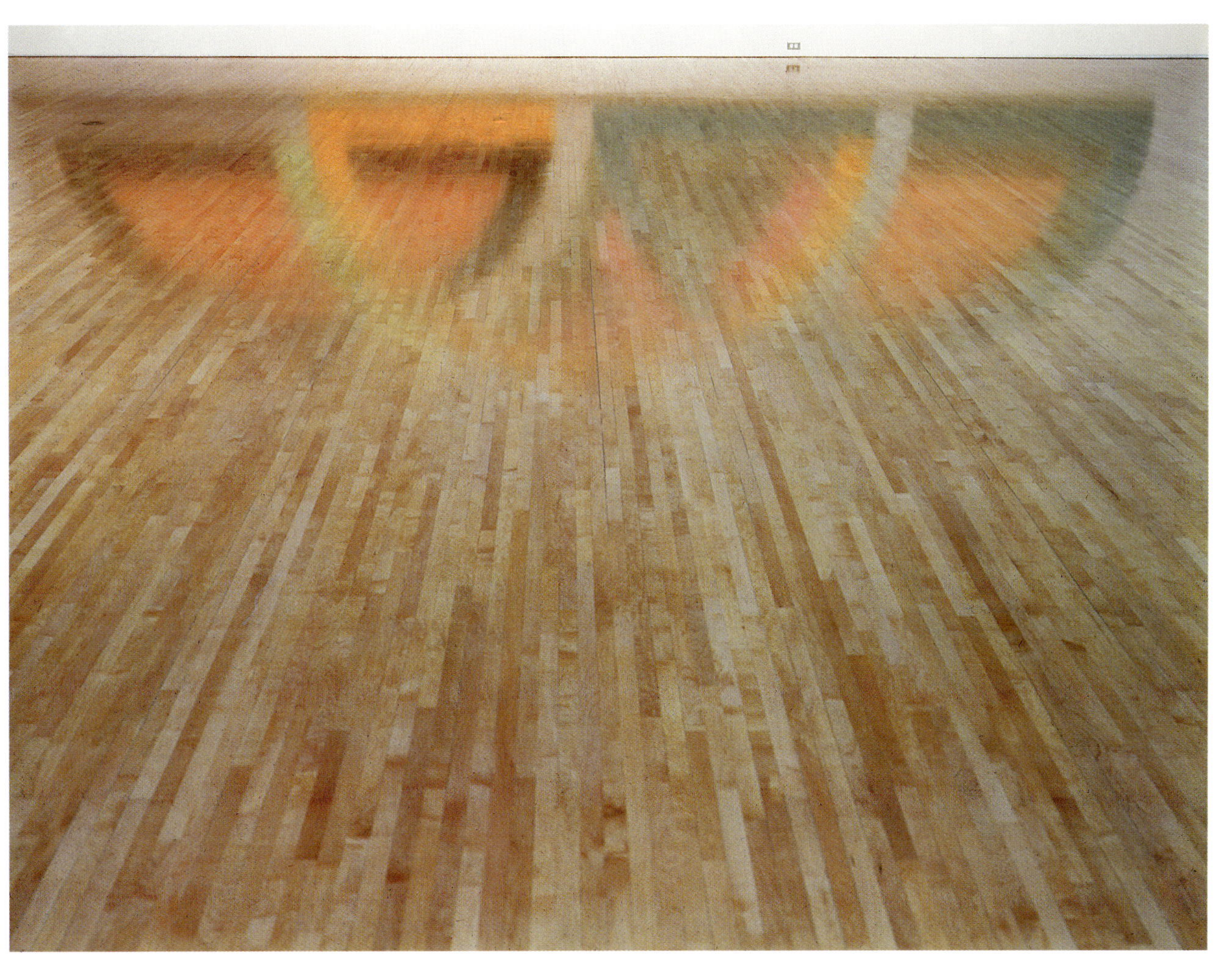

serial project NO. 1 (ABCD)

Gloss paint on aluminium, 51 x 414 x 414 cm
The Museum of Modern Art, New York

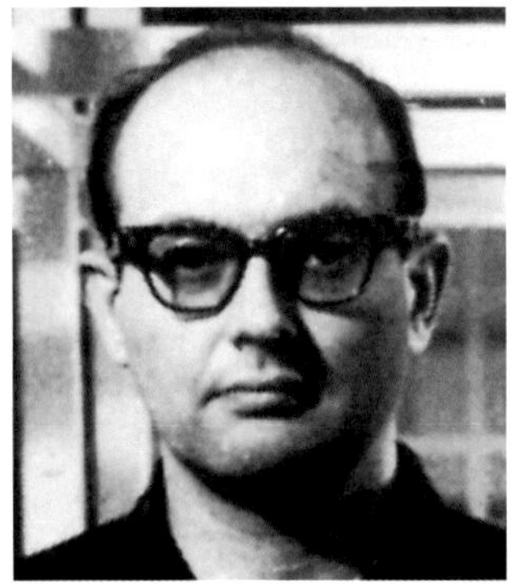

b. 1928 in Hartford (CT), USA
d. 2007 in New York (NY), USA

More obviously than almost any other artist, during the 1960s Sol LeWitt developed his work from a Minimal Art position in a Conceptual direction. Between 1963 and 1965, LeWitt worked on singular objects, which he mostly constructed from plywood. Painted in gloss in a single colour, these reduced sculptures either stood against the wall, or entered into a direct relationship with the exhibition room, being placed on the floor without a plinth. In 1965 LeWitt constructed his first modular structures and began to have his sculptures produced industrially. From now on, his three-dimensional works were mostly of aluminium or steel, and painted in immaculate white gloss. Just a year later, his first serial works appeared, executed by the artist according to conceptions defined in advance: these represented his definitive abandonment of Minimalist sculpture.

Starting from the basic geometrical forms of the cube and the square, the *Serial Project No. 1 (ABCD)* introduces "all the relevant combinations" of closed and open cubes and squares, which in their turn contain open and closed cubes and squares. On a surface area of more than four square metres, there extended an apparent chaos of square and cubic forms, the criteria of whose arrangement were difficult to make out just by looking. In an accompanying text, LeWitt described how serial compositions bring forth their own modification, as it were, of their own accord. The permutations and deviations within a concept laid down in advance thus become the actual theme of LeWitt's serial projects.

While in 1966 LeWitt still saw himself as a "serial artist", by the following year he seems already to have revised this self-assessment. For in 1967 he published the "Paragraphs on Conceptual Art", the first theoretical manifesto of the movement, albeit perhaps better understood in the spirit of an explanation of his own specific approach, in view of obvious differences with other artists. In his "Paragraphs" LeWitt makes it clear that the mental conception of a work is at least of equal status with its realization, whereby the idea underlying a work need be neither logical nor complex in order to be the successful starting point of a work. Succinctly, he notes furthermore: "What the work of art looks like isn't too important," and attributes the same status to ideas, sketches, models and conversations as to the work as executed. Unlike Joseph Kosuth or Lawrence Weiner, however, LeWitt did think it was necessary to realize the concepts, in order to judge the quality both of the work and the idea.

In 1968 LeWitt executed his first wall drawing in the Paula Cooper Gallery. Later works executed by assistants and fellow artists, or else by the staff of the exhibition rooms, on the basis of clear and not infrequently extremely detailed instructions. Because of its relationship to its location, and also on account of the clear division between conception and execution, one and the same work by LeWitt can, depending on the skill of the people involved and the concrete situation of the exhibition room, take on numerous, in some cases clearly different, forms.

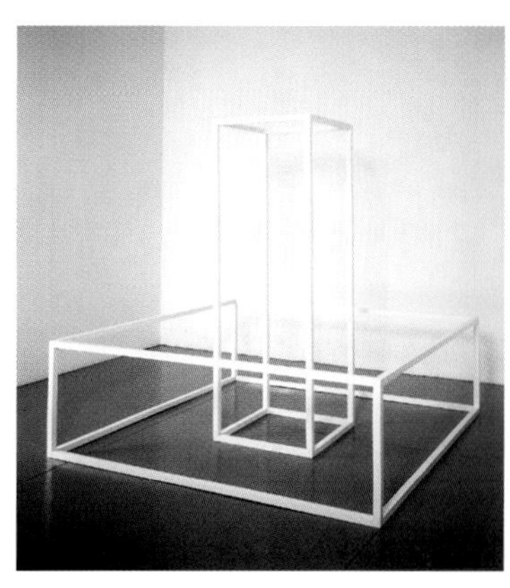

A#6, 1967

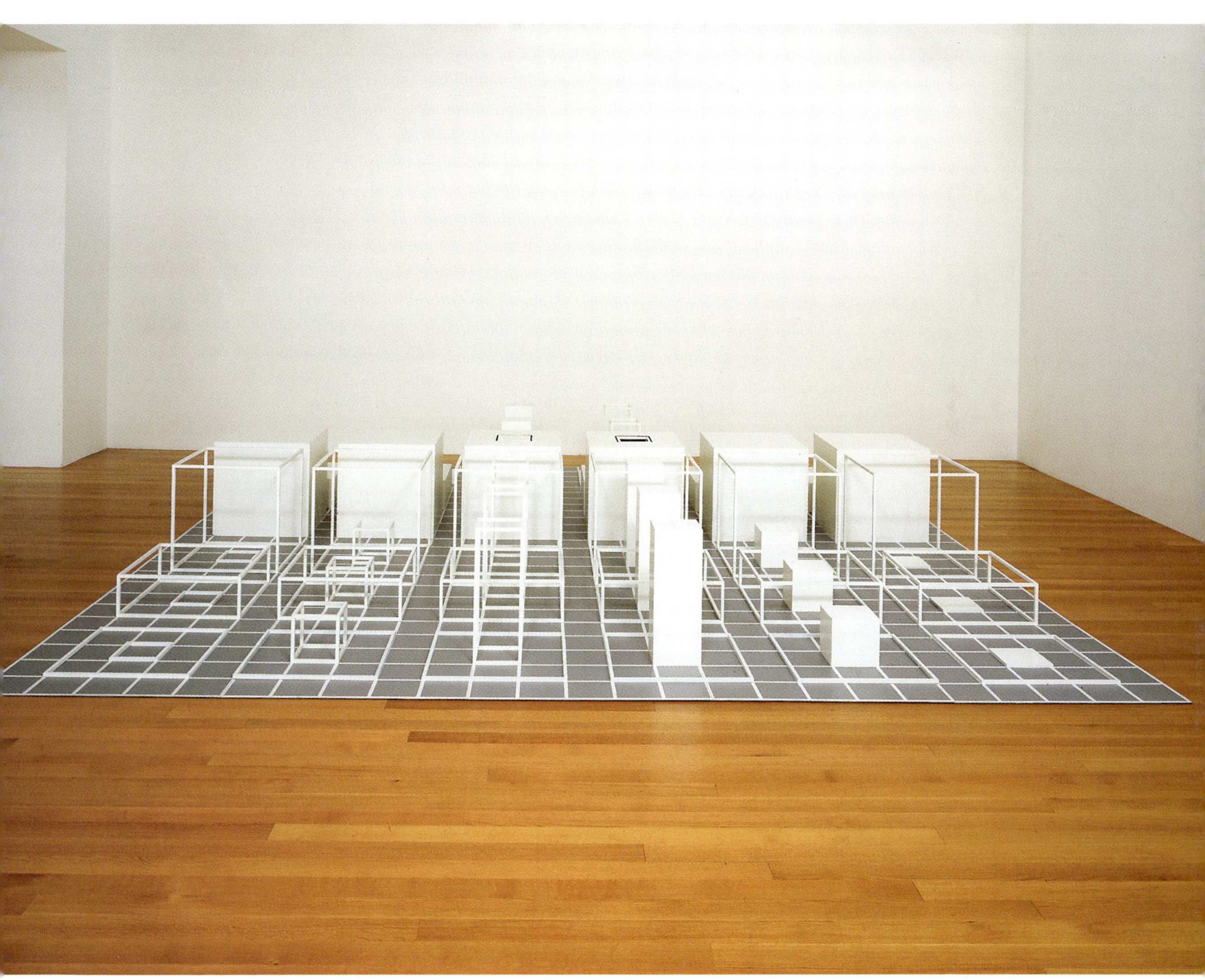

splitting

Photomontage, no dimensions given
Courtesy David Zwirner Gallery, New York

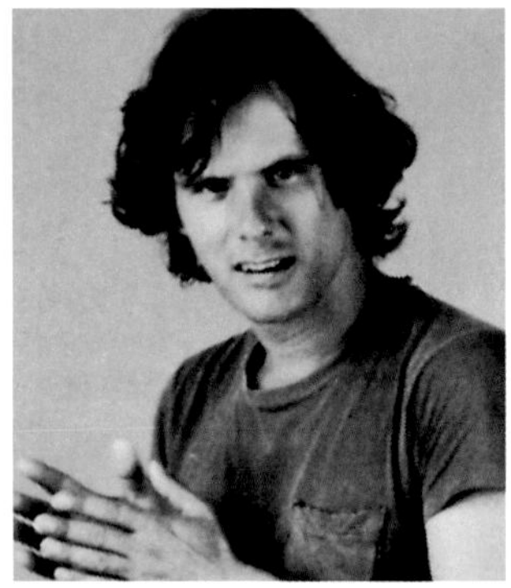

b. 1943 in New York,
d. 1978 in New York (NY), USA

As a student, Gordon Matta-Clark worked as Dennis Oppenheim's assistant on a number of Land Art projects. In 1968 he graduated in architecture from Cornell University, and a year later went to New York, where at first he devoted himself to various different activities. In the early 1970s, alongside his artistic activities, he worked on the alternative exhibition project 112 Greene Street, and was involved in the foundation of the co-operative restaurant Food, likewise in SoHo, which was chiefly frequented by artists. This soon became the regular meeting place for those artists who had joined together to form the Anarchitecture group, of which Matta-Clark was destined to become the outstanding member.

While Matta-Clark's early projects already revealed an interest in the phenomenon of transformation, they were however not yet integrated into the architectural context which was to be characteristic of his works post-1972. Thus for *Photo Fry* (1969) in the John Gibson Gallery he had photographs fried in hot fat, or, for *Cherry Tree* (1971), he planted a cherry tree in a dark cellar, and its death a few months later, was the completion of the process that represented the work.

From 1972 Matta-Clark started to concentrate his activity on architectural interventions. It was not the invention and erection of new structures, but the deconstruction of existing architecture, often incorporated into unambiguous urban contexts, that characterized his approach. Matta-Clark regarded empty buildings not just as material, but as a metaphor for social and political conditions, which he implicitly criticized with his work on and in architectural complexes which were no longer of any value to the community.

The earliest works that he realized actually on a building include *Pier In/Out* (1973), for which he used a metal cutter to remove a large rectangle from a corrugated iron wall together with part of a window. Alongside photographs documenting the operation on this warehouse, *Pier In/Out* also exists as a sculpture: Matta-Clark mounted the fragment of wall on a metal plinth.

With the support of the gallery-owner Holly Solomon and her husband Horace, Matta-Clark was able in 1974 to execute *Splitting*, his largest project to date. In that year, the couple bought a piece of land in Englewood, New Jersey, with the intention of demolishing the suburban house that stood on it. At Matta-Clark's request, Holly Solomon agreed to allow the building to be used for a major project. Matta-Clark's work on *Splitting* took some four months, and the result was the transformation of a prime example of anonymous architecture with no distinguishing features into a spectacular manifestation of contemporary sculpture. In time-consuming and laborious procedures, Matta-Clark split the house vertically into two halves. In order to make this incision even more visible, he lowered the level of one half, so that the crevice broadened into a wedge-shaped opening affecting the whole façade. Later he cut off the four corners of the house at second-floor level, and displayed them as sculptures at a number of exhibitions. In addition he documented his operation on the unassuming house at 322 Humphrey Street, which was definitively demolished two months later, in photographs and photo-collages.

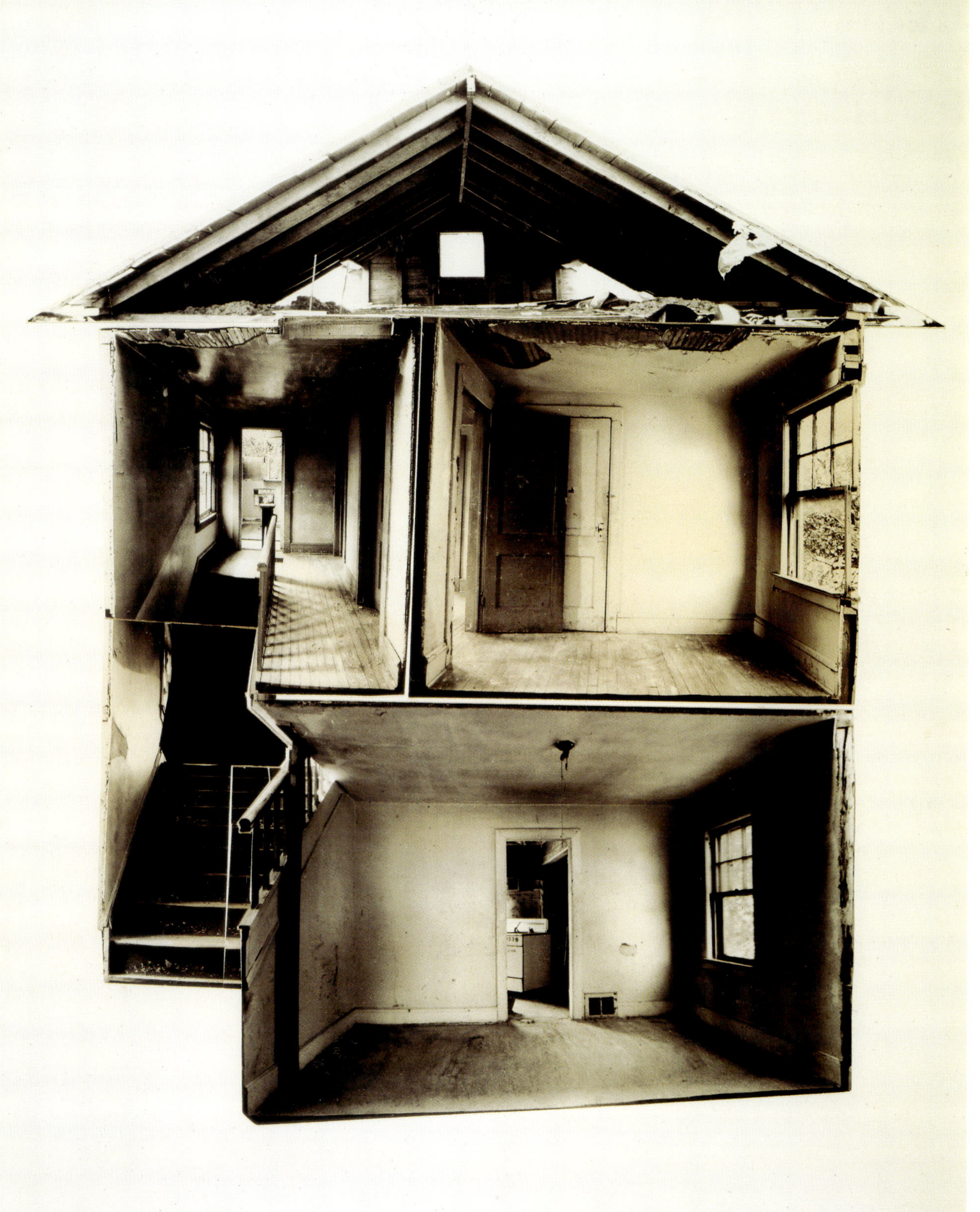

Facial Hair Transplant

Performance
Photography: Courtesy Galerie Lelong, New York

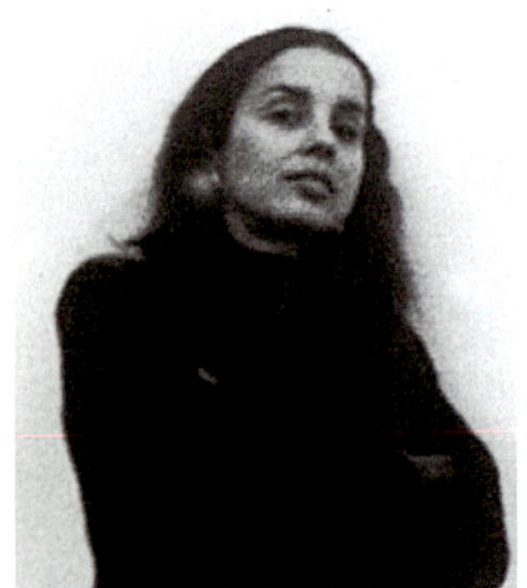

**b. 1948 in Havana, Cuba,
d. 1985 in New York (NY), USA**

After Fidel Castro came to power, Ana Mendieta was sent by her parents with a church-organized children's transport to the USA in 1961, where she grew up in an orphanage. She studied at the University of Iowa, where she conducted her first performances, such as *Death of a Chicken*, *Feathers on a Woman* and *Facial Hair Transplant* in 1972. In early works, Mendieta also thematized her relationship to nature, for example using various techniques to inscribe her silhouette into natural contexts. In further performances, she experimented with blood. In 1973 she poured several litres on to the pavement in front of her apartment and photographed the reactions of those who happened to pass by.

Mendieta always denied that her work had anything to do with Conceptual Art, pointing out that her technique was very different from the clean aesthetic of the male-dominated movement. But for all the differences, conceptual tendencies can certainly be found in Mendieta's eccentrically broad understanding of the ready-made.

In the work *People Looking at Blood*, mentioned above, she had used blood in the spirit of a ready-made, and in one of her most controversial performances, *Rape Scene* (1973), which she repeated in a variety of places, she used her own body as a ready-made. After the rape and murder of one of her fellow-students at the University of Iowa, Mendieta's reaction was drastic: She invited friends and acquaintances to her apartment, where the visitors found the front door open, and after entering the premises found themselves the involuntary witnesses to a scene that centred on the blood-smeared body of the artist chained to a table. Around the motionless Mendieta were pieces of broken glass and still more blood, suggesting a rape. In Mendieta's mercilessly staged tableau vivant, her own body functioned as a critic-ally charged ready-made, which, by reason of the temporal and geographical proximity of the real sex murder, could hardly be interpreted by the beholders as an abstract symbol.

In *Facial Hair Transplant* (1972) Mendieta re-interprets Duchamp's concept of the ready-made in more humorous fashion. In allusion to the work titled *L. H. O. O. Q.* (1919), in which Duchamp had disfigured a reproduction of Leonardo da Vinci's *Mona Lisa* by adding a beard, Mendieta, in the context of a performance, stuck the hairs of a friend's beard on to her face and thus acquired a perfect beard herself. It was no longer the reproduction of a picture or a mass-produced object, but the real hairs of a beard that in Mendieta's work acquired the status of a ready-made, in that she extricated it from its usual context, a man's face, and transferred it to a different one. The transfer of the male attribute onto her female body was evidently understood not only as a symbolic act of appropriation of sexual identity, but also in the spirit of a literal and specific exchange of energy: "I like the idea of transferring hair from one person to another because I think it gives me that person's strength."

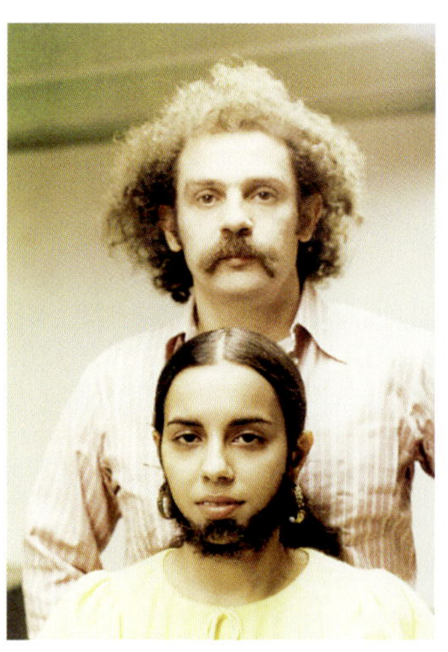

Facial Hair Transplant, 1972

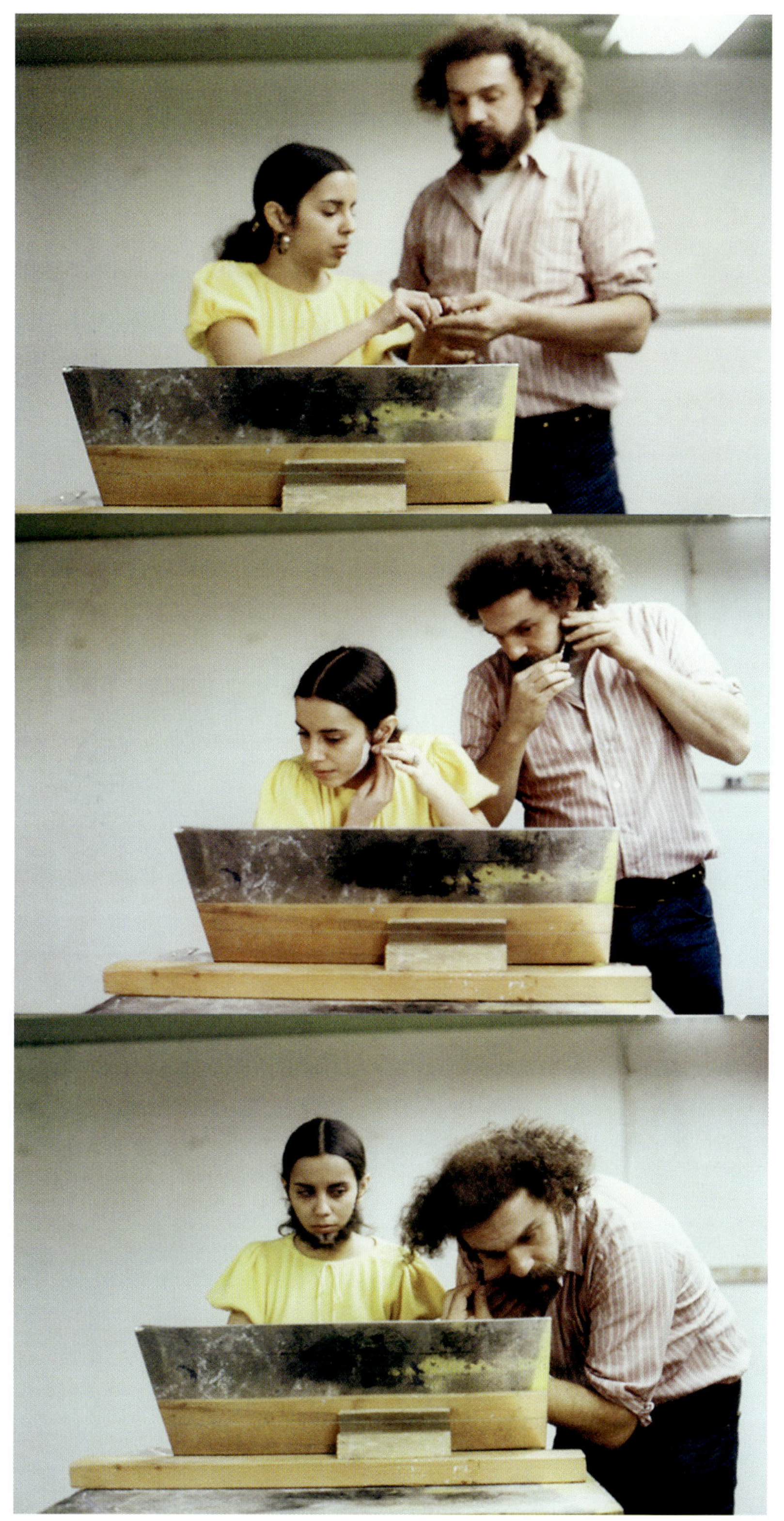

window or wall sign

Neon, 150 x 140 cm
Otterlo, Kröller-Müller Museum

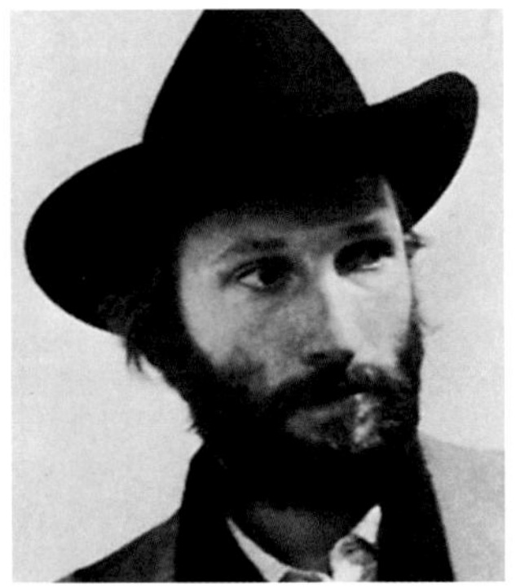

b. 1941 in Fort Wayne (IN), USA

Before Bruce Nauman earned his Master of Arts at the University of California in Davis in 1966, he had already studied mathematics and physics, and for a short while also music. While studying art, it soon became clear that Nauman was hardly interested in a continuation of artistic work within the traditional parameters.

1965 saw his first fibreglass sculptures, which leant against the wall in a fragile condition or else simply lay on the floor. Many of these early sculptures by Nauman are characterized by their unfinished state, as they were often only shaped to the point where the idea underlying the work became clearly visible. At the same time, the "raw state" of the work often emphasized the specific qualities of the respective material. Nauman thus distanced himself from Minimal Art, which, particularly on the east coast of the United States, was beginning to focus on the *production* of contemporary art. Nauman's early sculptures already show a pronounced interest in the possibilities of working with the body, many of the mysterious objects being casts of parts of the artist's own.

Physical activities of a wide variety provided the focus of numerous video works that Nauman made in his studio from 1968 on. In their absurdity and obvious meaninglessness, the filmed actions of *Bouncing Two Balls between the Floor and Ceiling with Changing Rhythms* or *Wall/Floor Positions* (both 1968) can be compared to the plays of Samuel Beckett. Often, a deliberately contrived aimlessness and senselessness determines the action. In any case, they bear witness to Nauman's creed that art was what the artist did in his studio. That the results of doing this need not always be planned is shown by Nauman's multipart photocollage *Composite Photo of Two Messes on the Studio Floor* (1967), which depicts materials heaped at random on the floor – in a sense left-overs of past activities.

In a series of photographic works dating from 1967, Nauman ironically confronted various aspects of the relationship between words and pictures. *Waxing Hot*, for example, shows two hands which are polishing a wooden sculpture consisting of the three letters H O T. In a literal and hence unexpected manner, the title of the work and its pictorial realization enter into an overlapping relationship.

Window or Wall Sign formulates a claim on art and the artist, which, in view of the other results of Nauman's investigations of the question of what art is, seems clearly obsolete. In any case, it remains unclear whether the message – The True Artist Helps the World by Revealing Mystic Truths – is to be taken seriously or ironically. The choice of the means with which Nauman brings his statement across, however, hints at an ironic parody of the formulation of artistic declarations of intents. For the garish neon sign, which originally hung in the window of Nauman's studio in San Francisco, competes for attention with any old colourful advertisement for beer or cigarettes.

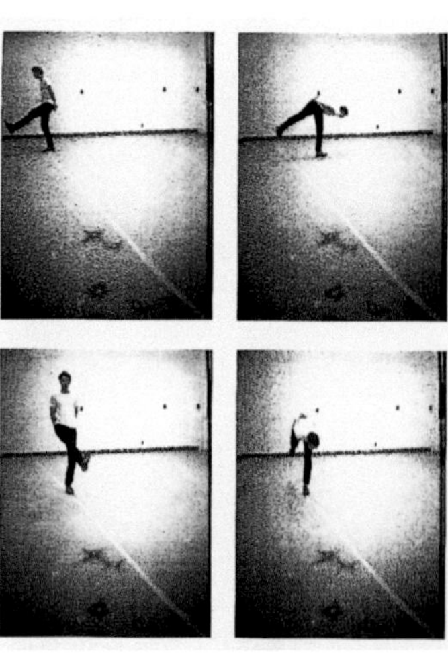

Slow Angle Walk (Beckett Walk), 1968

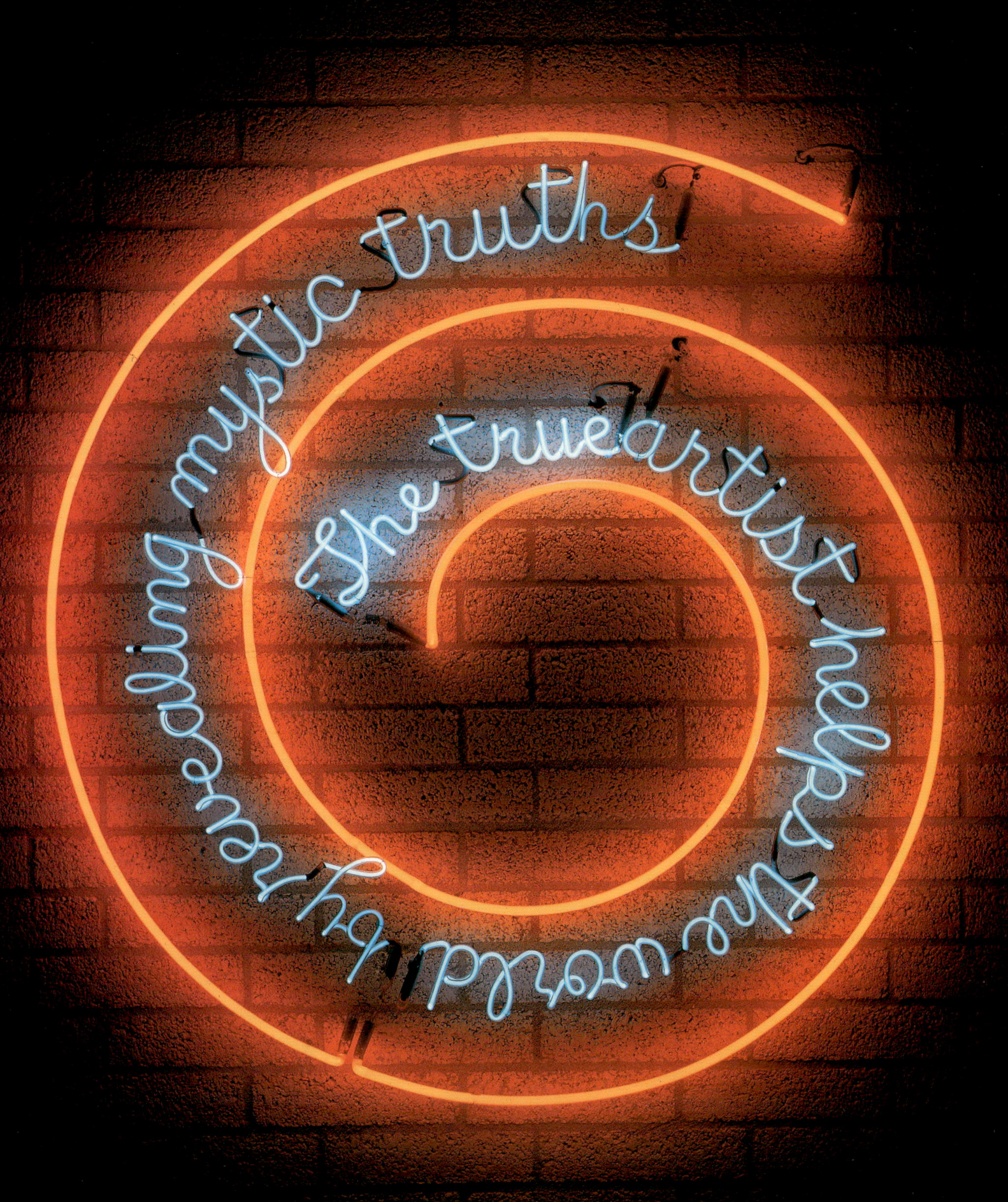
The true artist helps the world by revealing mystic truths

1965/1–∞ (Detail 1–35327)

Tempera on canvas, 196 x 135 cm
Lodz, Museum Sztuki

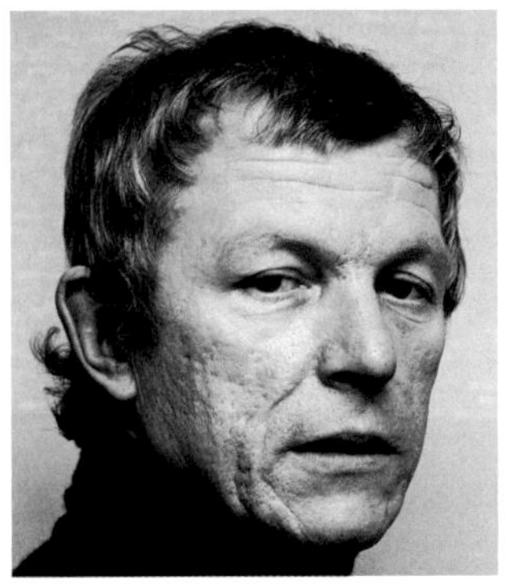

b. 1931 in Hocquincourt, France

Roman Opalka was born in France as the son of Polish immigrants; his childhood was marked by the politically unstable situation in Europe. Before the start of the Second World War, the Opalkas returned to Poland, but a few years later were deported to Germany, and only after the end of the war could they finally settle in Poland. After training as a lithographer, Opalka studied painting, graphic art and sculpture at the Academy of Fine Arts in Lodz between 1951 and 1956. While Opalka had already, in various series of works, confronted the phenomenon of time, from 1965 – the start of his project titled *1965/1–∞* – he concentrated exclusively on the depiction of time in painting. Unlike On Kawara, in whose *Today Series* the present takes on a particular status, Opalka seems more interested in actualizing the even flow of time.

The conception of Opalka's series of *Infinity Paintings* is based on the simple principle of progression. In 1965 he completed the first picture with the title *1965/1–∞ (Detail 1–35327)*, which begins in the top left with the figure 1 painted in white on a black ground and by the addition of 1 unit each time proceeds in rows of figures arranged one above the other as far as 35327. The following picture in the series – Opalka understands each of his pictures as a detail – continues at the top left with the number 35328, and so on. All the pictures in the series are the same size and are painted using the same technique. Opalka drenches the brush in paint only when the figures begin to get illegible. In the early 1970s, Opalka decided to increase the proportion of white paint from picture to picture in steps of 1%, so that the previously black backgrounds became grey. This procedure can at least theoretically lead to the numbers becoming indistinguishable from the now white background.

To accompany every picture, Opalka produces a tape-recording, in which he counts the numbers on the canvas in his native Polish. At the end of a working day, Opalka additionally takes a photographic self-portrait. By 1998, the artist, who continues the work *1965/1–∞* to this day without interruption, had got to five million. More than 200 pictures document the constant passing of time, something closely bound up with his biography. This passage of time is metaphorically preserved for posterity in the project. The ongoing act of painting/counting – in other words, the approach to infinity already hinted at in the title – stands in stark contrast to the continuous aging of the artist and the inevitable fact of his mortality.

"The problem is that we are, and are not about to be."

Roman Opalka

catalysis IV

Black-and-white photograph, no dimensions given
Courtesy the artist

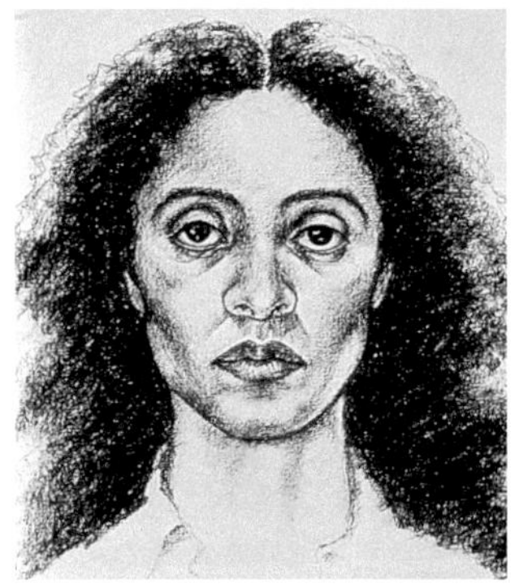

b. 1948 in New York (NY), USA

Adrian Piper was born in Harlem. After working for a short time as a painter, in 1967 she came into contact with the fringes of the New York Conceptual Art movement. Fascinated by the freedoms and possibilities of the recently tried-out forms of artistic expression, she turned to conceptual work in the form of projects that confronted various aspects of space and time. A large proportion of her early work consists of written pages of text, numbers or drawings, which she grouped thematically in ring-binders and presented at exhibitions. At the same time, she produced her first works with sound recordings.

For *Seriation #1* (1968) Piper repeatedly called up the automatic clock service. In addition to the announcement, updated and repeated at ten-second intervals, one also hears the ringing tone, which precedes every announcement of the time. Thus the work represents the continuous passage of time, which is also perceptible as a seriation of precisely denoted moments. Piper herself says that her interest was directed above all to those "objects that can refer both to concepts and ideas beyond themselves and their standard function, but at the same time refer to themselves".

The artist, who was at the time only 21, had considerable success with her mostly self-referential works. In 1969 and 1970, her work was shown at more than ten important exhibitions, such as "Konzeption – Conception" (Museum Morsbroich, Leverkusen, 1969) and "Information" (Museum of Modern Art, New York, 1970). Various social and political events as well as her exceptional position as an Afro-American woman artist in an art world dominated by white males, soon led to a palpable change in Piper's artistic practice, which became increasingly political. In retrospect, she described her concep-

tual early work as "the work I did in the Garden of Eden before I found out I was a black woman".

In 1971 Piper decided to shift her artistic activities from the galleries and museums to the public space. In the *Catalysis Series* she used the presence and perceptibility of her body in public in order to trigger reactions in chance encounters with passers-by. For *Catalysis IV* Piper stuffed a white cloth in her mouth until her cheeks were full, and a large piece of cloth was hanging out of her mouth. In this condition, she got on a bus and confronted her fellow-travellers with her demonstrative abnormality. Unlike most forms of performance, which are mostly anchored in the traditional art context, these actions on Piper's part are largely defined by the concrete reactions of their beholders.

As an artist, Piper continues to treat themes such as racism, xenophobia, or the social construction of identity in an openly political context. In this respect, for Piper, directly addressing her public, rather than the generalizations of many of her fellow-artists, is still of central importance.

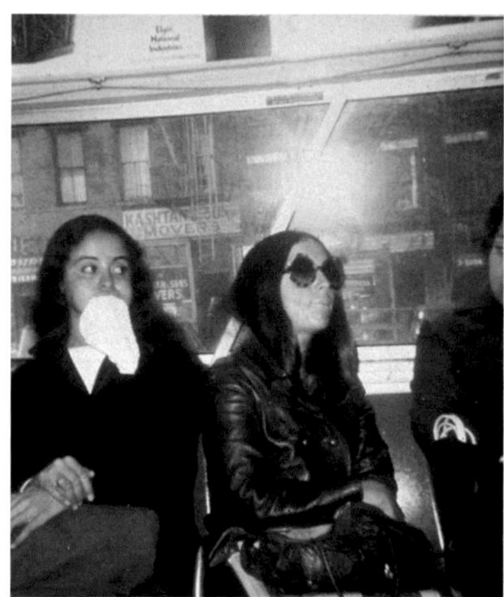

Catalysis IV, 1970/71

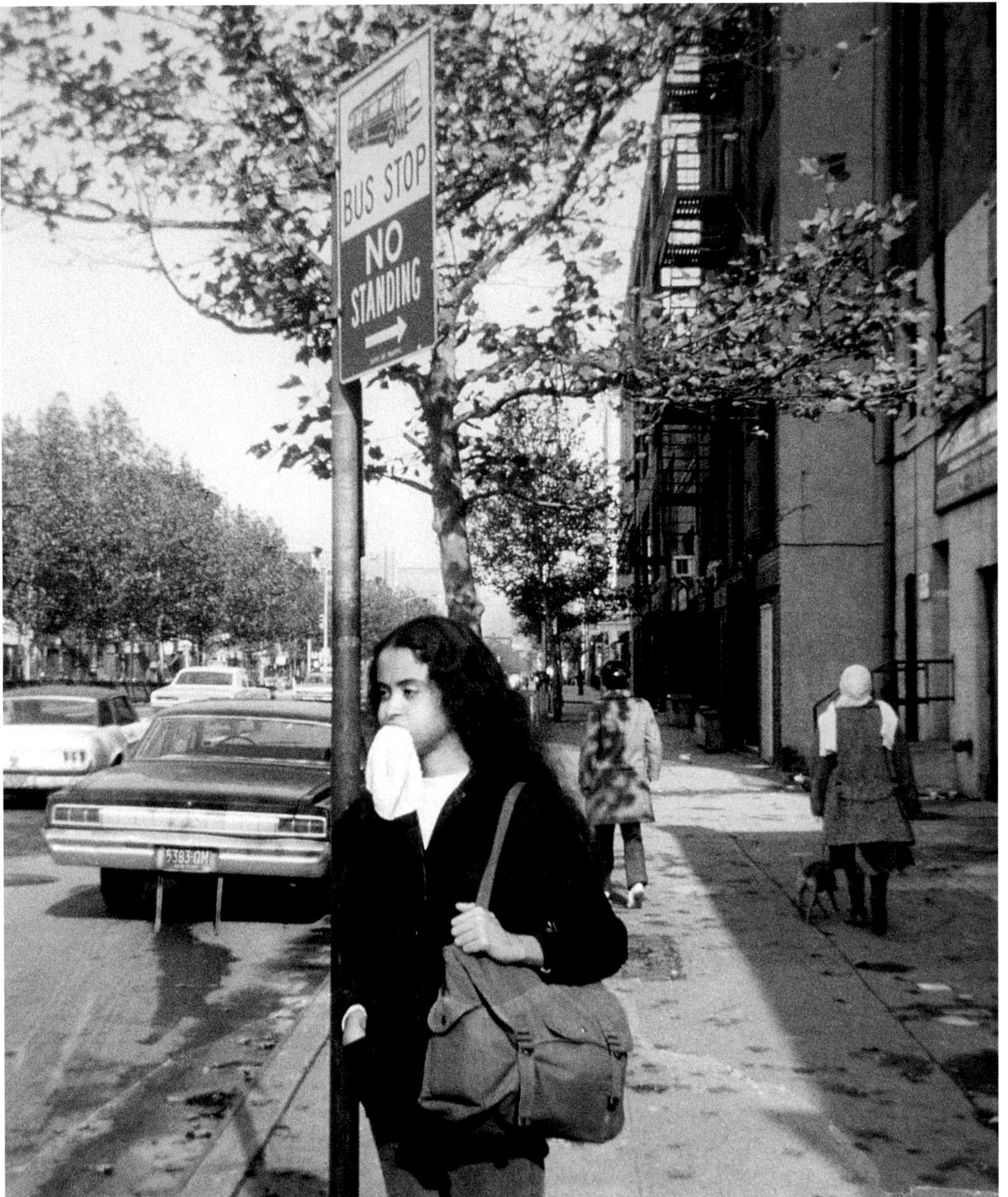
BUS STOP
NO
STANDING
5383-QM

vier verzinkte Elemente serie D

Galvanized steel plate, variable dimensions
Berlin, Staatliche Museen zu Berlin – Preußischer Kulturbesitz, Nationalgalerie, Marzona collection

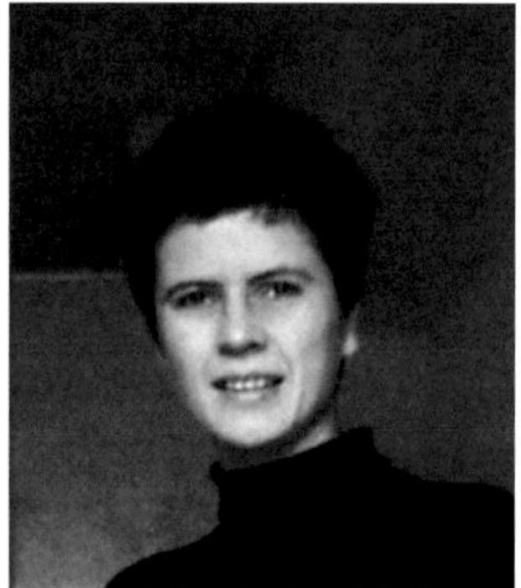

**b. 1930 in Wiesbaden, d. 1985
in Frankfurt am Main, Germany**

Charlotte Posenenske worked in the early 1950s for a time as a stage-set designer in various theatres before exhibiting her artistic works for the first time at the Galerie Weiss in Kassel in 1959. She developed her work consistently from the early painterly and graphic abstractions to the variable sculptures of the *Vierkantrohre* and *Drehflügel* of the years 1967/68. These minimalist and at the same time conceptual works, along with her decision to say goodbye to the art world in the middle of a promising career, were explained by nobody more clearly than the artist herself.

Posenenske went on to study social sciences and devoted herself in her later research work to issues that she had already raised as an artist – for example the effects of increasing mechanization and rationalization in an industrial society. Before her death, she specified what was to count as her work. The text printed here was published for the first time in the magazine "Art International" in May 1968.

The things I make are
variable
as simple as possible
reproducible.
They are components of space, since they are like building elements,
They can always be rearranged into new combinations or positions
Thus, they alter the space.
I leave this alteration to the consumer who thereby again and anew participates in the creation.

The simplicity of the basic geometric forms is beautiful and suited to demonstrate the principles of rationalized alteration.
I make series
Because I do not want to make single pieces for individuals,
in order to have elements combinable within a system,
in order to make something which is repeatable, objective,
and because it is economical.
The series could be prototypes for mass production.
Series DW (at Fischer's) is made of corrugated paste-board which is light and cheap: a material for consumption.
Often the elements or their combinations are very large in order to alter the spatial environment more thoroughly.
They approximate architectural dimensions and also for this reason differ increasingly from the former gallery objects.
They are decreasingly recognizable as 'artworks'.
The objects should have the objective character of industrial products.
They are not intended to represent anything other than what they are.
The former categorization of the arts no longer exists.
The artist of the future should have to work with a team of specialists in a development laboratory.
Though art's formal development has progressed at an increasing tempo, its social function has regressed.
Art is a product of temporary topicality, yet, the market is minute, and prestige and prices rise the less topical the supply is.
It is painful for me to face the fact that art cannot contribute to the solution of urgent social problems.

Offenbach, February 11, 1968

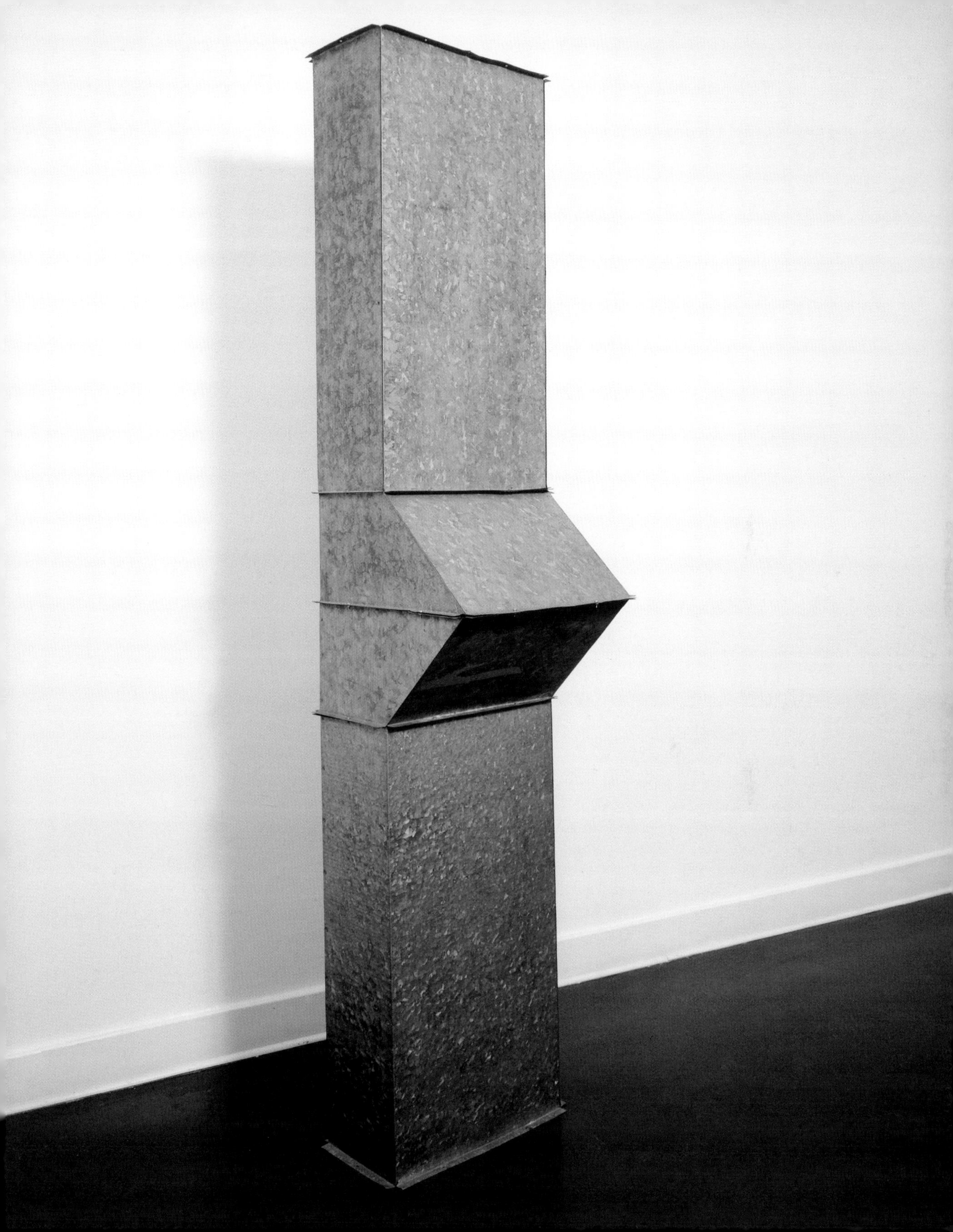

Nine swimming pools and a Broken glass

Artist book (details), 17.8 x 13.8 cm
Private collection

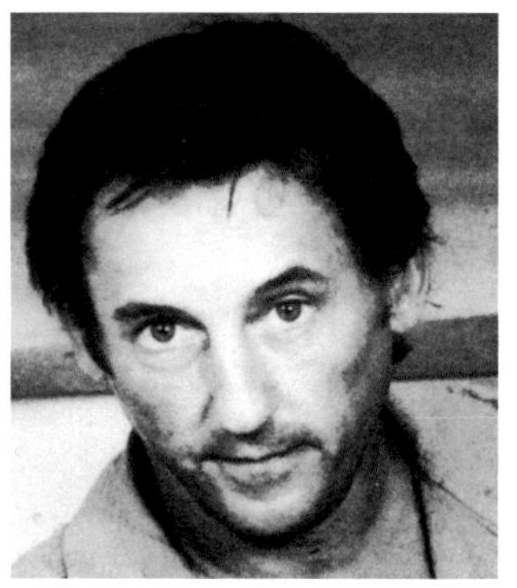

b. 1937 in Omaha (NE), USA

The artist Edward Ruscha, who lives in California, is regarded as one of the most important and earliest inspirations for the renovation of the tradition of the artist book, which was rediscovered and transformed by many artists in the 1960s. While the artist book had previously been an exclusive medium, accessible only to the few, and which contained mostly high-quality prints or original drawings by artists in limited editions, in the 1960s, the focus shifted to the utilitarian value and the inexpensive reproduction possibilities as the central aspects of the artist book.

Between 1962 and 1972 alone, Ruscha published 17 artist books. Apart from a few exceptions, he published them himself in unlimited editions, exclusively in paperback. Ruscha preferred neither to sign nor to number his books, precisely because he did not regard them as costly art objects, but rather used them as an innovative way of presenting and distributing his artistic ideas, which in addition had the advantage of being able to reach a broad spectrum of the public.

The simple and unpretentious format of his books matches their often quite banal content. Often they contain series of deliberately artless photographs depicting variations on one and the same theme. His first book project *Twenty-six Gasoline Stations* for example shows 26 black-and-white shots of filling stations along Route 66. The following publications are also clearly inspired by the lifestyle as well as the particular topographical and architectural features of California, particularly Los Angeles.

Some Los Angeles Apartments (1965), *Thirty-four Parking Lots in Los Angeles* (1967), *Nine Swimming Pools and a Broken Glass* (1968) and other books direct the beholder's attention willy-nilly to the uniform character of the urban structure of Los Angeles, where particular architectural types seem totally anonymized and interchangeable. To the extent that Ruscha's photographs precisely reflect, in their serial arrangement and basic interchangeability, the actual architectural characteristics of the city of Los Angeles, his books ironically draw attention to the stultifying unimaginativeness of modern city planning.

Alongside the artist books, since the 1960s Ruscha has been painting pictures often categorized as Pop Art, whereby he himself is interested first and foremost by the integration of language into painting. By his own account, however, Ruscha regards his photographs as ready-mades, whose aesthetic quality is a matter of virtual indifference to him. Thus in 1972 he stressed the expedience of his use of photography: "It's strictly a medium to use or not to use, and I use it only if I have to. I use it to do a job, which is to make a book."

NINE

SWIMMING

POOLS

Cover, 1968

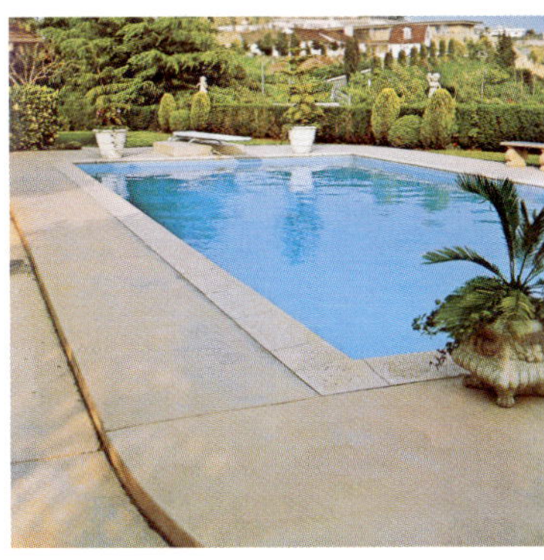
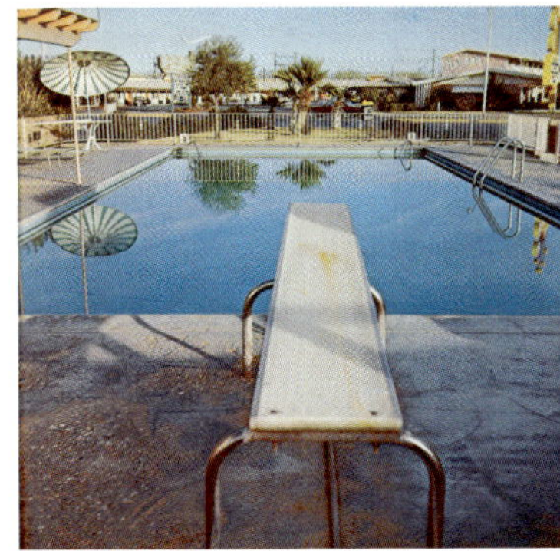
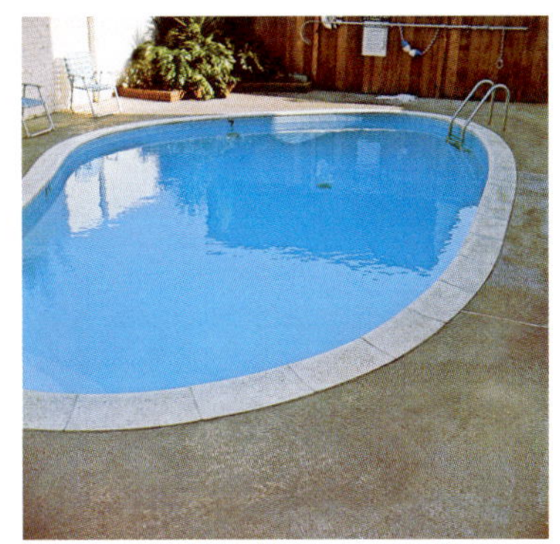
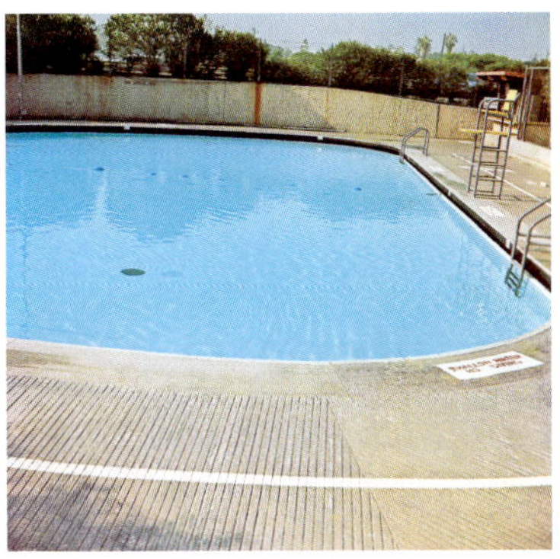
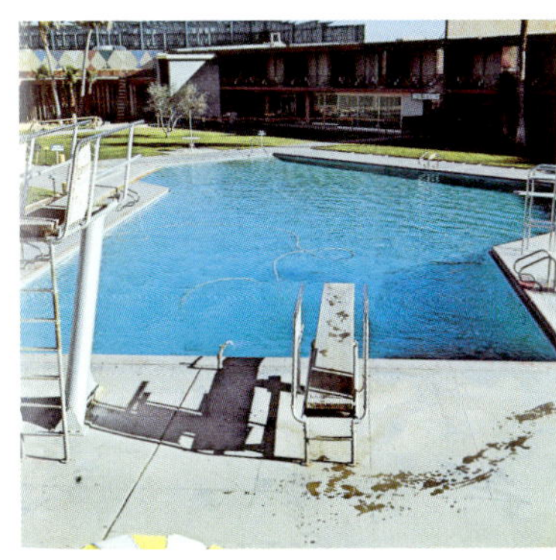
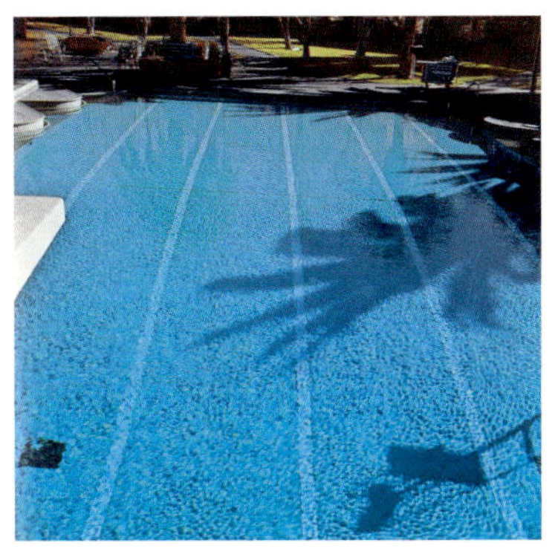
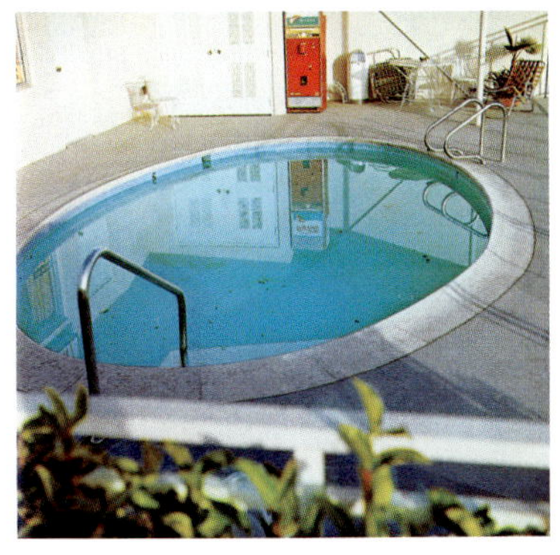
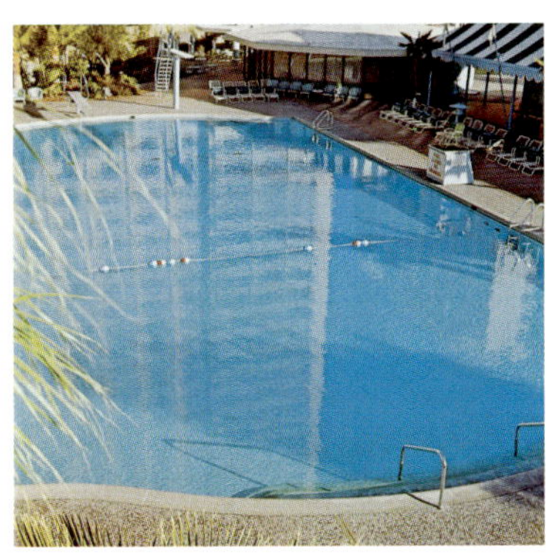
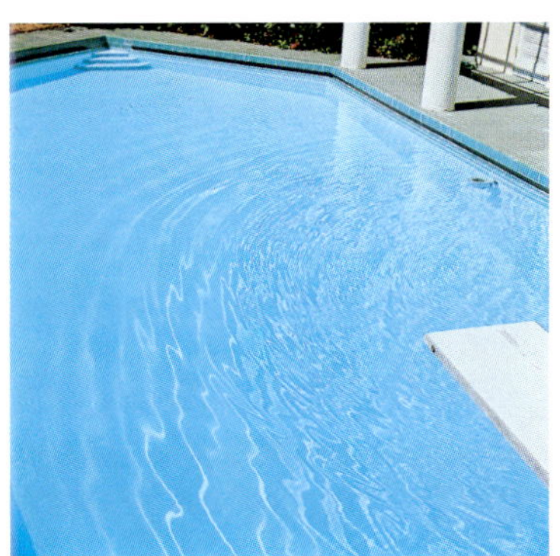
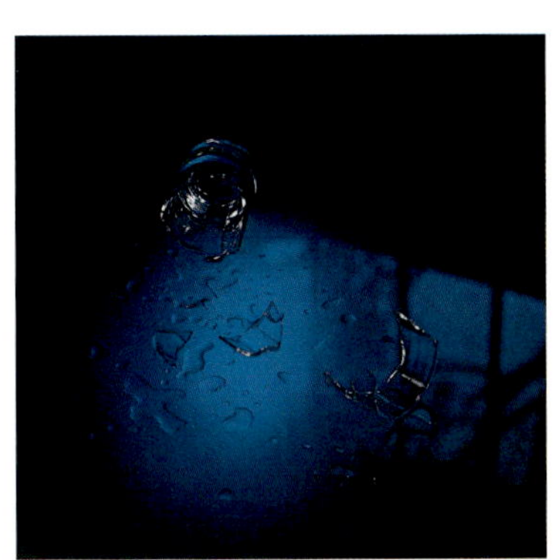

A SOUND GROWN SOFTER (diminuendo)

Writing on wall, variable dimensions
Berlin, Staatliche Museen zu Berlin – Preußischer Kulturbesitz, Nationalgalerie, Marzona collection

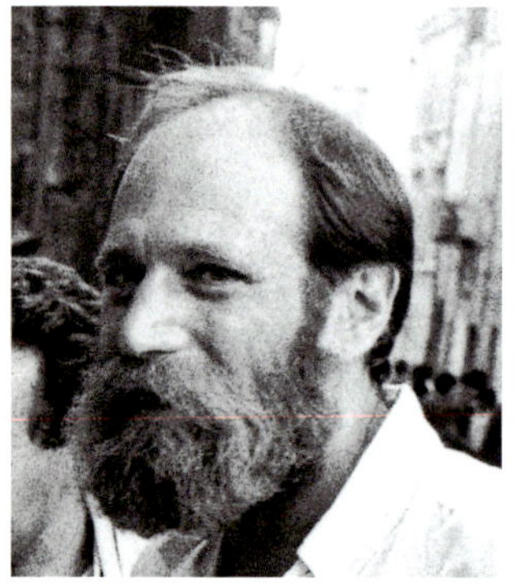

b. 1942 in New York (NY), USA

From the mid-1960s Lawrence Weiner worked on paintings – at first minimalist pictures, which took up not only Frank Stella's idea of "shaped canvases" but also the standardized production techniques of Andy Warhol. It was left to the collector or commissioner of his pictures to determine their coloration, and in order to continue to exorcize any subjective-expressionist content from his works, Weiner applies the paint in a standardized and always identical process. For the most part he refused to sign his pictures, because already at this point the conceptual component seemed to be of greater importance that the actual realization of the individual works.

In the spring of 1968, Weiner installed a sculptural work in the grounds of the campus of Windham College in Vermont for the group exhibition "Carl Andre, Robert Barry, Lawrence Weiner" organized by Seth Siegelaub. The work, with the descriptive title *A SERIES OF STAKES SET IN THE GROUND AT REGULAR INTERVALS TO FORM A RECTANGLE – TWINE STRUNG FROM STAKE TO STAKE TO DEMARK A GRID – A RECTANGLE REMOVED FROM THIS RECTANGLE* occupied the major part of a lawn and shortly after the exhibition opening was broken down by students. At first hurt by this event, Weiner soon realized that the work, in spite of its physical damage, was basically intact by reason of its verbal determination, for it could be replicated at any time in different conditions in accordance with the verbally formulated definitions.

On the basis of this insight, in the autumn of 1968 Weiner formulated his famous "Declaration of Intent", which since then has accompanied the presentation of his works. Theory and art-work in one, it states:

"1. The artist may construct the piece. / 2. The piece may be fabricated. / 3. The piece needs not be built. / Each being equal and consistent with the intent of the artist, the decision as to condition rests with the receiver upon the occasion of receivership."

Thus the principles which characterize Weiner's work to this day are clearly formulated. The actual execution of a work, the transition from the verbal-conceptual to some material form, is no longer a necessity, but merely an option of equal status, available both to the artist, and to the "receivers" of the work. Thus Weiner's work must be regarded as among the most egalitarian and open approaches to a renewal of art in the 1960s.

Weiner, who regards his works as being basically sculptures, often uses past participles to describe completed actions, processes or configurations of materials. Even though he did realize some of his statements himself – for the survey exhibition of contemporary art "Op losse Schroeven" (Amsterdam, 1969), for example, he burned a candle on a canal, in order to give concrete form to *THE RESIDUE OF A FLARE IGNITED UPON A BOUNDARY* – he presents the majority of his works in purely verbal form.

In artist books, on exhibition walls, or in the public space, Weiner's verbal sculptures urge the beholder to participate actively in the art process. Works like *A SOUND GROWN SOFTER (diminuendo)* exist at least virtually in infinitely many variations in the heads of the beholders, without ever taking on a definitive, let alone "correct", form.

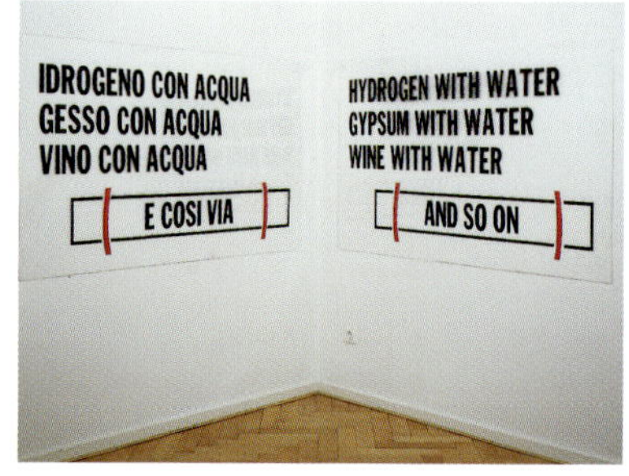

HYDROGEN WITH WATER, GYPSUM WITH WATER, WINE WITH WATER (AND SO ON), 1989

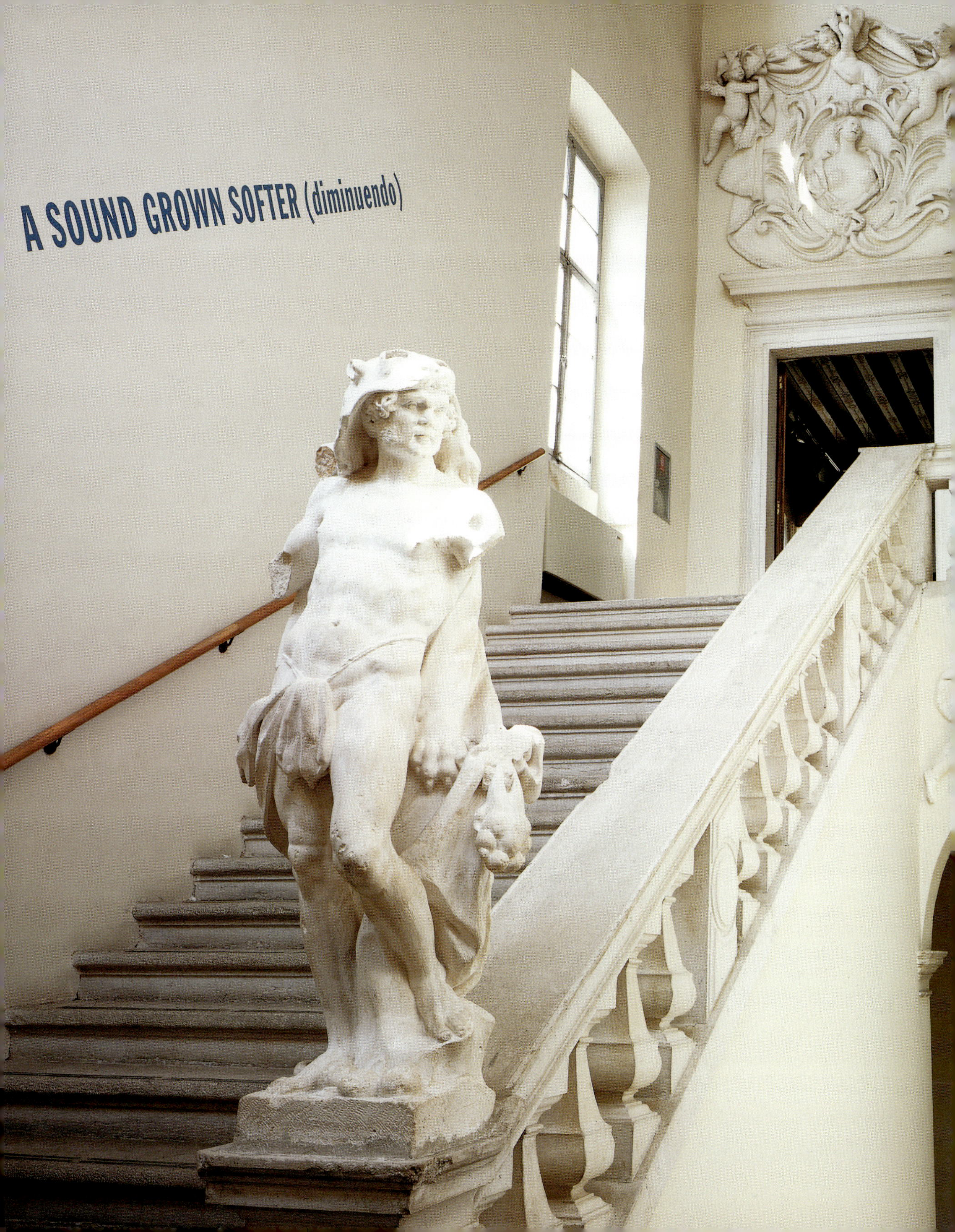

A SOUND GROWN SOFTER (diminuendo)

oral communication, ᴅecember 12 1970

With Michel Claura, Ian Wilson, Tommaso Trini
Photography: Berlin, Staatliche Museen zu Berlin – Preußischer Kulturbesitz, Kunstbibliothek, Marzona collection

b. 1940 in Durban, South Africa

If there was an artist in the late 1960s whose work accords with the tendency perceived by the critics John Chandler and Lucy Lippard towards the dematerialization of the art object, then it is Ian Wilson. While even such radical approaches as those of artists such as Robert Barry, Daniel Buren or Lawrence Weiner remain dependent on an – albeit often ephemeral – form of implementation and conveying of their ideas, in 1968 Wilson decided to embrace an artistic practice that rejected any form of materialization on principle. "Art spoken" was Wilson's exclusive artistic activity until the 1980s, when he started bringing out artist books.

At the start of the project, Wilson concentrates on the possible implications of the word "time". In mostly private talks, he turns the conversation deliberately to the subject of time, whereby what he is interested in first and foremost are the often unconscious philosophical and theoretical assumptions which go hand-in-hand with the use of the word. A little later, he replaces the word "time" by the words "oral communication", as he realizes that speaking itself is at the focus of his artistic work. As with the works based on the word "time", Wilson now makes the term "oral communication" the subject of countless conversations, which mostly take place unofficially in the context of daily meetings with his fellow human beings. At the same time, Wilson presented his idea of "oral communications" as an art form throughout the 1970s in the context of exhibitions. His contribution to the exhibition "Conceptual Art and Conceptual Aspects" at the New York Cultural Center in 1970 consisted of a statement printed in the catalogue, which revealed the political dimension of Wilson's project: "I present oral communication as an object, all art is information and communication. I've chosen to speak rather than sculpt. I've freed art from a specific place. It's possible for everyone. I'm diametrically opposed to the precious object. My art is not visual, but visualized."

No longer the production of art objects reserved to a small public, but a form of art accessible to all at any time in the context of open conversations: that was Wilson's declared aim. In 1972 Wilson's first officially announced "discussion" took place at the John Weber Gallery in New York; it was to be followed by numerous other discussions in museums and galleries. That Wilson's activities even in the allegedly liberal climate of the 1970s were by no means uncontroversial is demonstrated by a review of a "discussion" that took place at the John Weber Gallery in 1975. For the art magazine "Fox", Michael Corris wrote: "I don't like Ian Wilson and I thought his discussion was boring. As well as unimportant to anybody's idea of discourse."

This judgement is not capable of verification, as Wilson on principle never did, and still does not, allow recordings of his "discussions". As the only records of his "discussions", the artist draws up certificates, on which the place and date of the actions in question are noted. These can be purchased by museums and collectors.

"oral communication is a lot more than language; it is one of the best mediums for the dissemination of ideas."

Ian Wilson

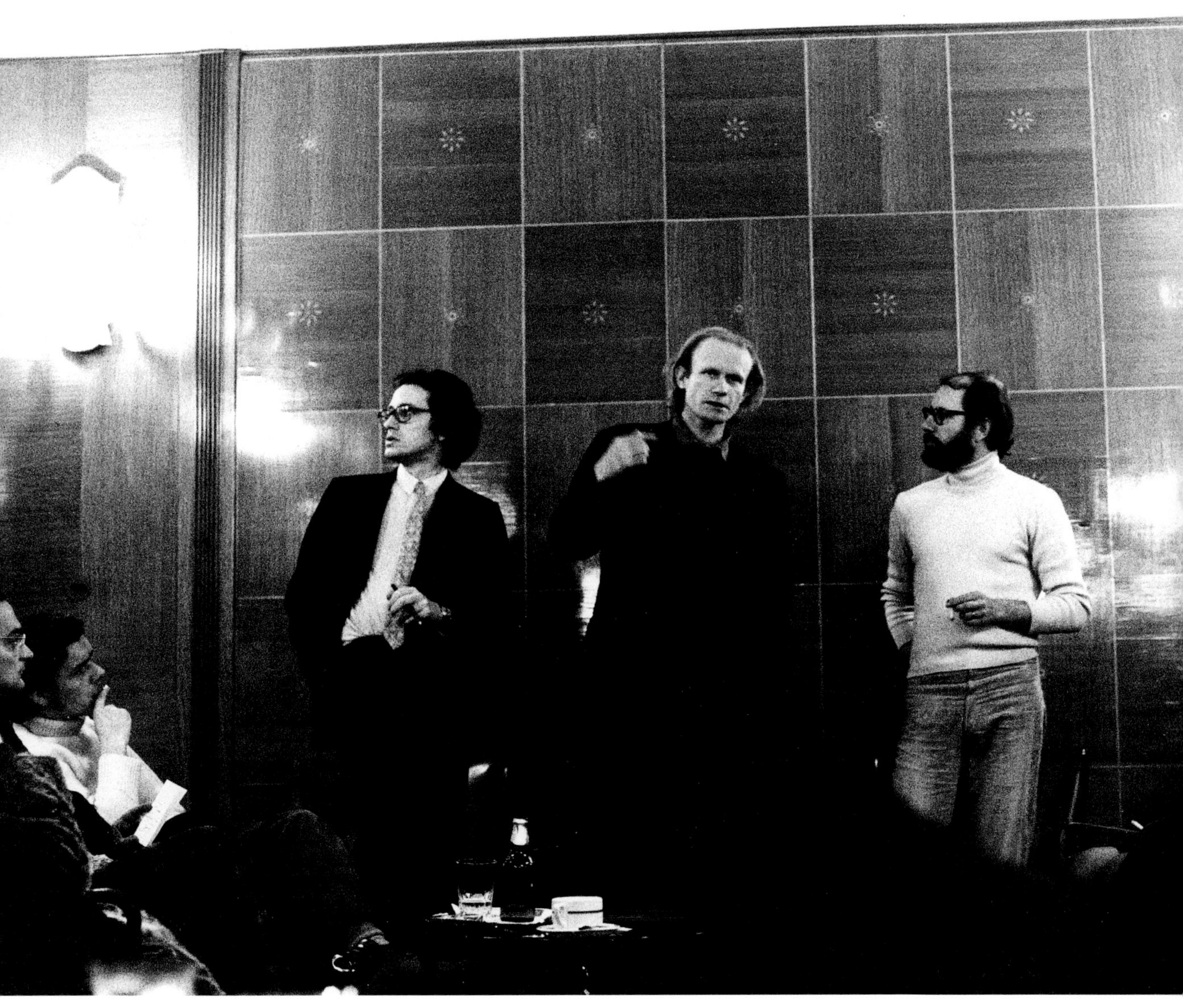

To stay informed about upcoming TASCHEN titles, please request our magazine at www.taschen.com/magazine or write to TASCHEN America, 6671 Sunset Boulevard, Suite 1508, USA–Los Angeles, CA 90028, contact-us@taschen.com, Fax: +1-323-463.4442. We will be happy to send you a free copy of our magazine which is filled with information about all of our books.

© 2006 TASCHEN GmbH
Hohenzollernring 53, D–50 672 Köln
www.taschen.com

Editorial coordination: Sabine Bleßmann, Cologne
Design: Sense/Net, Andy Disl and Birgit Reber, Cologne
Production: Ute Wachendorf, Cologne
Translation: Michael Scuffil, Leverkusen

Printed in Singapore
ISBN 978-3-8228-2962-2

Photo credits:
The publishers would like to express their thanks to the archives, museums, private collections, galleries and photographers for their kind support in the production of this book and for making their pictures available. If not stated otherwise, the reproductions were made from material from the archive of the publishers. In addition to the institutions and collections named in the picture descriptions, special mention is made of the following:
© Archiv für Kunst und Geschichte, Berlin: p. 13 right / Bridgeman Giraudon: p. 1, 4, 8 / Courtesy Cheim & Read, New York: p. 64 below / Courtesy Paula Cooper Gallery, New York: p. 20 right, 76 / Courtesy Konrad Fischer Galerie, Düsseldorf: p. 68 (photo: Stephen Kaltenbach) / Courtesy Marian Goodman Gallery, New York: p. 15, 61 / Courtesy Hans Haacke: p. 62 / Kröller-Müller Museum, Otterlo: p. 83 / Kunsthalle Düsseldorf: p. 44 below (photo: Klein) / Courtesy Galerie Lelong, New York: p. 24 right, 80 below, 81 / Courtesy Lisson Gallery and the artists: p. 31 / Courtesy Metro Pictures, New York: p. 75 / Musée de Grenoble: p. 67 / Museum Sztuki, Lodz: p. 85 (photo: Piotr Tomczyk) / Adrian Piper Research Archive, Berlin: p. 86, 87 / © Photo SCALA, Florenz/The Museum of Modern Art, New York 2005: p. 77 / Staatliche Museen zu Berlin – Preußischer Kulturbesitz, Sammlung Marzona: p. 17, 20 left (photo: Paolo Mussat Sartor), 21, 23, 24 left (photo: Betsy Jackson), 25 (photo: Philip Steinmetz), 28 below (photo: Kathy Dillon), 29 (photo: Kathy Dillon), 30, 33 (photo: Giorgio Colombo), 34 (photo: Giorgio Colombo), 37, 38, 41, 43 (photo: Jens Ziehe), 46 above (photo: Kramer), 46 below, 50, 53 (photo: Jens Ziehe), 54 below, 57 (photo: Jens Ziehe), 70 (photo: Giorgio Colombo), 71 (photo: Jens Ziehe), 73, 89 (photo: Jimbo), 93 above (photo: Paolo Pellion di Persano), 95 (photo: Giorgio Colombo) / Staatliche Museen zu Berlin – Preußischer Kulturbesitz, Sammlung Marzona: p. 2, 7 right, 14, 19 right, 22, 47, 48, 49, 58 below, 60 below, 65, 69, 92 below, 93 (all photos: Marcus Schneider) / Courtesy The Siegelaub Collection & Archives at the Stichting Egress Foundation, Amsterdam: p. 18 (photo: Seth Siegelaub) / Courtesy Sperone Westwater, New York: p. 52 / Courtesy David Zwirner Gallery, New York: p. 79

Reference illustrations:
p. 28: Vito Acconci, *Step Piece*, 1970 (February, April, July, November, every day 8 a.m.), performance 102 Christopher Street, New York, photography: Staatliche Museen zu Berlin – Preußischer Kulturbesitz, Kunstbibliothek, Marzona collection / p. 30: Art & Language, *Map to Not Indicate…*, 1967, letterpress print on paper, variable dimensions, photography: Berlin, Staatliche Museen zu Berlin – Preußischer Kulturbesitz, Kunstbibliothek, Marzona collection / p. 38: Bernd and Hilla Becher, *Schieferhaus, Giebelwand Siegen*, 1971, black-and-white photography, 60 x 50 cm, Berlin, Staatliche Museen zu Berlin – Preußischer Kulturbesitz, Nationalgalerie, Marzona collection / p. 42: Alighiero Boetti, *Mappa*, 1971, embroidery, 90 x 130 cm, Private collection / p. 44: Marcel Broodthaers, *Musée d'Art Moderne, Département des Aigles, Section des Figures* (detail), 1968–1972, Kunsthalle Düsseldorf / p. 46: Stanley Brouwn, *This Way Brouwn*, 1964, felt-tip pen and rubber stamp on paper, each 24.4 x 32 cm, Berlin, Staatliche Museen zu Berlin – Preußischer Kulturbesitz, Nationalgalerie, Marzona collection / p. 48: Daniel Buren, *Pour* (detail), 1973, painted cloth, 12 parts, each 320 x 140 cm, total dimensions variable, Berlin, Staatliche Museen zu Berlin – Preußischer Kulturbesitz, Nationalgalerie, Marzona collection / p. 50: Victor Burgin, *All Criteria*, 1970, mixed technique on cardboard, 2 parts, 30 x 21 cm each, Berlin, Staatliche Museen zu Berlin – Preußischer Kulturbesitz, Nationalgalerie, Marzona collection / p. 52: Hanne Darboven, *Leben, Leben/Life, Living*, 1997/98, 2,782 works on paper, 2 dolls' houses, total dimensions variable, each sheet and each photograph 30 x 20 cm, Courtesy Sperone Westwater, New York / p. 54: Jan Dibbets, *Shadow Piece* (detail), 1970, adhesive tape on wall, installation in the Galerie Yvon Lambert, Paris, photography: Berlin, Staatliche Museen zu Berlin – Preußischer Kulturbesitz, Kunstbibliothek, Marzona collection / p. 56: Hans-Peter Feldmann, *34 booklets*, 1968–1974, offset printing, grey cardboard, stamped, various dimensions / p. 58: Gilbert & George, *A Portrait of the Artists as Young Men*, 1972, video sculpture (certificate), Berlin, Staatliche Museen zu Berlin – Preußischer Kulturbesitz, Nationalgalerie, Marzona collection / p. 60: Dan Graham, *Bisected Two-way Mirror Triangle*, 1998, aluminium and reflective glas, 230 x 652 x 652 cm, Private collection / p. 62: Hans Haacke, *Condensation Cube*, 1963–1965, Plexiglas cube with distilled water, 76.2 x 76.2 x 76.2 cm, Ottawa, National Gallery of Canada / p. 64: Jenny Holzer, *TRUISMS: ABUSE OF POWER COMES*, 1977–1979, pencil on transparent paper, 106.7 x 180.3 cm, Courtesy Cheim & Read, New York / p. 68: Stephen Kaltenbach, *Time Capsule – Open After WW III (2)*, n.d., steel, 29 x 11.5 cm Ø, Courtesy Konrad Fischer Galerie, Düsseldorf / p. 70: On Kawara, *One Million Years – Past*, 1969, installation in the Galleria Toselli, Milan, 1971, photography: Berlin, Staatliche Museen zu Berlin – Preußischer Kulturbesitz, Kunstbibliothek, Marzona collection / p. 76: Sol LeWitt, *A#6*, 1967, baked enamel on aluminium, 2 parts, 213.4 x 213.4 cm, Courtesy Paula Cooper Gallery, New York / p. 80: Ana Mendieta, *Facial Hair Transplant*, 1972, photography, Courtesy Galerie Lelong, New York / p. 82: Bruce Nauman, *Slow Angle Walk (Beckett Walk)*, 1968, performance, black-and-white video, 60 min. / p. 86: Adrian Piper, *Catalysis IV*, 1970/71, black-and-white photography, no dimensions given, Courtesy the artist / p. 90: Edward Ruscha, *Nine Swimming Pools and a Broken Glass*, 1968, cover of the artist's book, 17.8 x 13.8 cm, Private collection / p. 92: Lawrence Weiner, *HYDROGEN WITH WATER, GYPSUM WITH WATER, WINE WITH WATER (AND SO ON)*, 1989, writing on wall, variable dimensions, Berlin, Staatliche Museen zu Berlin – Preußischer Kulturbesitz, Nationalgalerie, Marzona collection

page 1
BRUCE NAUMAN

Studies of Holograms (detail)
1970, silk-screen print, 66 x 66 cm
Hamburg, Kunsthalle Hamburg

page 2
DANIEL BUREN

Pour (detail)
1973, painted cloth, 12 parts, each 320 x 140 cm, total dimensions variable
Staatliche Museen zu Berlin – Preußischer Kulturbesitz, Nationalgalerie, Marzona collection

page 4
JOSEPH KOSUTH

Five Words in White Neon
1965, neon, 8 x 150 cm
Private ownership